Up Where We Belong

Helping African American and Latino Students Rise in School and in Life

Gail L. Thompson

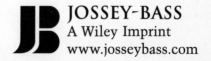

JOSSEY-BASS
A Wiley Imprint
www.josseybass.com

Published by Jossey-Bass
A Wiley Imprint
989 Market Street, San Francisco, CA 94103-1741   www.josseybass.com

Jossey-Bass books and products are available through most bookstores. To contact Jossey-Bass directly call our Customer Care Department within the U.S. at 800-956-7739, outside the U.S. at 317-572-3986, or fax 317-572-4002.

Jossey-Bass also publishes its books in a variety of electronic formats. Some content that appears in print may not be available in electronic books.

ISBN: 978-0-7879-9597-3

Library of Congress Cataloging-in-Publication Data has been applied for.

Printed in the United States of America
FIRST EDITION
HB Printing   10 9 8 7 6 5 4 3 2 1

The Jossey-Bass Education Series

Contents

Part Two: On the Schoolyard

Part Three: Out in the World: Beyond the Classroom and the Schoolyard

Acknowledgments

I am grateful to the Haynes Foundation for awarding me a research grant so that I could spend a summer working on this book. As always, I thank my husband, Rufus, for his comments and for proofreading part of this book, and my children, Nafissa, NaChe', and Stephen; my son-in-law, Derrick Spires; my great-niece Jayda for patience and for granting me time to write; my cousin Bobbie Timberlake for her ongoing encouragement; my sister Tracy for offering her proofreading services; and Dr. David Drew for his ongoing support and encouragement. I'm also very grateful to the principal, teachers, and students who participated in the study described in this book; to Mike McLinn, executive director of the Central Cities Gifted Children's Association in Los Angeles, and his wife, Dr. Claudette McLinn; to Katie Sample, director of the African American Academy for Accelerated Learning in Minneapolis; to Freddie Gray and the African American Achievement Council in Omaha; to LAUSD's Mary Lewis, Peggy Taylor Presley, Donna Simien, LaRoyce Bell, Sheila Smith, Pansy Rankin, and Arlene Fortier; to Dr. Melody Lark; and to every single person who has shared my work with teachers and who has given me words of encouragement. Last but not least, I wish to thank my agent, Djana Pearson Morris of Pearson Morris Belt Literary Agency, for her enthusiasm and great advice; and my editor, Lesley Iura, and her staff, Dimi Berkner, Kate Gagnon, and the entire Jossey-Bass team for their hard work, enthusiasm, and support for this project as well as for *Through Ebony Eyes*. . . .

About the Author

Dr. Gail L. Thompson, an associate professor at the Claremont Graduate University, has written three books: *African American Teens Discuss Their Schooling Experiences; What African American Parents Want Educators to Know;* and *Through Ebony Eyes: What Teachers Need to Know but Are Afraid to Ask About African American Students,* a book that has received a considerable amount of attention from educators, talk show hosts, and news reporters across the nation. She co-wrote her fourth book, *Exposing the Culture of Arrogance in the Academy: A Blueprint for Increasing Black Faculty Satisfaction,* with Dr. Angela Louque. Recently, a chapter that she wrote was published in an edited book, *From Work-Family Balance to Work-Family Interaction: Changing the Metaphor;* one of her essays was published in *USA Today;* and her work has been published in numerous academic journals. Dr. Thompson has appeared on PBS television's *Tony Brown's Journal,* National Public Radio, WURD, KPCC, WBAI, WSOU, and KXAM, and has been quoted in several newspapers. She has reviewed scripts for the Educational Broadcasting Corporation and several academic journals, and has done presentations, keynote addresses, workshops, and consultant work throughout the United States, as well as two presentations in Canada.

Dr. Thompson is married to Rufus, an educator, and they have three children: Nafissa, a doctoral student; NaChe', a college undergraduate; and Stephen, a high school senior. Her great niece Jayda also lives with her.

Up Where We Belong

Introduction

Several decades ago, my classmates and I were required to pass a U.S. Constitution test in order to graduate from the predominantly black, low-income high school that we attended. In terms of achievement, our school had one of the worst reputations in the city. Our U.S. Government teacher, a white man from suburbia, who was supposed to prepare us for the test, had low standards, assigned little useful work, and spent most of the class period talking about sensational current events, showing movies, or playing a game called "Baffa Baffa" with us. In spite of the limited curriculum in his class, all of us ended up passing the U.S. Constitution test. Later, I learned why. One of my friends said that when she returned after class one day to retrieve a forgotten item, she'd actually seen this teacher erasing incorrect answers and replacing them with correct ones. Instead of teaching us what we needed to know to pass the test, he cheated for us; at the same time, he cheated us out of valuable information that we needed to know. Was he too lazy to teach us the information that we needed to know in order to pass the test on our own, or did he believe that poor black kids from southeast San Diego didn't have the aptitude to learn? Today, I still don't know the answers to these questions.

This story is relevant to the ongoing national debate over the federal government's No Child Left Behind Act (NCLB), which links school promotion, high school graduation, school funding, and teacher and administrator job security to standardized test and High School Exit Exam (HSEE) scores. As a result of NCLB, teachers throughout the nation are feeling unprecedented pressure to ensure that students do well on standardized tests. Not only have many teachers felt compelled to "teach to the test," to the exclusion of other important topics, but many have become so obsessed with testing outcomes that they have found little time and few incentives to prepare creative, meaningful, and culturally relevant lesson plans. Others, like my former teacher, have actually resorted to cheating.[1] Several news reports during 2004 revealed that even the Houston School District, which had formerly been praised for having high test scores and narrowing the achievement gap, had misled the public about its test scores. In a 60 Minutes expose, Dan Rather said that district officials had "lied about dropout rates." According to Rather, the actual dropout rate was "somewhere between 25 and 50 percent. . . . Some of Houston's claims of success were just plain phony."[2] The Houston case is all the more alarming because Texas became the model for NCLB, and its former superintendent, Rod Paige, became the national education secretary as a result of the school reform miracles he had supposedly worked in Houston.

Just as the high-stakes testing movement has placed a lot of pressure on teachers, it has also placed a tremendous burden on students. In urban schools, for example, many students—particularly African Americans and Latinos—are failing exit exams and underperforming on standardized tests at alarming rates. For example, in August 2004, the California Achievement Test (CAT 6) scores were published for the 4.7 million California students in grades two through eleven who were tested. As usual, when they were disaggregated by race and ethnicity, the scores of black and Latino students trailed those of whites and Asian Americans.[3] Unlike the disappointing CAT 6 results, California HSEE results showed that some improvement had been made. Most of the high school students who were tested passed the English language arts and math portions of the exam. However, much lower percentages of black and Latino students did so. In fact, whereas 62 percent of the black students passed the English language arts portion of the exam, only 54 percent passed the math portion.[4] In response to the overall dismal results, Jack O'Connell, state superintendent of public instruction, said, "These scores should be viewed as a wake-up call for us all."[5] More recently, at the end of the 2006 school year, more than forty-two thousand California seniors hadn't passed the HSEE.

School districts throughout the nation are in a similar predicament, as educators scramble for solutions to improve scores, narrow the achievement gaps, and thereby prevent a state takeover and a loss of federal funding.

Besides cheating, the standardized test mania caused by NCLB's pressure on educators and students to raise test scores has led some officials to resort to additional extreme measures. South Carolina hired Edison Schools Incorporated, a "for profit company," to help "a poor rural district entering its fifth school year under state control."[6] In addition to helping the district align its curriculum to state standards, Edison provided teachers with classroom management and technology training.[7] However, the South Carolina plan appears minor when compared to the drastic action taken in Chicago.

In June 2004, officials of the Chicago Public Schools (CPS) announced that low-performing schools would be closed or downsized and one hundred new schools would be created. The National Teachers Academy is an example of one school that experienced the consequences of CPS's and the mayor's frustration over low test scores. This state-of-the-art, relatively new school located next door to the Ickies and across the street from the Hilliard Homes, two of Chicago's most notorious public housing projects, was placed under the control of a local university after failing to make enough progress on its standardized test scores. If the latest CPS reform is successful, by 2010, one-third of the city's schools will be charter schools, one-third will be controlled by CPS, and one-third will be run independently by businesses and religious organizations.[8]

The standardized test mania has also generated more research about ways to close the achievement gaps. For example, some studies say that the use of vouchers leads to higher test scores; others say that charter schools are the answer, which has resulted in an increase in the number of charter schools. According to the *Boston Globe*, "Charter schools are self-governing public schools. They are often operated by private companies, which do not come under the authority of local school boards. They also retain more flexibility than traditional public schools in areas such as policy, hiring, and teaching."[9] CNN reported that since 1991, nearly three thousand charter schools have opened throughout the nation.[10] Although President George W. Bush promised to increase funding for charter schools, the quality of these schools has been questioned. One reason is that a higher percentage of charter school teachers and principals are underqualified when compared to their counterparts in regular public schools.[11] Moreover, although charter school students are expected to outperform students in regular public schools, some reports have indicated that this doesn't always happen. In fact, a *Boston Globe* article stated that "fourth graders at charter schools lagged about six months behind students in regular public schools in reading and math."[12] Interestingly, at the same time that Chicago officials were planning to create more charter schools, California officials were closing many of its charter schools as a result of mismanagement.[13]

America's Stepchildren

Even though they are located in different states and different communities throughout the United States, most low-performing schools tend to have three things in common: they have a high percentage of minority students, they have a high percentage of low-income students, and they tend to be located in neighborhoods where most middle- and upper-class whites would never live. In other words, these schools are usually attended by what I call America's stepchildren. Throughout this book, I use the term *stepchildren* to refer to African Americans, Latinos, Southeast Asians, Native Americans, and sometimes even low-income whites, because members of these groups are often marginalized and treated as second-class citizens in schools and the wider society. My goal in this book is to describe some of the ways that this marginalization occurs—particularly for African Americans and Latinos; how it can affect students' schooling and life experiences; and how educators, parents, and policymakers can improve low-performing schools—and hopefully, the future of America's stepchildren.

How This Book Came About

The catalyst for this book was an invitation I received from a principal of a low-performing California high school that I shall refer to as "American High School" throughout this book. I selected this name because I believe that the school is typical of many U.S. high schools that are attended by America's stepchildren.

In 2002, the principal of American High School asked me to help him identify the reasons that the African American students at his school were continuing to perform poorly on standardized tests. Because of NCLB's stipulation that "subgroups" also demonstrate progress on standardized tests, the African American students' low scores placed the school in danger of a state takeover and a loss of federal funding.

During the previous year, for a separate project I had collected questionnaire data from most of the teachers at American High School in order to determine areas of professional growth they needed (see Appendix A). When the principal contacted me in 2002, although the original goal was for me to return to the school to collect information from the African American students, the plan changed after he accepted a job at a new high school in the same district. His successor, who had previously been the school's vice principal, had reservations about having an African American researcher (me) come to the school to collect data solely from African American students, because he feared that there might be a politically motivated public backlash that could harm his career. After all, racial issues still make many Americans uncomfortable. He also pointed out that other groups, including some white students at the school, had underperformed on standardized tests. Consequently, we decided that I should expand the scope of the study to include all students who wanted to participate, regardless of race or ethnicity.

Therefore, in May 2003 I returned to the school and spent four days collecting questionnaire and focus group data from students in the ninth, tenth, eleventh, and twelfth grades. Of a total school population of approximately 3,200 students, 268 completed questionnaires for the study, and 146 questionnaire respondents participated in the focus group discussions. Fifty-two percent of the questionnaire respondents were females, and nearly half the focus group participants were females. Although the three major racial and ethnic groups at the school (Latinos, whites, and African Americans, respectively) were well represented in the study, African American students were overrepresented in both the focus groups and among the questionnaire respondents, and whites were underrepresented (see Appendix B). This could be attributed to the fact that I'm an African American and that during my time at the school, I strongly encouraged African American students to consider participating in the study. After all, I had initially been invited to the school to examine African American student achievement. However, as a result of the overall low participation rate among all student groups, I also urged all students, regardless of their race or ethnicity, to encourage their friends and classmates to participate. (See Appendix C for more information about the questionnaire respondents.)

Although white students were underrepresented in this study, I wanted to include their feedback in this book for two reasons: first, I believe that including the feedback from whites, Latinos, and African Americans can illustrate whether or not students' schooling experiences, perceptions, effort, and attitudes about school might differ along racial lines, even when they attend the same school. Second, I believe that the feedback can show whether or not white students who attend a low-performing school are subjected to inequality of educational opportunity in the ways that African Americans and Latinos historically have been. In other words, I wanted to know whether or not attending a low-performing, predominantly minority school also meant that white students would be treated like stepchildren.

The student participants in this study reflected the total school population in that they represented the different academic tracks at the school at all grade levels, students who were extremely involved in extracurricular activities and those who weren't, and students who had a positive opinion of the school and those who did not. Regarding the number of participants, several students informed me that many students had not heard about the study, even though school officials assured me that they had publicized it during a school assembly and over the P.A. system and had promised to reward participants with a coupon for a free individual-size pizza and a raffle ticket for a yearbook drawing. Other students told me that some students felt so hopeless about the school that they didn't believe their participation would make a difference, and even the promise of receiving a pizza coupon and raffle ticket for participating in the study couldn't convince them to do so.

Nevertheless, nearly three hundred students accepted the invitation to participate, and the student questionnaire and focus group data proved to be rich sources of information about American High School. The students spoke about many aspects of their schooling that clearly explained why underachievement and student apathy were rampant at this high school. I was surprised to find, however, that the picture the students painted was extremely different in many ways from the one that their teachers had painted through the questionnaire data I had collected from them the previous year. (Teacher questionnaire results appear in Appendix D and are cited throughout the book.) The portrait that many of the students painted indicated not only a wide gulf between student and teacher perceptions but also that the school many students experienced appeared to be totally different from the one described by most of their teachers.

In the remaining chapters of this book, I do three things: first, I present the teachers' and students' often conflicting portraits of American High School, illustrating the magnitude of the disconnect between the two groups and revealing some of the reasons for students' low achievement, apathy, and beliefs and attitudes about standardized tests. I also describe the role of race, culture, and gender in the quality of students' schooling experiences, in terms of teacher and counselor expectations, discipline practices, the type of curriculum students received, and cross-cultural interactions among students and adults on campus. Although I set out to discover the reasons for the students' low standardized test scores, I ended up with a multidimensional portrait of the ways in which inequality of educational opportunity continues to be perpetuated in schools.

Second, I explain what I've learned about school reform, student underachievement, and related issues. When I first conceived of this book, I thought I would be drawing primarily from the data provided by the students who participated in the study and comparing their views with those of their teachers. But as I began to write, I found myself remembering stories from my own teaching experiences, workshop presentations, and parenting experiences, and stories that individuals have shared with me about the same topics that I was addressing in the study. I've incorporated these stories into this book because I feel that they enhance the messages emerging from the questionnaire and focus group data.

Third, at the end of each chapter, I make recommendations to school administrators, teachers, parents, and policymakers about specific ways that they can improve low-performing schools.

I believe that this book is a much-needed resource. At a time when President George W. Bush has vowed to reform the nation's high schools, and several politicians have either taken over school districts, tried to, or are in the process of attempting to do so, this book shows policymakers and state and national education officials how students and teachers can derail NCLB and other school reform ventures that are based exclusively on standardized test scores. This book also shows policymakers, parents, and educators how low test scores can merely be symptoms of larger problems in schools and with education reform. Further, the book shows teachers how their own attitudes and behaviors can contribute to student apathy. Moreover, by providing a holistic perspective of the schooling experiences of students at a racially diverse high school that in many ways is typical of thousands of low-performing schools throughout the nation, particularly those that are attended by large numbers of

America's stepchildren, this book provides parents, educators, and policymakers with a candid look at many of the factors that contribute to the decades-old problems of achievement gaps and poor student performance—problems that continue to plague schools throughout the nation.

PART ONE

In the Classroom

1

"You Can Tell If They Care"

Why Students Need Caring and Highly Qualified Teachers

I've spent much of my life in classrooms: first as a K–12 student, next as a college undergraduate, then, eventually, as a master's student, and much later as a doctoral student. More than two decades ago, as a Peace Corps volunteer in Africa, I also visited an elementary and a secondary school and observed what was going on in classrooms there. When I returned to the United States, I spent fourteen years teaching in "urban-fringe," predominantly minority junior high and high schools, and since 1998, I've taught graduate students—mostly individuals earning education degrees—full-time. Moreover, a few years ago, I created and ran an after-school literacy program for struggling third, fourth, and fifth graders at two schools, including a low-income, predominantly black school. Despite the extensive amount of time I've spent in classrooms, teaching wasn't my first career choice; writing was. The truth is, I entered the teaching force out of necessity at a time when I was a single parent who needed a steady income in order to feed my child.

So, thinking that it would only be a temporary job, I started working as a substitute teacher in 1984. After I "subbed" for a semester, a junior high school principal offered me a long-term position that was contingent on my immediate enrollment in a teacher certification program at a local university. Because her offer equaled job security, a regular monthly paycheck, and medical benefits for my daughter and me, I couldn't refuse it. But even though I became a full-time teacher "by accident," when I accepted the principal's offer, I made two promises to myself.

First, I would strive to provide my students with the best education that I could. Back then, and even today, my model of outstanding teaching was wrapped in nostalgic memories of my sixth-grade teacher, Mrs. Susan Tessem. Not only was she effective in making the curriculum comprehensible to the students at our predominantly black elementary school, in which many of us—including myself—were on welfare and from single-parent homes, but more important, Mrs. Tessem had a lifelong impact on me and others. In fact, even though I was only in elementary school, she was instrumental in convincing me to go to college, which changed the course of my life.[1] What is most interesting about Mrs. Tessem is that as a young white woman from suburbia who taught at a low-performing inner-city school, she faced many of the work-related problems that numerous current teachers aren't able to handle.[2] Yet, in spite of these problems, she made a decision each day to teach to the best of her ability. She refused to let the problems plaguing our community, and inner-city communities nationwide, prevent her from doing an outstanding job, or force her to lower her expectations. Neither poverty, community problems, the low prestige of our school, the low expectations of many of her colleagues, nor widespread teacher apathy could convince Mrs. Tessem that we were anything less than "college material."

The second promise I made to myself when I accepted the job offer was to set a personal goal related to payday. Each month when I collected my paycheck, I wanted to be able to look squarely at myself in the mirror and say honestly, "I *earned* this paycheck. I'm not merely *collecting* money that I don't deserve."

Even though my K–12 teaching career was often rocky, painful, and disillusioning, for the fourteen years that I taught, I tried to keep these two promises foremost in my mind. For me, they were the "big picture," and despite the fact that I made many mistakes during my journey to become an effective teacher, when I left the K–12 system to teach full-time at the university level, I left with my head held high and the belief that I'd lived up to Mrs. Tessem's example of excellence—but not perfection. Perfection is an elusive goal for human beings, for none of us is perfect. This is an important message for all teachers, especially idealistic new teachers, to remember.

Today, in my graduate school classroom, I continue to hold the same definition of teaching excellence that I learned from Mrs. Tessem: subject matter competency; a cohesive, comprehensible, challenging, and relevant curriculum; high expectations for students; multiple means of assessment; an engaging style of delivery; and the overall objective of not only equipping students with the skills they need to advance toward their personal goals but also encouraging them to use their education to bring about social justice—especially for America's stepchildren. Of course, not everyone agrees with my definition of excellent teaching.

In fact, the list of definitions of what constitutes effective teaching is quite extensive. For example, in "Good Teachers, Plural," Cruickshank and Haefele described ten different models of good teaching and noted a lack of consensus on which model is best.[3] Darling-Hammond, who has done extensive research on teacher quality, found that teachers with full certification who also majored in the subjects they teach are more likely to produce high-achieving students than teachers without full certification and those who didn't major in the subjects they teach.[4] Haycock, the director of the Education Trust, said that among other characteristics, good teachers have strong verbal and math skills and extensive knowledge about their subject matter.[5] In the Carnegie Challenge 2001 report, *Higher Education's Challenge: New Teacher Education Models for a New Century*, Grosso de Leon maintained that effective teachers must have subject-matter mastery and be knowledgeable about curriculum, instruction, classroom management, and learning theories. They must also have an understanding of their students' community, beliefs, concerns, and interests; an ability to evaluate students' learning; clinical training; technological training; and a ". . . set of metaphorical bridges between the teacher's subject knowledge and the implicit understandings brought to the classroom by the learner."[6]

One of the most recent models of what is required to become an effective teacher was created by the U.S. Department of Education as part of NCLB. In *Meeting the Highly Qualified Teachers Challenge*, Rod Paige, former secretary of education, defined a highly qualified teacher as one who "has at least a bachelor's degree, has obtained full state certification or licensure, [and] has demonstrated subject area competence in each of the academic subjects in which the teacher teaches." All teachers should be "highly qualified by the end of the 2005–2006 school year."[7]

Like NCLB itself, the U.S. Department of Education's definition of a "highly qualified" teacher and its related timelines generated controversy and disagreements.[8] However, even though policymakers and researchers may fail to agree on a uniform model or definition of effective teaching, the "experts" tend to agree on two points: there are too many underqualified teachers in classrooms, especially in low-income and high-minority schools, and there is a strong connection between teacher quality and student achievement.

The U.S. Department of Education has repeatedly emphasized that "Good teaching lasts a lifetime. . . . A teacher's mastery of the academic content of what he or she teaches is critical to engaging students and inspiring them to academic excellence."[9] In her extensive study on teacher quality, Darling-Hammond made a similar point. She found that teacher quality had a stronger link to student achievement than teacher salaries, class size, or spending levels.[10] In his Carnegie Challenge report, Grosso de Leon put it simply: ". . . good teaching is the single most important element in determining student achievement."[11] In another Carnegie report, deCourcy Hinds wrote, "Several bad teachers in a row can derail a child's education, and research also indicates that teachers are so influential that variations in teacher quality alone can explain the differences in achievement of children from different socioeconomic backgrounds."[12] In "Good Teaching Matters . . . a Lot," Haycock said candidly, ". . . much of what we have blamed on children and their families for decades is actually the result of things we have done to them. As a nation, we have deprived our neediest students of the very ingredient most important to learning: a highly qualified teacher."[13]

Like Haycock, education "experts" and policymakers throughout the nation, by and large, agree that there are too many underqualified teachers in schools and that these teachers have a negative effect on student achievement. Of course, the "neediest students" and the ones who get the least from K–12 schools tend to be America's stepchildren. Haberman, for example, concluded that only 5 to 8 percent of teachers who teach low-income students are "stars" or exemplary teachers.[14]

Convinced that true school reform must begin with teachers, numerous politicians have begun to spread the same message. For example, at the beginning of 2005, in California, Tennessee, Texas, and Washington, D.C., among other places, government officials rang in the New Year with the message that America's public school system is in need of additional reform, and reform must begin with improving the quality of our teachers. In his State of the State Address, Governor Arnold Schwarzenegger of California vowed to "expel" ineffective teachers and implement a merit-pay system for teachers. The governor referred to California's public school system as an "educational . . . and institutional disaster," and said, "The more we reward excellent teachers, the more our teachers will be excellent. The more we tolerate ineffective teachers, the more our teachers will be ineffective."[15] In Tennessee, Governor Phil Bredesen promised to create a program that would not only "teach teachers how to teach" but also catapult his state—which has one of the worst-ranked K–12 systems in the nation—to educational prestige.[16] In Texas, Governor Rick Perry also promised to reform the public school system by instituting a merit-pay system for teachers.[17]

These politicians' and others' plans to reform the public school system at the state level may have seemed ambitious, and they had their share of critics. But shortly before his second inauguration in 2005, President George W. Bush introduced a new reform plan that made the politicians' plan seem modest, to say the least. Bush vowed to reform the *nation's entire high school system*. To do this, he promised to increase funding for NCLB and require more mandatory testing of high school students.[18]

Although Bush and other politicians may have had good intentions, like other policymakers and some "experts," they failed to realize an important point: true and lasting school reform can occur only with the cooperation of teachers and students, and history has shown that when people are forced to do things they don't want to do, they can retaliate and derail even the best plans. A recent example of this phenomenon occurred at one of the lowest-performing high schools in Los Angeles. The Bill and Melinda Gates Foundation offered to give this school more than $1 million to implement their talent development model. Despite the fact that the school principal was eager to receive this assistance, many teachers believed that their concerns were being ignored. The teachers voted against the plan, and the school lost the opportunity to receive a huge amount of money that may have benefited America's stepchildren.

What is most interesting to me about my decision as an adult to look to my sixth-grade teacher, Mrs. Tessem, as an exemplar of good teaching is that even as a child, I could tell the difference between a good teacher and a bad one. Yet as researchers, policymakers, and others continue to argue over what constitutes good teaching and what should be done to reform the K–12 public school system, they rarely seek the input of students (or even of teachers). If they did, they would learn that students (and teachers) have plenty to say.

I learned this during my own years as a junior high school and high school teacher, and I am constantly reminded of this when I hear my own children describe their teachers. Further, when I collected data for *African American Teens Discuss Their Schooling Experiences*, the students from the seven participating high schools were quite certain about what differentiated good teachers from bad ones. The students at American High School who completed the questionnaire and who participated in the focus groups were equally as opinionated about good and bad teachers. In the next section, we hear what they really thought about their teachers and their instructional practices.

What the Students Said

Most of the teachers at American High School rated themselves as outstanding teachers. Most said they loved their job, had a positive perspective of the school, and still planned to be teaching there three years later. The majority of these teachers also said that most of their students viewed them as outstanding teachers. In other words, most of the teachers undoubtedly would have labeled themselves as "highly qualified," even though at the time that they completed the questionnaire, many had taught for five years or less, and only 42 percent were fully credentialed.

Like the teachers at American High School who participated in the first part of the study, the majority of students said that most of their teachers were good teachers. However, students were less likely than teachers to rate the teachers as good. Furthermore, white students were more likely than Latino and black students to state this; black students, particularly males, were the least likely group to rate most of their teachers as good. (See Appendix E for the student questionnaire results that I describe throughout this book.)

Although the majority of students rated their teachers as good, more than half the black and Latino students said they wished they had better teachers. African American females and Latinas were a lot more likely than whites to want better teachers, and white males were least likely to hold this view. Most students also said that they got along with most of their teachers, but a lower percentage of black and Latino students did in comparison to whites. Latino males were the least likely group to say they got along with most of their teachers. In terms of fairness, black students, especially males, were less likely to say their teachers treated them fairly.

Teacher Quality

The focus group participants made many statements about their teachers. Some of these statements illustrate why more than half of the African-American and Latino questionnaire respondents wanted better teachers. Numerous students complained about teachers having bad attitudes, abusing their authority, taking their personal problems out on students, engaging in unfair practices, using ineffective instructional methods, having poor classroom management skills (a topic I will say more about in Chapter Four), and wasting class time. For example, an African American student stated: "I think that a lot of the teachers misuse their authority. Like, me and another black student gave the teacher a pass to come here [to the focus group discussion] today, but just because the pass was wrinkled, the teacher sent us to the office. She could see that the pass is dated for today, but she had to create a big ordeal about it. She has a bad attitude."

Another African American female said:

> There's this one P.E. coach that threatens students. She says, "If I was younger, I'd beat you up." She gets a lot of kids suspended because if you come late, she'll yell at you. Then you'll say, "Well, I'm not late." Then she'll say, "Are you getting smart with me? I'm calling the principal." One day, it was real hot, and you could walk the track for extra credit. A group of black people were sitting on the bleachers. She said, "You're bothering my class." They were playing tennis and we weren't even doing nothing, but she called security on us.

Another focus group participant said, "They should check the credentials of some of the teachers. There's better teachers teaching math. Last year, in one class, all of the kids got A's but none of them passed the AP test. I don't want that same teacher teaching me next year. So, they should check the credentials, and some of these teachers are child rapists. They should check them too."

A girl said, "In my math class, we have personal tutoring available after school. But everyone's scared of the teacher and intimidated by her, because she's mean. If you don't understand something, she gets frustrated and says, 'What don't you understand?' or 'How could you not understand *that?*' She makes you feel stupid."

A high school senior said: "You think as a senior that you have two main classes and you think everything else is easy and fun. I have this English teacher. She's really mean. She's a witch with a 'b.' She doesn't care. They'll give you the work. Once in awhile, you do a project, present it in class, and that's it. But more than half the time, you ask for help and she says, 'Come after class, because I'm not repeating things.' So, why is she here then? You go to a school to teach because maybe you like students and you like to help them out, but I don't see any of that."

Another student summarized what many focus group participants implied: "They expect us to trust them, but how can we trust them if they're just gonna blow up in our face and we can't even ask them anything?" Several focus group participants agreed with the student who made the following comment: "They need to learn different ways of teaching, because they're stuck in their learning. There's different types of learning for different students. They need to learn different ones. That way, they could teach and help all the students and not just those with a certain learning style."

The qualifications of Senior Seminar teachers, in general, were criticized by some seniors. At American High School, seniors are required to take the Senior Seminar, which includes the creation of a portfolio and a presentation. A senior remarked bluntly: "[The Senior Seminar teachers] are retarded. They have no clue what they're doing. You ask them, 'What is this?' 'Oh, I don't know; I'm gonna have to ask somebody else.' If you're teaching Senior Seminar, then you should know what you're doing. They give [that class] to teachers, like coaches and any teacher who would take the class. . . . They have no idea. So then, when we come to turn in our portfolio or go do our presentation, we're lost, because our teachers didn't know anything."

Another senior gave a mixed rebuttal to complaints about the Senior Project and Senior Seminar teachers, arguing, "It's actually a good learning experience for you guys because it does take you out into the real world. It shows you what you're gonna be doing; it shows you what you need to do. The class is pathetic because the teachers don't know what they're doing. But once you get out and actually do your project and do your paper, you learn a lot and you actually get out into the real world. It's a good experience."

How Their Teachers Perceived Them

Most students who completed the questionnaire believed that the majority of their teachers liked them personally, but black students, especially females, were almost twice as likely as whites to believe that most of their teachers didn't like them. Black and Latino males were also more likely than other students to say their teachers viewed them as troublemakers. Among the three major racial and ethnic groups of students in the study, in general, males were more likely than females to say their teachers viewed them as trouble-makers, and black females and white females were less likely than Latinas to say their teachers viewed them as troublemakers. I will return to this topic in Chapter Seven.

In the earlier phase of the study, almost all the teachers said they believed that teachers' attitudes and expectations can affect student achievement, that they wanted all their students to succeed in their classes, and that they cared about students' academic and personal welfare. The overwhelming majority of the teachers said they believed that most of their students would become successful adults; however, nearly one-fourth admitted that they believed some students weren't capable of passing their classes, and more than one-fourth said that most of their students wouldn't reach grade-level standards by the end of the school year.

The majority of the students who completed the question-naire also said that most of their teachers believed they had the potential to be good students, but Latinas and white males were less likely to agree that this was true. Most students also said that the majority of their teachers believed that they would become successful adults, but black females and white males were less likely than other students to say this.

Caring Teachers

Although many of the students who participated in the study had a favorable opinion of their teachers, it was obvious that many others didn't. This was especially true when the students spoke about the topic of caring. In the earlier phase of the study, nearly all the teachers said they cared about their students' academic and personal success, but in the student phase of the study, nearly 40 percent of the questionnaire respondents said they didn't believe that most of their teachers cared. Blacks and Latinos were more likely than whites to believe that most of their teachers didn't care about them. Latinas were more likely than any group to believe that their teachers didn't care about them, and white males were the most likely to believe they did. During the focus groups, several participants commented on "teacher caring." One participant described her idea of a caring teacher as follows: "Caring teachers talk to you. My first period teacher, if she sees that you're sad, she'll ask you, 'What's wrong?' And she actually shows interest, not like some teachers that will say, 'What's wrong?' Then they cut you off halfway through when you're talking to them. She actually listens to you and she'll compare her own experiences with yours if she actually went through the same thing. She acts like a friend, but then, when she needs to be a teacher, she will be."

Another student equated caring with good instructional practices. She stated: "It's also the way they teach you. If they don't care, they'll just assign work, and then, they'll go to the back room, and do whatever. But if they actually stand up there and teach you, and you ask them something, they can be funny and sarcastic with you, but they will still help you, if they care."

Some focus group participants described teachers who actually admitted to students that they didn't care about them. For instance, one student remarked, "They'll tell you, 'I don't care. It's up to you to pass your classes. If you don't, I'll still keep my job.'" Another student complained, "My math teacher screamed at the whole class that she didn't care if we failed; all she cared was that she was getting paid." One student summarized what many focus group participants expressed: "You can tell when they like teaching. You can tell the way they teach and the way they speak. You can tell that they're interested in wanting to teach you."

Teachers' Instructional Practices

Most of the teachers at American High School who participated in the first phase of the study had a very favorable opinion of their instructional practices. During the student phase of the study, several questionnaire items gave students an opportunity to share their views about specific aspects of their teachers' classroom practices that they liked or that they felt needed improvement.

Make the Course Work Comprehensible. Although the majority of the students said that most of their teachers did a good job of explaining class assignments, one-third disagreed; African Americans and Latinos were more likely than whites to disagree. In fact, black students were almost twice as likely as whites to say that most of their teachers didn't explain class assignments well.

Of the students who completed the questionnaire, 41 percent said that they were often confused about the work their teachers assigned. More than half the Latinas and nearly half the black females said they were often confused by the work their teachers assigned. During focus group discussions, several students made related comments. For example, one participant said, "My Health teacher, she just sits down, gives us the work, and she doesn't teach us nothing." A girl who participated in one of the first focus groups remarked, "People have different learning styles. So not everybody learns at the same rate or they learn different types of ways. The teachers should be able to explain it, because that's what they come to work for."

Another student stated:

I would like for her to explain things, but she doesn't do that. Some of the teachers can explain the work to a point where you get it. Then, there are some teachers that just don't explain the work. They give you a page number and tell you what to work on and expect you to just go and work on it. Then, when you go ask them questions they say, "I just told you what to do and how to do it." But you just told me the page number to go work on. You didn't explain how to do it.

One focus group participant made a complaint that was common among students: "We need teachers who have patience in explaining things. I have a sixth-period math teacher. I asked her for help and she just read the directions from a paper. Every day, when we come to class, she looks like she's tired of seeing us and she wants to go home and not help us."

Give Extra Help. In the earlier phase of the study, nearly all the teachers said that their students knew they were available to give extra help on a regular basis, but one third of the students disagreed. White students were more likely than blacks and Latinos to say their teachers were willing to give extra help during class time. Females tended to be less likely than males to agree that this was true, and white males were most likely to agree. At the same time, African Americans and Latinos were more likely than whites to admit that they were often too embarrassed to ask their teachers for help. In fact, Latinos were four times more likely than whites, and blacks were three times more likely than whites, to say they were often too embarrassed to ask their teachers for help.

Respond to Students' Questions During Class Time. Nearly all the teachers claimed that they encouraged their students to ask questions on a regular basis, but one-fifth of the students believed that most of their teachers were not willing to answer questions if they didn't understand an assignment. Once again, white students were more likely than students of color to agree that most of their teachers were willing to answer questions, and black students were least likely to agree. In fact, black students were eight times more likely and Latinos were seven times more likely than whites to indicate that most of their teachers weren't willing to answer questions if they were confused about class work.

Numerous focus group participants complained about this issue. For example, one student stated, "What I don't like is how the teachers will assign you work and then they'll get on the phone and talk to people and pay their bills. Then, when you ask a question, they'll say, 'Can't you see I'm on the phone?' That's not cool to me."

One girl remarked, "They should actually go over the stuff and answer questions. Some of them, if you ask a question, because you don't understand, they get irritated and they just don't want to answer your questions. They'll be just like, 'Oh, you should know.'"

Patience. A similar pattern emerged among the questionnaire results regarding patience. Although the majority of student questionnaire respondents agreed that their teachers were patient with them when they didn't understand an assignment, nearly 30 percent disagreed. Once again, there was a noticeable difference between the percentage of students of color who agreed and the percentage of whites, in that Latinos and blacks were a lot more likely to disagree.

According to one focus group participant, "They need to also have patience with students, because some teachers give up. They get into their teaching and they probably see students aren't taking it seriously. So, they're like, 'Fine, it's your grade, not mine. You do it.' They give up. A lot of teachers do that. I think they need to have more patience with us. It's not the whole class that doesn't want to learn. There are some students who do want to learn."

Another student summarized what many focus group participants implied: "They expect us to trust them, but how can we trust them if they're just gonna blow up in our face and we can't even ask them anything?" Another focus group participant made a similar comment, stating, "Sometimes, the kids get out of control. That's why they lose their patience, but some of us, we need that patience, because some of us don't learn as fast."

Tying It All Together

Based on the study results that I presented in this chapter, it appears that most teachers at American High School had a favorable view of themselves and their students, and most students in the study had a favorable view of their teachers. However, students were less likely than teachers to have a positive impression of teachers. In some cases, there were distinct gender differences in how students responded to various questionnaire items, and in many cases, there were noticeable racial and ethnic differences, with higher percentages of African Americans and Latinos holding negative views of their teachers than whites. In other words, in a number of instances, students appeared to be having racialized and noticeably different schooling experiences and receiving differential treatment from teachers based on students' race and/or gender.

Two of the most troubling findings discussed in this chapter reveal that more than half the black and Latino students who completed the questionnaire said they wanted better teachers, and more than 40 percent didn't believe that most of their teachers cared about them. This first finding is especially important because it suggests that many teachers at American High School were not as effective as they thought they were or needed to be. In other words, they failed to meet the students' standard of "highly qualified" teacher even if they did meet that of the U.S. Department of Education.

The second finding is also noteworthy because some researchers have argued that students of color are more likely to be motivated to achieve academically when their teachers care about them on a personal and academic level. For example, in its study of high-performing, high-poverty schools in Kentucky, the Prichard

Committee for Academic Excellence identified seven common characteristics of high-performing schools. One of these characteristics involved relationships on campus. At the high-performing schools, "Respectful relationships were observed among adults, between adults and students, and among students."[19] Although this second finding may or may not have been correlated to the widespread student underachievement at American High School, the first undoubtedly was. As I stated earlier in this chapter, numerous researchers have maintained that teacher quality and student achievement are linked, and students know the difference between a good teacher and a bad one.

What We Can Do

In the next sections, I offer recommendations to administrators, teachers, parents, and policymakers.

Administrators

The research on high-performing, high-minority, high-poverty schools indicates that in these schools, administrators play an important role in improving students' academic performance. Most high-performing schools are led by effective school leaders who take a holistic and comprehensive approach to improving their schools. Providing adequate support for teachers and students is one way in which they do this.[20] Administrators must ensure that teachers have the resources, information, and technical assistance they need in order to teach well. But this isn't enough. They must also ensure that teachers have the right mind-set and attitudes about their students. To do this, administrators must first do their own personal and professional growth work in this area. If a school administrator, especially the principal, fundamentally believes that African American, Latino, Southeast Asian, Native American, and low-income white students are inferior to middle- and upper-class whites, this leader won't be effective in urban schools or schools that are predominated by these groups—America's stepchildren. For one thing, such an administrator won't have high expectations because he or she believes that these groups aren't capable of academic excellence. Having high expectations is one of the hallmarks of high-performing schools.[21] An administrator with low expectations of students won't expect much from teachers either, and teachers with negative beliefs about these groups of students will be permitted to continue to promote inequality of educational opportunity through their low expectations. So before school administrators can create a school environment in which every student has caring and qualified teachers, each school administrator must do what I call "a checkup from the neck up": each administrator must examine his or her own mind-set about students, by asking the following questions:

- Do I truly believe that *all* students, regardless of race, ethnicity, gender, or socioeconomic background, are capable of being academically successful?

- Do I believe that *all* students deserve outstanding teachers?

- Do I have negative beliefs about the students' home life and community that prevent me from seeing their academic potential?

- Do I treat students in the manner in which I would want my own children to be treated by educators?

- Do I treat students' parents respectfully, or do I try to intimidate them or minimize their concerns?

- Am I strongly committed to finding the information and resources that are necessary to improve student achievement at my school?

- Am I familiar with the research on high-performing, high-poverty, high-minority schools?

- What can I do to change any of my beliefs that might prevent me from truly improving student achievement at my school?

- Am I willing to continue to work on my own beliefs, attitudes, and behaviors on an ongoing basis?
- What individuals, books, articles, and other resources might help me improve in these areas?

After each administrator has begun to examine his or her personal beliefs that might keep him or her from becoming an effective school leader and has created a related action plan, the second step is to begin to help teachers improve specifically in the area of their beliefs and attitudes about students. A teacher who believes that certain students are lazy, dumb, culturally deprived, and undeserving of an outstanding education won't ever become a caring and effective teacher. Unfortunately, because of the strong influence of teachers' unions, rotten teachers who are ineffective and who have bad attitudes and negative beliefs about students are often permitted to spend their careers indulging in unprofessional and destructive behavior, especially in urban schools and high-poverty, high-minority schools—in other words, in schools that are predominated by America's stepchildren.

Ideally, principals should hire teachers who have good teaching skills and great attitudes about students. In reality, of course, some principals are placed at schools where there is already a strong and powerful contingent of negative teachers. Other principals are duped into hiring teachers who know the right things to say during a job interview but who show their true negative colors after they get hired. Negative teachers can thwart even the most well-meaning principal's school reform efforts. Therefore, principals must do their best to help these teachers become effective or, in the case of teachers who refuse to change, help them leave the school permanently. This requires courage and persistence on the principal's part. It may also require battling the teachers' union.

The principal should also address teachers' mind-sets and attitudes through mandatory professional development workshops that focus on these topics and through the principal's behavior and the messages that he or she gives to teachers about students and expectations. After realizing that a teacher or group of teachers isn't willing to improve in these areas, the principal should start creating a paper trail by documenting negative comments and behaviors that go against the school's explicit vision statement for student achievement. Teachers' attitudes and behaviors should also be addressed during formal and informal evaluations conducted on a regular basis. One of the main reasons bad teachers are able to shortchange students academically is that in too many schools, the administrators rarely visit classrooms and are out of touch with what is really going on behind closed doors. Administrators should visit classrooms regularly, give deserving teachers positive feedback, and provide teachers who are struggling in any area—including their beliefs and attitudes about students—with the assistance they need.

Another way that administrators can help teachers improve in these areas is to believe students and parents when they complain about negative and ineffective teachers. When a pattern of complaint about a teacher's negative behavior begins to emerge, the worst thing a principal can do is to ignore the complaints. As the designated school leader, the principal has a professional obligation to investigate these complaints and help the teacher rectify counterproductive behaviors stemming from the teacher's negative beliefs.

Teachers

Like school administrators, teachers must be willing to examine their beliefs and attitudes that impede their efficacy with students. Teachers shouldn't wait until they're required to attend professional development workshops or conferences that address these topics. Every teacher walks into the classroom with a set of beliefs and attitudes that are a product of his or her socialization and upbringing, the media, and other influences. Because most Americans have been socialized to believe that whites are superior to people of color, and most teachers in the United States are white, teachers are very likely to bring negative "mental baggage" into the classroom with them that can have a detrimental effect on student learning and their relations with students. Sadly, this problem is prevalent among teachers of color as well as white teachers. For example, on several occasions, various educators have complained to me about black teachers who didn't want to teach black kids and who made derogatory comments about the home lives of low-income black students. In *Black Students/Middle Class Teachers*, Jawanza Kunjufu writes extensively about black and white teachers who are ineffective with black students for a number of reasons.[22] This book should be required reading for all teachers, including Asian American and Latino teachers.

The first thing that teachers can do is to be honest with themselves as they examine their baggage. Many teachers remain in denial about their negative beliefs, but students can detect the truth. The three-part, long-term professional development plan that I included in *Through Ebony Eyes* is one resource that teachers can use in the privacy of their own home. Another is *Overcoming Our Racism: The Journey to Liberation*. In this outstanding book, Derald Wing Sue, a Chinese American professor who has studied racism for more than thirty years, includes many great exercises that educators can use to uncover their baggage and improve their teaching efficacy. Teachers should also read Gary Howard's *We Can't Teach What We Don't Know*.

One of the best strategies that teachers can use to work on their mind-sets and attitudes is to listen to messages from students and parents. When a parent or student accuses a teacher of being racist or uncaring, for instance, the teacher can choose to ignore the allegation, become defensive, or use it as an opportunity for personal and professional growth. Of course, parents and students can be wrong, and teachers can be falsely accused. However, when there are patterns and the same complaints keep surfacing, a wise teacher will examine his or her own behavior to try to identify the source of the problem.

Finally, to become highly qualified, teachers must

- Know their subject matter well
- Know how to make the subject matter interesting and comprehensible to students by using diverse teaching strategies

- Be well prepared on a daily basis
- Know how to write good lesson plans
- Write their objectives and agenda on the board each day
- Make their objectives clear to students
- Be willing to give extra help
- Have good classroom management skills
- Be patient with struggling students
- Give a "reasonable" amount of homework that is relevant to class work, tests, and quizzes
- Understand their students' cultures
- Genuinely care about students' personal and academic welfare

Teachers who need help in any of these areas must be honest with themselves and seek related information by reading professional literature; attending conferences and workshops; and requesting assistance from mentor teachers, good veteran teachers, and school administrators.

Parents

Parents should know their children well enough to be able to determine when a child is telling the truth and when he or she is lying. If a child who has previously loved school and loved his or her teachers starts to complain about a specific teacher, a parent should pay close attention. Parents who are able to visit the classroom and observe what's going on should do so. Asking the child for specific reasons why he or she dislikes a teacher is another strategy. Sometimes a child who has been subjected to low expectations by teachers in the past may assume that a teacher with high expectations and a rigorous curriculum is being mean. In that case, the parent should explain that the teacher with high expectations believes that the child is smart enough to rise to the challenge. If the child is struggling, the parent should find ways to assist the child through tutoring, helping with homework, buying related workbooks, and so on, and asking the teacher for additional strategies. However, if a child says that a teacher is singling him or her out, engaging in unfair disciplinary practices, making racist or sexist comments, not giving extra help to struggling students, or embarrassing students who ask for help, the parent should be assertive. Contacting the child's counselor or the school principal, and even insisting that the student be transferred to another class are options that the parent should consider.

Policymakers

One specific way that policymakers can increase the likelihood that students will have caring and effective teachers is to enact policies that make it easier for school principals to get rid of bad teachers. Another is to make the improvement of low-performing schools—which of course are usually situated in high-minority, low-income communities and populated by America's stepchildren—a national priority in word and deed. This is a recommendation that I will make repeatedly in the remaining chapters of this book.

Policymakers must be willing to address systemic problems in the communities surrounding underperforming schools. These problems often affect students' learning and behavior at school, and increase the likelihood of teacher attrition. When a low-performing school has a high rate of teacher turnover, principals become desperate to hire teachers and often have to settle for underqualified candidates. Underqualified teachers are unlikely to have the knowledge, skills, and experience needed to prepare students for standardized tests or to offer them an outstanding quality of instruction. As long as policymakers refuse to provide adequate funding to resolve many of the problems in low-income communities and their schools, true reform will never occur in America. Instead, America's stepchildren will continue to be viewed and treated as second-class citizens and forced to attend second-, third-, and fourth-rate schools.

A Final Word

In every profession and organization, many employees would be considered average in terms of their productivity and the quality of their work. There are also employees who are slackers. These people do mediocre work or the bare minimum required to keep their jobs. Then there are the overachievers—employees who go beyond the call of duty. They work hard and try to do their very best. I have met numerous educators who fall into each of these three categories.

Recently, after one of my presentations, I met an individual with a negative attitude toward students. This new teacher, a young white man, taught at a predominantly Latino school. Throughout my presentation, I had noticed that he looked bored and sometimes even downright hostile. Afterwards, he approached me to tell me that he hadn't learned one valuable thing during the entire four-hour presentation. Why he chose to stay for the duration when he could have walked out is a mystery to me. As I listened to him speak, I gradually learned more about his background and how his own schooling experiences had affected his attitude toward his students.

He said he'd grown up in a farming community in the northwest and had had a difficult childhood. At school, he was a marginal student who felt that his teachers didn't care about him. In spite of this, he had somehow eventually gotten his life together, earned a college degree, and entered the teaching force. For some reason, the difficulties he had experienced during his own childhood hadn't created a sense of caring or empathy in him toward other students who were experiencing hardship. At the time of our discussion, he was teaching at a high-poverty school in a community in which unemployment and crime rates were high. When I told him that he was in a position to make a lasting positive impact on his students, he coldly replied, "No one helped *me* when *I* was growing up. *I* had to do it all by myself. Why should *I* help *them?*"

His reply unnerved me, but it also convinced me that there was no way that I'd be able to change this man's mind-set about his students. After all, if he had "listened" to a four-hour presentation that I'd just given and hadn't learned anything useful from it, how likely was it that the follow-up conversation would really matter? His mind was made up, and at best all I could do was give him advice that was in his students' best interest: "You teach at a school where the kids really need good, caring teachers," I said. "Please do me a favor and leave that school. With your attitude, you're going to do a lot of damage, because I'm sure your students have already realized that you don't care about them."

In the twenty-four years that I've been an educator, I've met many teachers who behaved as if they didn't care about students' personal or academic welfare, especially students from low-income backgrounds and black and Latino students. But these were usually veteran teachers—teachers who were suffering from burnout, hopelessness, and an underlying fear that they weren't effective. Of course, some of these individuals were color-blind racists—teachers who were in denial about their own fundamental belief that blacks and Latinos are cognitively inferior and culturally deprived, and who engaged in grade inflation and had low expectations as a result of their deficit mind-set. But I'd never heard a *new teacher* say outright that he didn't really care about his students.

Although there are far too many educators who have negative attitudes about their students and aren't willing to go the extra mile, I'm grateful that there are countless others who choose to be different. Of all the presentations that I'm invited to give at schools and conferences throughout the nation, my very favorite presentation is called "Becoming a Life-Changing, Powerful, Influential Teacher of Children from Challenging Backgrounds." During this resiliency presentation, I get to describe educators who try to make a lasting impact on students. One of my favorite stories is about a white vice principal who became a strong advocate for children who were being mislabeled and mistreated.

When I first met him, he worked at a predominantly white school that had an unwelcoming attitude toward black children who were bused to the school from a low-income neighborhood.

Predictably, the same things that happen at schools throughout the nation began to occur quickly at that school: black students, especially boys, were labeled as troublemakers, and teachers were kicking them out of class on a regular basis. But the vice principal decided to become proactive. Although he didn't receive extra pay for choosing to go the extra mile and becoming an advocate for the children who were being mistreated, he made a choice to do so anyway. Besides trying to serve as a mentor to several of these students, the vice principal tried to help teachers see when they were unfairly targeting black students and overreacting to behaviors that they ignored in white children. He also created a formal mentoring program in which he encouraged retired adults to come to the school to work one-on-one with struggling students.

During my resiliency presentation, I tell many similar stories about great educators. My goal is to convince the audience that each teacher and administrator can *choose* to make a positive impact on students. In addition to telling them about educators who have done this, I also tell them about students who benefited from having powerful, influential, life-changing teachers. I tell them about Mrs. Tessem, my sixth-grade teacher, and about how her dedication changed the course of my life, and I tell about many others, such as Gavin De Becker.

De Becker had a horrific childhood. His mother was not only addicted to drugs but also mentally unstable, and got involved with a string of abusive and dysfunctional men. At an early age, like many children from troubled homes, De Becker had to find a way to survive in the midst of this turmoil. One of his teachers stood out above the rest and changed his life. Today, instead of being a failure, De Becker is an extremely successful business owner and author, and is an expert on stalkers and serial killers.[23]

All students deserve to have great teachers and an outstanding K–12 education. Unfortunately, this is not the experience of countless students throughout the nation, especially America's stepchildren. Instead of shaking our heads and ignoring the situation, there is much work that each adult can do to bring about reform.

2

"It Would Be Nice to Learn Something About My Culture"

A Plea for a Culturally Relevant and More Interesting Education

Many years ago, an African American professor told me an interesting story. At the time when the incident occurred, she was sitting in a meeting that was presided over by the president of the university where she worked at that time. The meeting was well under way, when another professor arrived. Because the late arrival, a middle-aged white woman who taught dance classes at the university, was clearly out of breath, the other meeting participants couldn't help but notice her. Out of concern, the president stopped the meeting to ask why she was out of breath. At that point, according to the African American professor who recounted this story to me, the dance instructor gushed to the president, "Oh, President _____: I've just come from *Watts*, where I've been teaching the children to dance!" On hearing this, the president commended the woman not only for going to Watts—a city with a negative reputation stemming from the notorious riots of the 1960s—but for going there with the "noble" purpose of teaching the children, mostly poor blacks and Latinos, to *dance*.

The African American professor didn't share the president's enthusiasm, and when I heard the story, I didn't either. "The last thing the kids in Watts need," she told me, "is for someone to teach them how to dance. Most of them already know how to dance. The real issue is that the way *they* dance wasn't acceptable to that white woman, so she went there to teach them modern dance." In other words, the white professor went to Watts to teach "culture"—her own—to children of color.

Despite the fact that the professor and I laughed sarcastically about this incident, the deeper message angered us, and this issue of determining or judging what knowledge and behavior is of value, often referred to as "the culture wars," continues to cause disagreement in schools and other segments of U.S. society. Although Nuala O'Faolain was referring specifically to the quality of literary works, her words summarize the subject of the debate: "I recognise that there is a hierarchy. There is great and less great and so on, down to trash. I think classic literature is deservedly so-called. . . . I don't have any objection to the art made by dead white males. . . ."[1] And neither do most teachers. The problem is that many whites view the literature and other contributions of nonwhites as less important, unimportant, or even trash.

The culture wars, which position the traditional Western curriculum against multiculturalism—the contributions of nonwhites—have a long history. According to Noll, the tone was set during the early 1970s. Since then, many educators, authors, and public figures have taken strong stances either in favor of or against diversifying the curriculum. In *Taking Sides*, Noll referred to the culture wars as ". . . an educational battlefield that extends from kindergarten to graduate school."[2] In an article titled "Battle over Multicultural Education Rises in Intensity," Viadero remarked, "Two decades after educators and politicians began calling on schools to teach more about the contributions of blacks, Hispanics, Native Americans, and other ethnic and racial groups long absent from the curriculum, the debate over how best to do that is reaching new—and sometimes bitter—levels of intensity in schools across the country."[3]

Viadero's article was published more than a decade ago, but her words are still timely. The debate over what information is of value and what should be included in school curricula continues today. In *Through Ebony Eyes*, I made a related point: "Although multicultural education and culturally relevant teaching have been discussed in academic circles for decades, they are still topics of debate, confusion, and resistance among educators. There are several reasons why. Among them are cultural insensitivity, cultural ignorance, and teachers' resistance."[4]

In *And Still We Rise*, Corwin illustrated this debate well and personified the culture wars through his contrast of two teachers at Crenshaw High School in Los Angeles.[5] Both teachers, Toni Little, a white woman, and Anna Moultrie, a black woman, taught English courses in the school's gifted magnet program during the year that Corwin observed and interacted with students, teachers, and administrators at the school. Because Moultrie's eleventh graders would have Little as a teacher during their senior year, she and Little could have been working very closely together to design a cohesive curriculum. However, several factors prevented them from working as a team. In fact, school politics, personality differences, racial issues, and their beliefs not only prevented them from working collaboratively but actually made them arch enemies. Consequently, on numerous occasions, their students were caught in a culture-war crossfire. According to Corwin, "Little's reading list for her AP class contains no works by black writers . . ." because she believed that it wasn't the school's job to teach students about their culture or race. She also believed that teaching the classics was the best way to prepare students for college and the AP exams they would be required to take during their senior year.[6]

Conversely, Moultrie taught ". . . some classics . . . but also [felt that it was] important to expose her students to black authors. And she frequently [integrated] current events and societal issues into her discussions."[7] When criticized by Little, Moultrie defended her curriculum by saying that ". . . her goals [were] greater than merely lecturing and giving exams."[8] In other words, she believed that she was teaching ". . . the *whole* child. . . ."[9] and ". . . not merely preparing students for college, but for life."[10]

During my own years as a junior high school and high school teacher in urban-fringe schools, my teaching motto was similar to Moultrie's and that of celebrated educator Marva Collins in that I tried to teach my students both academic skills and life skills.[11] I used a variety of strategies to do this. Like Moultrie, I used multicultural literature, the classics, and current events in my lesson plans. Because I taught at a high school that was nearly 80 percent Hispanic, the inclusion of multicultural works in the curriculum made perfect sense to me. My job was made easier because the district- and state-recommended reading lists included numerous multicultural works.

Like many other educators and researchers, I strongly believe that *all* students can benefit from a curriculum that stresses both academic *and* life skills and that includes both the Western or classic canon and multicultural works. Because we live in a diverse world, all students, including white students, need to hear about the contributions that marginalized groups have made to world advancement.[12]

Experts on culturally relevant pedagogy, such as Lisa Delpit, Gloria Ladson-Billings, Beverly Cross, Asa Hilliard, Geneva Gay, Janice Hale, and others, underscore the fact that such pedagogy is mutually beneficial for students and teachers, primarily through improving student achievement.[13] In *The Dreamkeepers: Successful Teachers of African American Children*, Ladson-Billings summarized the definition and goals well by stating, "Specifically, culturally relevant teaching is a pedagogy that empowers students intellectually, socially, emotionally, and politically by using cultural referents to impart knowledge, skills, and attitudes."[14] Cross emphasized that in culturally responsive teaching, "Sources of knowledge are not limited to textbooks, teachers, and the written curriculum, but instead include the knowledge and experiences students gain outside of school"; such teaching is participatory, personal, situated around big ideas, and built upon emotional and societal issues.[15] Gay said that among other benefits, culturally responsive teaching requires teachers to use a variety of instructional strategies so they will target all learning styles.[16]

In spite of the strong arguments that the aforementioned scholars and other researchers have made about the advantages of diversifying the curriculum and the benefits of culturally responsive teaching, the controversy continues over what knowledge is most valuable and what students should be taught. As Corwin's portrayals of Moultrie and Little illustrate, culture-war battles are often played out in the classroom, and students can get caught in the middle. While the "experts" continue to debate this issue, not enough attention has been given to the voices of students and how the culture wars affect them. So, in the next section, we will listen to what students at American High School said about the curriculum.

What the Students Said

Numerous questionnaire items gave the students who participated in the study at American High School opportunities to express their views about the school's curriculum. Some questionnaire items pertained to students' overall attitude about the curriculum; others were more specific. Although nearly 70 percent of the students said they learned a lot of useful information in most of their classes, Latino students were more likely than whites and blacks to say this. Black females and white males were least likely to say they learned a lot of useful information in their classes. For many students, boredom, low teacher expectations, and an irrelevant curriculum were related problems.

Boredom

Boredom was a problem for nearly 60 percent of the students in the study, yet the majority of the teachers had said that most of their students enjoyed their classes. Black females and Latino males were more likely than others to say that their classes were boring.

Teaching Standards and Expectations

During the earlier phase of the study, nearly 40 percent of the teachers said that they sometimes had to lower their academic standards, and 80 percent said that some of their colleagues had low expectations. In the student phase of the study, nearly 40 percent of the students said they wanted a more challenging curriculum, but black students were less likely than Latinos and whites to say this. For each racial group, females were more likely than males to say they wanted more challenging classes.

Several focus group participants explained why many students wanted more challenging classes. As one student stated, "There are certain classes that are so easy to get an A in but you don't even learn anything the whole year." Another student said, "I think that it's obvious: when you're in honors and AP, they're challenging, but when you're in regular classes, sometimes it feels like you're in Special Ed. There's a big difference." A female focus group participant remarked, "I don't know. It doesn't seem like we are in high school to me. It feels like we are just learning everything we have already learned before. I have some advanced classes. Right now, I am just in Honors classes, and they are a little bit more challenging, but they don't really offer that many honors or Advanced Placement classes."

Cultural Relevance

In the earlier phase of the study, almost all the teachers said that they made the curriculum relevant to their students' lives, but many students at American High School disagreed. The student questionnaire contained two statements about the cultural relevance of the school curricula. More than half of the students said that in most of their classes they hadn't learned as much as they would like to learn about their own culture. Black students were much more likely than Latinos and whites to say this. Black females were more likely than any group to say they had not learned as much as they would like about their culture, and white males were the least likely to say this.

Nearly 60 percent of the students said that they wanted to learn more about their culture in their classes. Whereas the overwhelming majority of black students (75 percent) and nearly 60 percent of Latinos indicated that this was true, only 36 percent of the white students concurred. Once again, black females were more likely than other students to express this desire, and white males were the least likely to do so.

During the focus group discussions, many students elaborated on why they wanted to learn more about their culture in their classes. The recurring theme from numerous African American students was that they were exposed to only a limited amount of black history at school, and what they were exposed to in class tended to be negative. For example, an African American male summarized one of the main themes when he stated, "You learn about negative black culture. You learn about slavery. You don't learn about positive black people." Another student added that in his history textbook, "There's a little paragraph about Martin Luther King." Numerous focus group participants agreed with an African American girl who said, "Most of the stuff that they talk about is slavery and how it was back in the old days. Then, I heard someone talk about Martin Luther King, but when they do talk about him, it's like around a certain time, not all the time."

The majority of the African American focus group participants said that one of the main reasons they objected to how black history was being taught in their classes was that "they make it seem like black people haven't done anything but be slaves." Another girl added, "It's annoying to always keep reading about slavery, because you end up always reading about the same thing. They don't move on." One student summarized the feelings of many African American focus group participants by stating, "They act like [slavery is] all we come from, when we have great black poets. We have civil rights leaders, we have great black lawyers, authors, all kinds of black people, and they act like all we come from is cotton fields." Another African American focus group participant made the following comment: "It's not so much that I don't want to learn about slavery, but *all* they do is talk about slavery. They need to talk more about black accomplishments, see how we *rose* from slavery. All they have is slavery and that's it. Blacks were slaves.

That's it, but we've accomplished so much. There's so much in American culture that black people have contributed to."

One African American male focus group participant said that he didn't have a problem with being taught about slavery, but did have a problem with the way other students behaved when slavery was being taught in his classes. He explained, "I really personally don't have a problem with watching those movies but there's other nationalities in the class, and they like to make little smart comments, and it's not funny. It ain't funny at all." Another participant agreed that students did need to learn about slavery, but like many focus group participants, she stressed that the positive aspects of black culture also needed to be included in the curriculum. She said, "I think that not only do people just know about slavery, but they only know about certain black people, like Martin Luther King and Rosa Parks. There's other people than just them [who] are black." An African American student, who was grateful that her mother had exposed her to aspects of her culture that the school system had neglected to teach her, remarked, "If it hadn't been for my mom teaching me from the time that I was five, I would not know half of the great black people in America or all the stuff they accomplished. I'd be thinking that Harriet Tubman, Martin Luther King, and Sojourner Truth are the only three that did something great."

Some focus group participants also complained about the way that Black History Month is observed at American High School. For example, one African American student remarked, "They only dedicate one month to black history when history is supposed to be taught throughout the year. So, if there was black history, why can't we learn it throughout the year, not just in February?" Although some students complained that only one month was devoted to black history, others said that they didn't have any classes that even devoted one month to it. As one focus group participant explained, "I don't even have a class that teaches black history. Last year, I had U.S. history, and we didn't learn anything about black history, not even during Black History Month. They didn't even talk about it." Another African American student remarked, "They feel like they can baby us by just saying on the PA system, 'Oh, well, this person did this,' and that's supposed to just keep us quiet, and we're supposed to just be okay with that. But we don't learn anything about our own culture at all. I'm a junior now, and I'm in Advanced Placement U.S. History, and I still haven't learned anything about my culture."

During some focus group discussions, several students became angry. For example, one African American girl complained:

> When it was Black History Month, February, none of the teachers said anything about that. We're learning that stupid book, *The Odyssey*, I think it's called. I was looking forward to Black History Month, reading some interesting stuff, like Maya Angelou, in our English class. But we're learning *The Odyssey* and Shakespeare and I'm like, "What does this have to do with me being a black child?" Me, personally, I like to read black novels because I can relate to the people in [those] books. I feel that the more you read something that you're interested in, the higher you'll go in your reading, and higher-level books pertaining to that subject, not necessarily just higher books, like Shakespeare.

Numerous white focus group participants also complained about how black history was taught in their classes. These students tended to believe that when slavery was taught, some of their African American classmates became angry and scapegoated all whites. As a result, white students felt uncomfortable. These students were also upset that their teachers usually ignored the racial animosity that surfaced in class at these times. For example, one white focus group participant stated:

> What I found interesting mostly is history class. That's when we start studying civil rights, which I feel is a very important part of history and stuff. The African American students in our class, all of a sudden get so defensive, especially when we talk about slavery and stuff. And if anything, they become more racist than the white people about it. Just because

of what our ancestors did, isn't necessarily what we represent, and they still think that is what we represent—that every black should be in slavery and shouldn't have rights. We'll talk about it in class, not ignorantly, but not know all of the facts and just generalizing [about] what had happened. But when they get mad, the teachers don't do anything.

The recurring theme among Latino focus group participants was that they rarely learned *anything at all* about their culture in class. For example, many focus group participants agreed with a Latina who stated, "I've already learned a lot of American history my whole life, because I've lived here my whole life. So, it would be nice to learn something about my culture, too. It wouldn't hurt, right?" An African American male, who noticed that the history and contributions of Latinos were absent from the curriculum, asked, "Where's the Mexican people in the history books? You don't be learning nothing about them." However, one Latina remarked, "I don't really care to learn about my culture. I live in America, and I'd rather learn about that. Right now, in eleventh grade English, we learn about Americans. I'd rather learn about that than the Mexican people who traveled across the country. I don't care about that."

Although three Latino students agreed with the previous statement, the majority didn't. Instead, most agreed with the following rebuttal of another Latina focus group participant:

People have ways of viewing everyone. If you're Mexican, they assume that you're a "beaner," or there [are] certain ways that they view you. So maybe, if the intelligence of Mexicans or the intelligence of Puerto Ricans, or whatever was brought up, people wouldn't be negative about each other. White people wouldn't say, "Oh, beaners," or Mexicans wouldn't say, "Oh, white people," or whatever. . . . Intelligence about everybody in all the different cultures [needs to be shown], and everybody needs to realize who they are and what they are, and love yourself for who you are and where you come from.

In summarizing the benefits of learning more about his own culture, an African American male student spoke for many Latinos and African Americans by stating, "I have AP History, and I find myself doing better on tests when I'm reading and writing about stuff that pertains to my culture. If they incorporated more of that, then maybe I could do better in that class."

The Relevance of the Curriculum to the Community and the "Real World"

Several questionnaire items gave students an opportunity to discuss additional aspects of the curriculum. In the earlier phase of the study, nearly all the teachers said that their curricula and instructional practices would improve the quality of students' lives, but in the student phase of the study, nearly half the students said that most of their classes weren't really teaching them what they needed to know to survive in their communities; a higher percentage of students of color said this than whites. Black females were more likely to say that the curriculum wasn't teaching them what they needed to know, and white males were more likely to agree that it was.

Furthermore, nearly 60 percent of the students who completed the questionnaire said that most of their classes weren't preparing them for the "real world." Half the white students agreed with this statement; a noticeably higher percentage of blacks (60 percent) and Latinos (61 percent) did. White females were almost twice as likely as white males to agree with this statement.

Homework

Regarding homework, nearly half the students said that most of the homework that was assigned to them wasn't very useful. A slightly higher percentage of whites than blacks and Latinos felt this way, but there was little difference among the percentages of students from the three racial and ethnic groups in their attitudes about the benefits of their homework. (I will return to this topic in the next chapter, because it also appeared to be related to students' attitudes about state-mandated exams.)

The School's Reading Program

Even though there wasn't a formal questionnaire item about the school's reading program, students made it clear during the focus group discussions that they wanted to discuss it. American High School had recently begun requiring that students use the Accelerated Reader (AR) program, and the English teachers had stipulated that 15 or 20 percent of the students' course grade would be based on the number of points they had accumulated by reading AR books and passing the related tests. This requirement not only added to students' testing woes but also caused many to become resistant. Students complained about the culturally limited selection of books they were required to read, the unfairness of the tests, and also the unfairness of having a course grade linked to reading assignments that had to be done outside of class on a limited number of books.

A male student, who suspected that trickery was involved in the AR testing program, remarked: "Half the time, you read the book and it'll be a huge boring book. Then, the test will point out something in the book that you weren't even paying attention to." A student who agreed with this point made the following accusation: "I also feel that they try to ask trick questions to see if you really paid attention to the book. Like, they'll ask something like, 'Say a [person] in the book went to the store. Who did he walk with? Why did he go there?' Who cares? We just know he went there." One student commented, "It's easier to talk about the book if you like it and tell them, and get them to know that you did read it, than to sit there and answer questions about the book. They go after the little bitty details that you're not going to remember about the book."

Another student said, "I think that if everyone chose a book that they wanted to read and then took a test on it, they would do much better and get more points, even if the questions are hard. If you're reading what you like and then taking a test on it, you might have a better chance of getting a good grade."

A student who didn't understand why the tests were even required remarked, "I don't get the AR tests. We're supposed to read at our reading level, but some of the higher reading levels, to me, it's like boring books. Like, the lower reading levels are more interesting. So, I read one and they told me not to read those books anymore, but how you gonna read a boring book?"

Because so many students were upset about being "forced" to read books that many of them didn't want to read in the first place, plus the fact that their English grade was tied to AR points, several focus group participants said that cheating had become common at the school. Students found "creative" ways to outsmart their teachers and the AR program in order to earn points for books that they hadn't actually read. The topic of cheating will also surface in the next chapter.

Tying It All Together

Many years ago, during a presentation at a large reading conference, I shared a story from my childhood that is related to the themes that surfaced in this chapter. I told the audience that my elementary school teachers came close to making me dislike reading, because I hated the required reading books: the Dick and Jane basal reading series, which were considered to be ". . . a hallmark of American education in the 1950s and 1960s. . . ."[17] The preface of the *Storybook Treasury of Dick and Jane*, a reissue of the original stories, states, "Generations of American children learned to read with Dick and Jane and many still cherish the memory of reading the simple stories on their own."[18]

During my presentation, I told the audience that I'm not one of those individuals who "cherish the memory." In my opinion, the books were terribly boring, bland stories about children whose world was totally unrelated to my own. It was actually my mother, instead of my teachers, who motivated me to become an avid reader. Even though she had only a high school education and was a single parent on welfare, my mother constantly read when I was a child. She loved reading her *True Romance* and *True Confessions* magazines, but warned us that they were off-limits to us; we were not to touch her magazines. Being the curious children we were, my older sister and I wanted to know why we couldn't touch her magazines. So, behind my mother's back, we would "borrow" them and hide in a bedroom closet as we tried to make sense of them. This is how we became excellent readers. The juicy content of the magazines was so interesting that we became intrinsically motivated to read.[19]

At the end of my presentation in Sacramento, a middle-aged white teacher approached me. She wanted me to know that my story about my dislike of the Dick and Jane books had offended her. "*I* grew up reading Dick and Jane," she said, and "*I* loved them!" She turned on her heels and left in a huff.

Since then, I have recounted both stories—the one from my childhood and the one about the middle-aged teacher—to numerous graduate students, educators, and other conference attendees. Each time, I try to illustrate two points. First, I emphasize that there wasn't necessarily anything wrong with the Dick and Jane books and that my goal is not to offend individuals who loved the series. My point is that the books were boring to me because I couldn't relate to the main characters' experiences or lifestyle. Second, I express my opinion that the angry conference participant demonstrates how difficult it is for some individuals to understand the importance of a culturally relevant curriculum for all students, but particularly for those from marginalized groups, such as African Americans and Latinos—the two groups of students who are most likely to underperform in school. As one of the students at American High School remarked, "I have AP History, and I find myself doing better on tests when I'm reading and writing about stuff that pertains to my culture." Although there is no guarantee that test scores will improve if students are given a more interesting, meaningful, and culturally relevant curriculum that is taught in an inclusive, culturally sensitive manner, I believe that at the very least the boredom and student apathy about class work that abounded at American High School and that is common at other schools nationwide would decrease.

In the meantime, as long as the contributions and experiences of marginalized groups continue to be excluded from the curriculum or only incorporated into the curriculum during Black History Month and Cinco de Mayo, many students will continue to behave in passive-aggressive, if not outright aggressive, ways to express their displeasure with a school system that excludes them and that is out of touch with their real-world needs and interests. In fact, student resistance is one of the main themes of the next chapter, and in this current chapter, I mentioned that students had found ways to cheat in order to get AR points.

School reforms that are out of touch with students' needs will continue to fail as long as policymakers remain oblivious to teachers' needs as well. For example, in the first phase of the study, nearly 30 percent of the teachers at American High School admitted that they didn't use enough innovation or creativity in their lesson plans, and 21 percent said they hadn't received adequate training to teach the majority of their students. The truth of these admissions was borne out by the high percentages of students who were bored in class, who wanted better teachers, and who were dissatisfied with the curriculum and instructional practices.

In sum, one of the main messages that surfaced in this chapter and the previous one is that although most of the teachers thought they were outstanding, in reality they weren't meeting many students' academic needs as well as they could have. All the teachers had at least a bachelor's degree, many had a graduate degree, and most had served in a leadership capacity as a lead teacher, department chair, or mentor teacher at some point, but many weren't "highly qualified" by students' standards, and they weren't that effective. The U.S. Department of Education's definition of a highly qualified teacher doesn't encompass certain aspects of teaching, such as caring and the ability to create a culturally relevant curriculum, that many students at American High School equated with effectiveness, and NCLB ignores students' need for a culturally relevant, empowering education that prepares them for the real world. Until these problems are rectified, lasting high school reform won't occur.

What We Can Do

The recommendations that follow can help administrators, teachers, parents, and policymakers improve school curricula.

Administrators

In order to improve the curriculum, administrators must set a schoolwide tone about learning which emphasizes that every teacher should spend the majority of class time on *instruction*. Providing teachers with adequate professional development workshops covering the following topics should be helpful:

- How to create interesting *and* relevant lesson plans
- How to tie lesson plans to state standards
- What culturally relevant teaching entails and why it's important
- Strategies to make lesson plans culturally relevant and relevant to the real world

Second, administrators can sponsor field trips to cultural museums and host school assemblies that allow students to showcase their talents and that bring community-based cultural groups to perform traditional songs and dances, recite poetry, and so on. Another way that administrators can make schools more culturally inclusive is to invite guest speakers from all cultural and racial groups into the school to speak about topics of interest to students, share stories about resiliency, and explain how students can improve society.

Third, administrators should ensure that the school library is well stocked with a diverse, interesting, and extensive selection of books, magazines, films, and other resources. Teachers should be able to borrow multicultural materials throughout the school year, and students should have access to a wealth of multicultural reading material. The library should be decorated with multicultural posters, and the librarian should be adding new multicultural books and magazines to the school's collection on an ongoing basis.

Fourth, the principal should do his or her best to hire a racially and ethnically diverse staff. School custodians, security, and cafeteria workers shouldn't be the only adults of color on any K–12 campus in America. Administration, staff, and the teaching force should reflect the diversity of the U.S. population. When there is only one African American, Latino, or Asian American teacher at the school, that individual carries the heavy burden of having to be the resident expert about diversity issues. He or she will find it difficult to educate colleagues, administrators, students, and staff about the importance of a culturally relevant curriculum. Principals should therefore be careful not to engage in tokenism in their hiring practices. Having one token person of color from each racial and ethnic group is not fair to teachers or to students.

Finally, another way that school administrators can make their schools more inclusive is to use parents as a resource. Principals can begin this process at the very beginning of the school year by finding out which parents are willing to visit the school later in the year to do "cultural awareness" presentations. Sending notes, flyers, and verbal messages to parents is a simple way of letting parents know that their participation and expertise are welcome at the school. At several designated times throughout the year, small groups of parents can perform and share their knowledge during assemblies or host a schoolwide cultural awareness day, or they can be invited to visit classrooms on a rotating basis.

Teachers

As I often say, when the classroom door is closed, every teacher is a powerful person who can use her power for good or for bad purposes. A teacher who is naïve, culturally insensitive, racist, or ignorant about racial and cultural groups other than his or her own can do a lot of damage to students through words, behaviors, and both the hidden and the formal curriculum.

As I will say repeatedly throughout this book, effective teaching starts with the teacher's mind-set about students. That mind-set includes the teacher's beliefs about students' home life, community, style of discourse, and cultural background. Teachers who subconsciously or consciously believe that black, Latino, Native American, Southeast Asian, or other marginalized groups—including low-income whites—are inferior to middle- and upper-class whites will never be effective with most students in these groups. Like a police radar gun detecting a speeding driver, students will be able to detect the teacher's true feelings. As I will repeat later, this can lead to passive-aggressive behavior, apathy, blatant resistance, and confrontations. So first and foremost, teachers must examine and deal with their mental baggage.

Teachers must also set the appropriate tone in their classroom regarding inclusiveness. No student or group should ever be marginalized, denigrated, or ridiculed in the classroom. The only way that this marginalization can occur is if the teacher has conveyed the message that he or she condones such behavior.

Each teacher should also make the curriculum culturally relevant *throughout the academic year* by including the contributions and experiences of people of color in lesson plans on an ongoing basis. A good way to do this is to teach thematically. Teaching around "big ideas" is a highly recommended comprehension strategy that many reading experts recommend. When I taught high school, I usually designed all my lesson plans around one or two themes or big ideas per quarter. For example, during one quarter, the theme was poverty. Therefore, the literature that I assigned, essay topics, quizzes, tests, class discussions, class projects, mock trials, debates, and so on were all related to this theme in one way or another. Requiring students to read Francisco Jimenez's *The Circuit,* Gary Soto's *Living up the Street,* and John Steinbeck's *The Grapes of Wrath,* and poems and short stories about poverty was an easy way for me to use a diverse array of literature without engaging in tokenism or making students feel that we were focusing only on one group's experiences while ignoring those of others.

Teachers should also make sure that the classroom walls display multicultural posters and that the classroom library contains a diverse selection of books and magazines. Teachers can improve their classroom library collection by asking their friends to donate books and magazines and by taking advantage of book sales at public libraries and the low prices at thrift shops.

Another important way that teachers can make the curriculum more inclusive is to ask students for suggestions and to seek out professional literature and professional development opportunities pertaining specifically to this topic. They can also visit the classrooms of exemplary teachers who are known to use culturally relevant teaching methods. This is especially important for teachers who come from cultural and racial backgrounds that are different from those of their students. Seeking advice from veteran teachers and adults in the community outside the school is a great way to increase cultural sensitivity and avoid blunders that can blow up in a teacher's face.

One of the best ways teachers can improve the curriculum and make it culturally relevant is to remember a point that I constantly stress in one of my presentations called, "What the Statistics Can't Tell You About African Americans and Literacy." The point is that just because a teacher loves a certain book or story, this doesn't mean that students will like it. In fact, students might actually hate the very same book, poem, or short story that the teacher thinks is wonderful. The following two examples illustrate this fact.

The first example pertains to one of my former graduate students. This sixty-five-year-old African American man told our class that during his youth, he was traumatized by being forced to read two so-called classics: *The Adventures of Tom Sawyer* and *The Adventures of Huckleberry Finn*. Although the teachers who required him to read these books that many Americans love probably had good intentions, this student said that the books evoked horrific scenes in his mind. "They reminded me of the images of black men hanging from trees that I used to see in the *Chicago Defender* newspaper," he told us.

The second example concerns my son, Stephen. During the summer before his junior year of high school, an AP English teacher assigned her incoming students to read *The Adventures of Huckleberry Finn* and to write a related essay. At the beginning of the school year, students were going to be tested on the novel. Throughout the summer, I kept asking Stephen about his progress in reading the book. I soon realized that something was wrong. My son has always been an avid reader. In fact, we once had a heated argument in a bookstore because he wanted me to buy more books for him than I wanted to buy that day. This child has always loved reading and receiving books, and I've never had to force him to read anything—that is, until the summer he was required to read *The Adventures of Huckleberry Finn*.

It seemed that the closer we got to the end of summer and time for him to return to school, the more he dragged his feet about finishing the book and essay. I was so perplexed about this that I told him that I wanted to interview him after he'd finished. Although he eventually finished the book, the essay that he wrote was a last-minute rush job that didn't reflect his capabilities. The entire ordeal had been so unpleasant for him that he refused to devote any more time to the assignment than he had to, and when he finished, he threw his copy of the book in a corner of his bedroom and left it there for months.

When we finally sat down for the interview, the reasons for Stephen's resistance became clearer to me. Regarding the subjective term *classic*, he explained, "Classic is such a relative term. To me, *Animorphs* [a series of science fiction books] are classics. I've been able to stay interested in *Animorphs* through all forty books [in the series] and I still want to reread them. I think that what people see as 'classics' [are books that you can] reread and they'll still be just as good [when you reread them]." Stephen shared several reasons why he had such difficulty forcing himself to complete this assignment: "*Huck Finn* is at the bottom of my list. It got all this hype . . . but the people who are giving those reviews are the same type of people. They're not like students, and I don't think that many students liked that book at all. . . ."

Regarding why he had such difficulty forcing himself to complete this assignment, he said:

> First of all, it was a pretty boring book. He was just going through random adventures at the beginning that were just petty, not that interesting. Second of all, they made Mr. Jim have a bad accent and sound stupid and illiterate. So that was just hard to read in general. And it made me angry that they would make him talk like that, but they wouldn't make any of the other characters speak like that. Everybody who wasn't black, spoke proper English or didn't speak anything like Jim spoke.
>
> The story line wasn't that potent. It didn't impact me at all. Huck was supposed to be doing the right thing by saving Jim and getting along with him, but most of it was being done from a racist point of view.
>
> When Huck made his final decision to save Jim, he was like "Okay then, I guess I'll just go to hell" because he was told he'd go to hell for saving a black person. . . . If he's under that impression then, just because he's saving a black person [doesn't make his actions] morally correct.

Unlike *The Adventures of Huckleberry Finn*, Stephen did enjoy reading another so-called classic. He told me: "*The Crucible* was action packed and had a drama-filled story line with all these twists and turns and back stabbing. Also, it didn't have clichés that are commonly found in classics. A cliché is when the good guy always wins. [In *The Crucible*,] the good guy ended up dying for his cause. It was historical fiction, and it had a deeper meaning in general. It was an allegory of the Red Scare."

The main point that teachers should remember from my graduate student's experience, Stephen's experiences, and from the messages that I emphasized previously is that they should give students options. Certain books that have historically been viewed as controversial, including *The Adventures of Huckleberry Finn*, are known to be offensive to African Americans. Why can't teachers give students a list of books or let them go to the school library and select literature that is less offensive yet addresses some of the same themes as the book in question? My friend the late Margaret Goss, a veteran and exemplary educator, ran into this problem many years ago when we both taught at the same junior high school. A parent who was a Jehovah's Witness objected to her daughter being assigned Greek myths to read, because the parent believed they promoted polytheism—the belief in multiple gods. Although Margaret didn't necessarily agree with this view, she thought of optional reading assignments for the student. In other words, she didn't *force* the student to read the myths.

Unfortunately, no matter how often it is revealed that certain literature and aspects of the standard K–12 curriculum may be extremely offensive to some groups, many teachers will never be able to get beyond their own biases to understand how these students feel. When I did a presentation in South Carolina in 2005, I learned this from an African American teacher. She said that when she was a teacher education student, no matter how often she and other blacks in the program tried to explain this issue to prospective white teachers, the white teachers never understood it, especially when it came to the controversy about *The Adventures of Huckleberry Finn*. The bottom line was, the *white teachers* loved the book, they felt that *everyone* else should love it, and that was *all* that mattered to them. After hearing this story, I could only feel sorry for any African American child who was misfortunate enough to end up in the classroom of such a narrow-minded teacher.

A final way that teachers can improve the curriculum and make it culturally inclusive is to make this issue a top priority. One of the main lessons that I've learned in life is that people find time to do what's important to them. When something is not a priority for them, they make excuses for not getting the job done, or ignore it completely. During many of my presentations, I've heard teachers frequently complain that they don't have time to try new strategies or to make the curriculum culturally relevant because they are under pressure from school administrators to teach the standards and follow a prescribed curriculum related to standardized tests.

What these teachers fail to realize is that multiculturalism and culturally relevant teaching aren't superficial, "touchy-feely" frills that waste time and detract from real learning. In fact, both Cross and Ladson-Billings underscore the fact that when true culturally relevant teaching occurs, students' skills improve.[20] At the 2006 annual conference of the American Educational Research Association, Jeffrey Duncan-Andrade, a professor at San Francisco State University, and Ernest Morrell, a UCLA professor, demonstrated how this happens. Both professors teach tenth-grade classes in addition to their university teaching. Their tenth graders tend to be students of color who would be viewed as "at risk." But through their culturally relevant lesson plans, Morrell and Duncan-Andrade have shown students how having good academic skills can empower them to improve social conditions. As a result of tying the curriculum to real-world problems, students' cultures, and topics that interest them, Morrell and Duncan-Andrade saw that the students became intrinsically motivated to learn; their political consciousness increased, and their academic skills improved. In fact, their students were reading college-level textbooks, analyzing Census Bureau data about poverty, and designing maps to identify where the most impoverished communities were located in their cities. Morrell and Duncan-Andrade's work illustrates how easy it is for teachers to teach reading, writing, and math standards through culturally relevant lesson plans. All it takes is commitment, adequate knowledge about culturally relevant teaching, and creativity on the teacher's part.

Parents

There are several ways that parents can teach their children positive messages about their culture. Ideally, this should begin when children are very young, and in some cultures it does. Some cultural groups even send their children to special schools that teach them about their heritage. In addition to teaching their children about their cultural history, ancestry, and positive role models through storytelling and personal examples, parents should also take their children to the public library and help them find multicultural books. Buying multicultural books for their children's birthdays and other special occasions is another useful strategy. It is also beneficial to take children to museums and cultural events and to expose them to movies and films that can broaden their cultural awareness.

Furthermore, parents can teach their children to be respectful of other cultural and racial groups. As I will emphasize in Chapter Five, many children learn to be racist and culturally insensitive because of messages they learn from their parents and other adult relatives. Throughout my career as an educator, I've often heard that students want to get along with and even socialize with their peers from different racial and cultural backgrounds. In many cases, the problem is that their parents convey negative messages to them, and in extreme—but not unusual—cases, parents will even punish them if they socialize with individuals from racial backgrounds that the parents disparage. By middle school and high school, the situation is worsened by peer pressure to stick with "one's own kind." When parents teach their children to judge people on the basis of their *individual* behavior and characteristics, instead of on stereotypes and racist beliefs that have been passed down through the generations, they are more likely to help their children develop into individuals who can function in a racially and ethnically diverse classroom, school, and society.

Another way that parents can help is to offer their advice and expertise to educators. Parents can plan multicultural school assemblies and class presentations; volunteer to serve as guest speakers;

make suggestions to teachers and school administrators about ways in which the school can become more culturally inclusive; and recommend and even donate multicultural books, posters, and other materials to be included in the classroom or school library.

Policymakers

There are at least two ways in which policymakers can make schools more culturally inclusive. The first is that they can give enough money to underperforming schools to ensure that school district officials and administrators are able to provide adequate professional development for teachers to learn more about how they can make the curriculum culturally relevant, as well as money for field trips, assemblies, and guest speakers. There must also be enough funding for school libraries, classroom libraries, and local public libraries to have plenty of multicultural materials.

The second way that policymakers can help is to be fairer and more inclusive when making decisions about textbook adoptions. Every textbook adoption committee should consist of a multiracial group of parents, teachers, and other community representatives. The committees should be careful to scrutinize the books for tokenism and for racist, white supremacist, and ethnocentric messages; and they should ensure that adequate space is devoted in textbooks to the histories, contributions, and experiences of the groups that have historically been left out of textbooks.

A Final Word

In spite of all the research that has been done to help educators understand what a culturally relevant education entails and why all students, including whites, need to hear about the contributions that marginalized groups have made to civilization, there is still a lot of ignorance and resistance from educators—particularly, but not exclusively, white educators. I was reminded of this during a presentation when a young white male teacher raised his hand and asked, "Why does it always have to be about *race?* Why can't it just be about *culture?* After all, America is still a young nation, and there's really no *one* American culture. So why does it *always* have to be about *race?*"

He was referring to the fact that throughout the presentation, I had repeatedly mentioned that *all* students need a culturally relevant education, but that one of the main reasons why many black, Latino, Native American, and Southeast Asian students perform poorly in school is that the curriculum is boring, irrelevant, and sometimes even offensive to them.

My response to this teacher was that as an American citizen, I wish that I could walk into stores, drive down the street, walk into buildings, go to work, and so on and be viewed merely as an *American.* But that has not been my experience. Because most Americans have been socialized by their parents, peers, and religious leaders and by the media to view African Americans as dangerous, evil, deficient, dishonest, lazy, and stupid, when I walk into stores, I am perceived to be a thief. I've been treated disrespectfully by police, not because of any crime or wrongdoing on my part, but simply because of my race. Although I have always wanted to be sweet, docile, and unassuming, I've had to be assertive and outspoken in the workplace and at my children's schools in order to demand respect and fair treatment. Why? Because the respect that most white people take for granted is not automatically given to someone like me. Like the students at American High School who described their experiences at an underperforming school, I am one of America's stepchildren, a second-class citizen who lives in a racialized society.

Regarding the teacher's claim that America doesn't really have any *one* culture, I disagreed. Everything in America—including standardized tests—tends to be "normed" according to white middle-class values and behaviors (see the next chapter for more information). This is the standard by which other groups are usually judged, and because of my background, the way I look, and the way I grew up speaking, I am viewed as deficient and inferior.

was explaining this to the young man, many of the teach-
in the audience tuned me out. Perhaps they would have
preferred for me to sugarcoat my answer and not speak about some
of the ways that racism continues to rear its ugly head in American
society.

In tuning me out, what they failed to realize was that they were
also tuning out some of their students. I believe that teachers and
others who are resistant to hearing the painful truths about the ways
in which racism and differential treatment affect the lives of countless Americans can never be effective teachers of America's
stepchildren, because these teachers aren't willing to open their
ears, hearts, and minds to the experiences that these students bring
into the classroom. As long as educators remain resistant to learning about these unpleasant topics, they will continue to blame kids
for not wanting to read *The Adventures of Huckleberry Finn,* for
having low test scores, for being apathetic and unmotivated, and
for having "parents who don't care about their education." These
teachers will never be able to look at how their own mind-sets, behaviors, boring lesson plans, and exclusionary curricula can contribute
to low student achievement.

3

"It Don't Make No Sense to Give Us All These Tests"

Student Effort, Achievement, and Attitudes About Standardized Tests

Long ago, when I was an elementary school student in southeast San Diego, I learned a very important lesson each spring when we took the required standardized test: test time meant nap time! So each day during testing week, after the teacher passed out the test materials, I quickly bubbled in answers for the section of the test that we were required to complete that day. Although I never paid attention to what my classmates were doing at the time (and I'm sure that many were doing the same thing I was), I'm certain that I was probably one of the first students to finish. The sooner I finished randomly bubbling in answers, the sooner I could lay my head on my desk, close my eyes, and take a long-awaited nap.

Although I did this throughout my elementary school years (with the exception of sixth grade), I don't ever recall any teacher objecting to my behavior. They didn't awaken me, and they didn't tell me to take the test seriously. More important, they failed to inform me that even though *I* didn't take the test seriously, some teachers did, and my scores could and would be used to determine my worth. Years later, and far too late, I realized that my standardized test scores may have been one of the reasons why most of my elementary teachers thought I was dumb. But then again, knowing what I now know about the view many teachers hold of America's stepchildren, I'm fairly sure they would've thought I was dumb no matter what.

My childhood experience was one of the reasons I tried my best as a K–12 teacher not only to prepare my students for all tests but also to make sure they understood that some individuals would use their test scores to judge their aptitude and potential for academic success. Of course, pressure from school administrators to raise test scores at the two underperforming secondary schools where I taught was another factor. It was never the main one, though. For me, the bottom line was that I believed my students could do well on the tests if they were adequately prepared. I wanted them to do their best, I wanted to do a good job of preparing them for the tests, and I didn't want to give any of my colleagues another excuse to say that low-income students and black, Latino, and Southeast Asian students aren't as smart as whites and certain Asian American groups.

I held tenaciously to these views in spite of my strong feelings about the origins and uses of state-mandated tests in schools, and my belief that we were required to give too many tests, a point that was echoed by Alfie Kohn, an education expert, who said, "Our children are tested to an extent that is unprecedented in our history and unparalleled anywhere else in the world."[1] I also believed that most of these tests had very little to do with the curriculum that we were required to teach. In fact, during a public speech that he gave several years ago, a high-ranking U.S. Department of Education official admitted that California was one of thirteen states whose K–12 curriculum was still not aligned with the state-mandated test. More recently, W. James Popham, a professor emeritus at UCLA, said, "As currently set up, most standards-based assessments don't really align with classroom instruction, and instruction doesn't significantly influence test scores."[2]

I also held on to my views about testing even after I eventually realized that standardized tests are overrated, culturally biased, and of limited usefulness. As I said in *Through Ebony Eyes*: ". . . effective teachers know that no test can truly measure the depth and breadth of students' knowledge, since many students suffer from test anxiety and have poor test taking skills. Therefore, they understand that multiple ways of assessing what students know through projects, writing assignments, individual and group presentations, portfolios, quizzes, and tests should be used."[3]

I also believe that the racist legacy of standardized tests continues to cast a dark cloud over the current overemphasis on them. This history encompasses the eugenics movement, biological determinism, hereditarianism, and other philosophies, theories, and movements whose goal has been to rank human groups.[4] Regardless of the fancy title of the underlying theory, the end result is that whites (and more recently some Asian American groups) are always deemed to have superior intelligence to Latinos and blacks. The periodic resurgence of these theories is often political and is tied to economics, as Stephen Jay Gould explained in *The Mismeasure of Man*, a book that summarizes many of these theories, details their origins, and provides a historical overview of the standardized testing movement in the United States.[5]

Popham has exposed some of the problems that arise when educators and policymakers overrate the importance of standardized test scores; for example, he states that ". . . many educators (and most laypeople) employ the term *achievement* interchangeably with *learning*," but "test performance does not equal learning."[6] To this point, I say "Amen!"

A second problem that Popham and others have identified is that *all* standardized tests, including the California Achievement Test (CAT), the Comprehensive Test of Basic Skills (CTBS), the Iowa Test of Basic Skills (ITBS), the Metropolitan Achievement Test (MAT), and the Stanford Achievement Test (SAT), are flawed. Moreover, both norm-referenced tests (which compare a "person's score against the score of a group of people who have already taken the same exam, called the 'norming group'"[7]) and criterion-based tests (which test students' mastery of specific skills or criteria) are biased. Criterion-based tests are used by about 50 percent of the states in the United States.

The biases in both types of tests are caused by an overreliance on questions, statements, and items that really measure students' socioeconomic status—what Popham refers to as "ses-linked" test items—rather than items that assess what students have learned in school. Middle- and upper-class students are more likely than low-income students to have been exposed to this information outside school. Popham found that 15 to 20 percent of the math items and 40 to 80 percent of reading, social studies, science, and language arts items on two popular standardized tests that he examined actually measure socioeconomic status. Popham stated, "Simply because of life experiences, youth from economically advantaged families will outperform less advantaged youngsters."[8] He elaborated further on the consequences of using "flawed measurement instruments" and of equating achievement with learning: "Because of the United States' social and economic history, minority students are more likely to be low-ses than nonminority students are. It should be apparent, therefore, that if many items on standardized achievement tests are more directly linked to students' scores than to what students have been taught in school, then the use of such tests will never reduce the difference in test scores between minority and white students. We are relying on tests containing ses-linked items to demonstrate that students can overcome ses-linked education deficits. This is really stupid."[9]

Kohn also described several problems that are inherent in the standardized testing movement. He maintains that the tests "were never intended to measure the quality of learning or teaching"; that the main objective is not to rate students but to rank them; and that the tests often "measure superficial thinking," "a shallow approach to learning," and the "skill of test taking." Like Popham, Kohn believes that biases in standardized tests give middle- and upper-class students advantages over low-income students: "For decades, critics have complained that many standardized tests are unfair because the questions require a set of knowledge and skills more likely to be possessed by children from a privileged background."[10]

For many years, Asa Hilliard, a highly respected scholar, has tried to expose the problems with standardized tests and has served as an expert witness in several cases regarding test bias. According to

Hilliard, the tests are culturally biased, and many of the same individuals who develop and promote the use of these tests are not willing to engage in open and honest dialogue about the ways these tests can harm students. "Many of the invalid and bad practices in testing and assessment, in particular, stem from the well-documented partnerships between many powerful people . . . and the forces of slavery, colonialism, segregation/apartheid, and white supremacy ideology," Hilliard states. To put it succinctly, Hilliard concludes, the current "one size fits all" testing model doesn't work, and "tests should measure what schools promise to teach."[11]

Like Hilliard, Kohn, and Popham, many researchers and educators have criticized the public school system's overreliance on standardized tests to label and sort students, and even some earlier supporters of NCLB later became its critics. As I mentioned in the Introduction, hundreds of teachers have resorted to cheating, yet the standardized testing movement continues to be the foundation on which NCLB and subsequent education reforms promoted by the Bush administration rests. Kohn maintains that "Many educators are leaving the field because of what is being done to schools in the name of 'accountability' and 'tougher standards.'"[12] Furthermore, in 2000, a bipartisan opinion poll of eight hundred registered voters revealed that many Americans aren't happy with an overemphasis on high-stakes testing. The poll results indicated that "Most American voters do not agree that test scores measure progress" or that students should be punished for their standardized test scores; further, "only 49 percent of voters [agreed] that 'When I took a standardized test, the score accurately reflected what I knew about the subject being tested.'"[13]

Despite the widespread criticism of NCLB and the standardized testing movement, standardized tests continue to be the foundation on which NCLB and subsequent education reforms promoted by the Bush administration rest. In fact, in 2005 President Bush announced his plan to expand NCLB by increasing funding for schools and requiring more testing in high school—three years rather than one.[14] The President's new plan to expand NCLB hadn't yet been implemented at the time when I collected data from the students at American High School. The students were already required to take numerous tests, however. During the previous year, they had taken the SAT 9, which was California's state-mandated test at the time, one that was widely criticized for not being aligned to the required K–12 curriculum. The year I collected data from students, they had just taken the California Achievement Test (CAT 6), which, in spite of its well-known inherent biases, became the new state-mandated test. Furthermore, students who hadn't already passed the California High School Exit Exam (CAHSEE) were also required to take that test. Honors and AP students also took the Golden State Exam and AP exams, and college-bound students had to take the SAT or the ACT. On top of all this, students had to take quizzes and tests, including regular Accelerated Reader reading tests in their English classes, and midterms and final exams in their core academic classes.

In this chapter, we hear what the American High School students who participated in the study said about their overall effort and achievement and about their attitudes toward the standardized tests they were required to take. Specific recommendations from the students are also included.

What the Students Said

In the earlier phase of the study, 63 percent of the teachers said that most of their students couldn't read at or above grade level; one-fourth said that most of their students wouldn't reach grade-level standards by the end of the school year; nearly 20 percent said that most students wouldn't pass their class with a C or higher grade; and nearly one-fourth said that some students weren't capable of passing their classes.

Again, there were discrepancies between the teachers' views and what students believed, for when asked to rate themselves, students thought more highly of their academic skills than their teachers did. For example, 84 percent of whites, 80 percent of blacks, and 67 percent of Latinos rated themselves as an outstanding or good student. The overwhelming majority of students in each group also said that they had good reading skills and that they could read and understand most of their textbooks. The majority of students in each group also said that they had good math skills, but a lower percentage did in comparison to the percentage who said they had good reading skills. A third of the students admitted that they had weak math skills, and a third said they couldn't understand most of the work in their math classes. White students were more likely than blacks and Latinos to say they had good math skills, and Latinas and black females were less likely than all subgroups to say they did.

Although most of the students viewed themselves as outstanding or good students, many admitted that they didn't always exert as much effort as they should. This might explain the discrepancy between the teachers' and students' views of the students' skill levels and capabilities. For example, half of the black and Latino students and more than a fourth of the whites admitted that they didn't usually take their classes as seriously as they should. Most of the students in each group also admitted that they would get better grades if they spent more time on their homework, and most admitted that they spent one hour or less on homework each night. In spite of their admission that they didn't always exert as much effort as they could, the majority of students said that getting good grades was very important to them and that most of their friends wanted them to get good grades, even though nearly 20 percent agreed with the statement "If I get good grades, I'm afraid people might think I'm a 'nerd.'" A higher percentage of black and Latino males than others were concerned about being perceived as a "nerd." This suggests that for some students, peer pressure may have affected their effort, achievement, and attitudes about school.

Failing Courses

Despite the fact that most students said they valued getting good grades, a third were failing at least one course, and a higher percentage of black and Latino students were failing in comparison to whites. More than half the students said that their personal problems often prevented them from earning good grades and doing well on tests. Latino students were more likely than blacks and whites to say this, but a much higher percentage of Latinas than Latino males agreed with this statement. This is an interesting point, because Latinas were also more likely than all other groups to believe that most of their teachers didn't care about them.

Students' Attitudes About the SAT 9 and CAT 6 State-Mandated Tests

Numerous questionnaire items pertained to the students' attitudes and beliefs about the SAT 9, the state-mandated test they'd taken the previous year, and the CAT 6, the test they'd taken shortly before I arrived at American High School to collect data from them. Although most of the students said they were serious about doing well on state tests like the SAT 9, nearly 40 percent said they weren't. There were no major differences in the percentages of whites, Latinos, and blacks who said they were serious about doing well on state-mandated tests, but white females were more likely than others to say this, and white males were less likely than other groups to say this.

Although most students said they were serious about doing well on the SAT 9, more than 40 percent admitted that in the past, they hadn't done their best on this test because they believed it was a waste of time. Black and Latino students, and black males especially, were more likely than whites to have this attitude; white females were least likely to agree. The focus group discussions revealed one major difference between students who were serious about the tests and those who weren't, which was that the possibility of earning a scholarship for high test scores was a motivating factor for some students. At that time, California awarded small college scholarships to students with high test scores, and this was an incentive for some, but not all, students.

The students gave numerous reasons for not taking these tests seriously. Many thought they were required to take too many tests and that they hadn't been adequately prepared for the state-mandated tests; many didn't believe they would receive enough benefit for putting more effort into doing well on the tests. For example, one student stated, "They don't really determine your grade. I didn't really think the tests were necessary. Plus, the things that were on there, I had no clue about the answers." Another focus group participant said, "We're tired of just taking all these tests all the time. We had the mid-terms or something, and right after that we had the SAT 9 test." A senior said that she wasn't serious about doing well on state-mandated tests because she didn't believe they were tied to her future goals. Another student, who felt that students were burdened with way too much work, exclaimed, "We have to take so many tests just to graduate. We have the High School Exit Exam, and now we have a senior project. What kind of crap is this? Oh, my God!" An African American male student admitted, "I didn't take it seriously at all because it don't count for our grades, and they give us twenty tests a year. It don't make no sense to give us all these tests. If they don't count, why take your time on it?"

A student who believed that apathy about the state-mandated tests was reflective of overall student apathy explained, "Some kids still don't care, because they don't like coming to school, and the majority of kids that come to school don't like taking the tests. So, they just sit there and go through it. Some people told me that they just bubbled in anything. They're bored when they come to school. They don't like having to sit at a desk and have [to take] a 100-question test in a certain amount of time and not be able to actually pay attention to the test. They just hate coming to school."

In explaining why he didn't take the tests seriously, an African American male student made a similar comment: "I didn't take it seriously because it didn't have anything to do with me as an individual. The school gets points, so the school won't get shut down. But it's like, sometimes, you feel that the school don't care about you, so why you gonna care about the school? By the time the state does come in, you gonna be gone anyway. It doesn't have anything to do with your grade."

In voicing his agreement with the previous statement, another African American male focus group participant said, "I read some of the test, and then I started getting tired. So I started thinking, 'The test is not going to do anything for me. So I might as well just mark any answer and then go to sleep.'" A white female stated, "I don't think that I personally have a clue as to what these tests mean. They [teachers] don't tell us what they mean. They just said, 'This is a very important test. You need to study for this test.' I think that if they want to give so many tests, they should make up one test. We should take it one time and everyone does their stupid statistics that way."

Another focus group participant who said that she had taken so many tests that she couldn't differentiate among them remarked: "I don't know what CAT 6 you are talking about or SAT 9. I seriously don't know. I just go in and take a test. I have no clue what name it is, and then they say, 'Oh what did you get on that?' and I am like, 'I don't know; I don't remember.' It seems like they give us all of the standardized tests and stuff that they need to, but it seems like it cuts down on the amount of time they have to teach us."

Many focus group participants made similar statements about the tests being too long, boring, and too time-consuming. The end result was that students either copied other students' tests or marked any answer and fell asleep. A student who admitted to cheating on tests said, "You have to think about why people cheat. I'm sure there's a reason why people cheat. Maybe they just don't understand. I know that I've cheated because I just didn't understand." However, a student who had previously done well on standardized tests said that he was insulted by the content of the test: "The CAT 6, it was a joke to me. They was asking a lot of stupid questions, like 'two plus two.' I was like, 'Come on now; I learned this in elementary.' And I already had a thousand dollar school grant from scoring high on another test."

The Connection Between Poor Reading and Math Skills and Test Scores

Two questionnaire statements provided additional information about students' attitudes about the standardized tests they were required to take. Nearly 30 percent of the students said that they could not read and understand most of the information on the state-required test during the previous year. Although there was no major difference between the percentages of students by racial or ethnic subgroup who said they could read and understand the test, a slightly higher percentage of blacks said they could in comparison to whites and Latinos.

In the case of math, nearly half the students said they couldn't understand most of the math problems on the standardized test during the previous year. White students were more likely than Latinos and black students, especially African American females and Latinas, to say they could comprehend the math problems.

Preparation for the SAT 9 and CAT 6

In addition to expressing their views about the state-mandated standardized tests in general, the students also spoke about how well their teachers had prepared them for the tests. Nearly half the questionnaire respondents said that most of their teachers had not done a good job of preparing them for state tests. White students were more likely to agree that their teachers had done a good job, and black students were the least likely to do so. In fact, less than half the black students agreed that their teachers had done a good job. However, black females and Latinas were a lot less likely than black and Latino males to agree.

Furthermore, nearly half the students said that during the previous year, their SAT 9 scores weren't very high because they hadn't been taught most of the information on the test. Latino students were more likely than others to state this, and white females were least likely to do so. Students who believed that their teachers hadn't done a good job of preparing them for the test also tended to believe that their teachers weren't doing a good job overall.

The focus group participants made many comments about how well their teachers had or hadn't prepared them for the SAT 9 and the CAT 6. Students said that some teachers made no attempt whatsoever to prepare them for the tests. Other teachers made an effort to prepare students for the tests, but didn't devote enough time to it. For example, a student remarked, "They don't even teach nothing that's going to be on the test. When we took those SAT 9 tests, we sat there and half of the stuff you don't know. They don't teach you nothing."

Consequently, many students inferred that if the tests weren't important enough for their teachers to devote a substantial amount of time to test preparation, then the students didn't have to take the tests seriously either. In fact, several students actually stated that some of their teachers indicated that they didn't care if students did well on the tests or not. Some students also said that the classroom environment wasn't conducive to students' doing well on the tests or taking the tests seriously. Some classes were noisy; in some classes, students were sleeping; in others, students who finished early had too much idle time on their hands. Several students also said that the tests were so different from the curriculum that they had never been exposed to any of the information on the tests. In many cases, this caused students to become resentful. For example, a senior exclaimed, "I don't think our teachers have adequately prepared us for this test because when I look at those tests, I'm like 'Dang! I didn't get none of it; I didn't understand it.' I don't know if it's because I'm not smart, but I didn't understand a lot of the questions that were on there. So, I basically decided 'Well, I'll just guess, 'cause I don't know none of this. So, I must be stupid.'"

In contrasting two of her teachers' attitudes about the state tests, another focus group participant said, "One of my teachers went on 'vacation' and just didn't care. The math teacher, he was all right. He gives some of the problems but not exactly. I know it's not supposed to be exactly what's going to be on the test, but it did help somewhat."

Another student, who complained that some teachers placed the burden of doing well on the tests solely on the students, remarked, "I'm in some Honors classes, and the teachers basically said, 'You should know what's on the test.' But you don't know what's on it. My math teacher didn't go over anything that was going to be on the test."

A focus group participant who received mixed messages from her teachers explained, "Freshman year, the teachers did pretty good, but then, after that, they'd say, 'You're taking the STAR Test.' That's it. [In] the class that we took it in this year, there were people talking and stuff. You really want people to be quiet when you're taking the test. Nobody cared. I don't think that we're doing good enough. I think that they gave up on us, really, some of them."

The High School Exit Exam

In addition to sharing feedback about the CAT 6 and SAT 9, the students also shared their thoughts about the High School Exit Exam (HSEE). In general, their attitudes about this exam were better. For example, only 12 percent of the students said that passing this test wasn't important to them. Most students (79 percent) also believed that they would pass the HSEE. A much higher percentage of whites (92 percent) than blacks (75 percent) and Latinos (71 percent) believed they would pass. Latinas were the least likely of all groups to believe they would pass the exam.

Many focus group participants had already passed the HSEE, but others had not. Numerous students said they were more serious about doing well on this exam because it was a graduation requirement. For instance, a male focus group participant said, "I took it seriously because you need it to get out of high school, basically. I was like 'why not knock it out?'" A student who made a similar comment said, "The only reason why I had to care for it is because I had to pass it in order to graduate. That is the only reason why I took it seriously."

However, some students said they had received mixed messages about the test, which affected their attitude about it. As one focus group participant explained, "I didn't get the whole concept of taking an exit exam. You have to pass this test to get out of high school, but how can you pass it as a sophomore? So, I was just like, 'This is a joke.' It was easy anyway, so I didn't really take it seriously." A student who made a similar comment said, "When we were freshmen, they said that it wasn't going to count toward anything. It was just to see if everyone knew the stuff. So I only took it somewhat seriously."

Several focus group participants also believed that having to take the test was unfair to students. For example, one female focus group participant complained, "I don't think it's fair that you have to pass it to graduate from high school. That's not fair because you be doing all that work and then you don't get your diploma; you get a 'completion.'"

Another student who felt the test was unfair questioned the relevance of the test: "I just want to know what is the point of taking a High School Exit Exam when our presence here as students—we're here. We are at high school, so why should we take a test? If we're doing good and we're passing our classes, why should we take a test?" In expressing her frustration about the exit exam, another focus group participant said, "They grade us on our test, when they should be grading us on our classes, you know? You pass all of your classes, but say you're not good at tests, what happens if you can't pass it? That is not fair when you went through four years and did well the whole time."

Some focus group participants also complained that the test was too easy, and that this affected students' attitudes. For example, one student said, "They made us take that test when we first got into high school, our freshman year, which means we really didn't have enough time to prepare and study for the test, which is supposed to help us for our whole four years. It was a waste of time. Most people passed it their first year, and that was it."

A student who described her friend's attitude about the test explained, "I have a friend who took it twice in a year, and he failed it purposely every year. He put A on all his answers, and the next day he put B on all his answers. I don't know why he did that, but all my other friends are like, 'We don't even know what the questions were and we never got any packets or anything.' The test didn't make any sense at all."

Despite the fact that many students complained about the HSEE, several thought that it was a good idea because too many students graduate with weak academic skills. For example, a focus group participant remarked, "I think it should count because the average high school graduate reads at like a fifth-grade level." Another student who defended the test said, "In a way, the test was, like, easy. Some people spend all of high school cheating off of the person next to them. Throughout high school, there are so many people who cheat and get A's but then, after they graduate, they're so stupid; they can't even get jobs." A third focus group participant also defended the test, stating, "I think the test, in a way, is a good thing. I think if you have a certain GPA, then you should be exempt from the test. But personally, the kids in the school that are going to be leading our society, they don't need to be leaving high school stupid."

Preparation for the High School Exit Exam

Half the questionnaire respondents said that most of their teachers had done a good job of preparing them for the test. In terms of race, African Americans were less likely to say their teachers had done a good job, but in terms of gender, black females and white males were the least likely to say so. The focus group participants explained why many students believed that their teachers had done a good job of preparing them for the exam and others didn't. However, focus group participants tended to have more to say about teachers who had done a poor job. Their comments were similar to those regarding teachers' ability to prepare them for the state tests.

One student remarked, "I had no preparation whatsoever from any of my teachers. All you got to do is read certain stuff and then answer the question. We don't do that in class. We do vocab, and then we might read a book. But that's not gonna prepare us for that test. Sitting there for three hours reading fifty million paragraphs and answering fifty million questions, that's not preparing us for nothing. That hurts me inside. It really does. I just want to go to sleep."

Some students complained that their teachers made excuses for their lack of test preparation. For example, one girl said, "Half of the teachers say they don't know what's going to be on the test. Then, I think that whoever is in charge, the government, or whoever, should make sure that the teachers know what to teach us before the test comes along."

Another student questioned why the curriculum wasn't tied to the exam: "Why don't they teach exactly to the curriculum that we need in order to pass the test? They're teaching all this other stuff that we don't need to know, that we don't care about, and that is unnecessary. Then, the test comes, and we're ill-prepared for it."

Several students also complained about differences among teachers in preparing students for the exam. Apparently, some teachers were willing to tell students when their answers on test preparation materials were wrong, but others were not. One focus group participant made a comment with which many students agreed: "Some teachers say that they can't give us the answers, but other teachers do give them."

Another student made a similar remark: "Our history teacher gave us a worksheet, and we had to get the answers from the book. But the problem with that is that if the answers were wrong, we couldn't go ask him for every answer." This concern was affirmed by a focus group participant who stated,

Other teachers give you the answers *and* the test, and you just have to match the answers with the test, but our teacher said, "Well, I can't risk my job." I said, "Well, if other teachers are doing it, how are you going to risk your job? They can't fire every history teacher at this school." He said, "I still can't risk it." We said, "If we find the answers can you tell us if they're right or wrong?" He said, "I can't tell you if they're right or wrong." Then, when we took the High School Exit Exam, none of the questions that we had studied [were] on that test. It was completely different.

The fact that students in certain grades got more or less preparation for the CHSEE was also a complaint that some focus group participants made, as indicated by the following statement: "The juniors this year, they took it freshman year, so we [freshmen] didn't get prepared. The only preparation we had was from junior high, and we didn't have high school teachers teaching us."

Students' Recommendations About How Teachers Can Better Prepare Them for State-Mandated Tests

When the students were asked how teachers can better prepare them for state-mandated tests, they made numerous suggestions, which we will review in the next sections.

Provide Tutoring. Half the questionnaire respondents said that if before- and after-school tutoring were available to help them prepare for state-mandated tests, they would attend the sessions. Black and Latino students were more likely than whites to say they would attend, and black females and Latinas were the most likely to do so. A focus group participant who made a related comment stated: "I feel like after-school programs that are interesting and fun—not just sitting there learning, but that will keep you interested and won't make you fall asleep—are needed. Teach us the stuff that they know is going to be on the test and that we haven't learned, and not cram all this studying in a week or three days before the test comes along. They should be teaching us this stuff three months before the test."

Spend More Time on Test Preparation. The most commonly cited recommendation from focus group participants was that teachers should spend more time preparing students for the tests. As one student explained, "The teachers teach stuff, but then, they'll stay on a subject for like two days, and then go on to something else, because they say the California requirements are somewhat different. But it don't make no sense to stay on a subject for two days and then move on to the next one. The next one that you move onto, you're going to stay on that subject for a week, and [we] don't even need to know that [information]. But the one that you really needed to know, you only stayed on for two days."

Another student advised teachers: "Maybe two weeks, three weeks in advance, sit down and explain it to us and go through each section. They know what areas and what kind of questions will be on the tests, so they could help us a little bit. Just review." This suggestion was echoed by a focus group participant who said, "They should review with us a little bit longer; stop rushing it. They should take the time that they're getting paid for to actually help us with the tests."

Provide Students with Information That Is Relevant to the Tests. Many focus group participants also stated that test preparation needed to include information that was actually relevant to the tests they would be required to take. As I already mentioned, numerous students complained that the curriculum was totally disconnected from the state tests. Most students agreed with the focus group participant who said, "For the exit exam, they need to give more and better examples from the test." Another student advised teachers to "Teach us things that are on the test. They might teach us things, but they don't teach us anything that's on these tests. When I look at the tests, and I look at some of the work that we have to do, none of this is familiar to me, because I've never seen it before. So, I just guess on it."

Do a Better Job of Preparing Students for the Math Sections of the Tests. As I mentioned earlier, nearly half the questionnaire respondents said they couldn't understand most of the math problems on the SAT 9 test the previous year. This indicates that at American High School, there was a strong need to improve the math curriculum, math instructional practices, and preparation for the math components of the state-mandated tests. The following comments by focus group participants were affirmed by many students: "Teachers need to prepare us more for the math portion, because that's the hardest part. I already passed the English portion of the High School Exit Exam, but the math one is just killing me." One student complained: "Most of the information on the High School Exit Exam is just algebra and basic English. So, if you're a junior, you're pretty much screwed because you've forgotten everything you learned in algebra." Another student made a similar observation: "The math portion was very difficult compared to the English. I think the English was easy because it was basically what you know, but the math is either right or it's wrong." This difference was also noted by a focus group participant who remarked, "The thing about the test is, the English is common sense. You already know some of the words that they ask you. The math, that's something that you actually have to learn."

Be More Patient and More Willing to Answer Questions. As we saw in Chapter One, students reported a need for patience from their teachers, especially with regard to answering students' questions, which clearly has implications for test preparation. This point was illustrated by the focus group participant who remarked, "Some people don't get it as quickly as other people. So, we need more time," and by the student who said, "They should actually go over the stuff and answer questions. Some of them, if you ask a question . . . they get irritated, and they just don't want to answer your questions."

Use Diverse Teaching Strategies. During my visits to American High School, I often heard students say that more teachers needed to use diverse teaching strategies. Some teachers at American High School also recognized this need, for nearly 30 percent admitted that they didn't use enough innovation or creativity in their lesson plans.

The focus group participants also stressed the need for teachers to use variety and innovation in their teaching and test preparation.

Three focus group participants spoke about specific strategies that were ineffective. One warned teachers, "Don't just hand out worksheets and expect us to do them. Worksheets are a waste of time." Another remarked, "The worksheets that come out on the computer, I think those are boring. You don't learn nothing, and you just gotta answer them." Another complained, "My English teacher didn't really prepare us; she just let us read poems and analyze them."

Stress the Importance of the Tests Through Teachers' Words and Actions. The focus group participants also said that teachers should spend more time explaining the importance and purposes of the tests through their words and their actions. A few focus group participants stated that most of their teachers had made an effort to do this. For example, one student admitted, "My teachers did a really good job of preparing me for the test, but I blew it off, because the test doesn't mean anything. . . . [I'm saying this because] I just wanted to defend my teachers." Another student said, "They gave us problems that were going to be on the test, and they asked questions, and gave us worksheets." Nevertheless, the following statement was more typical of most focus group participants' comments and experiences: "I feel like my teachers didn't prepare me at all. They didn't tell us how important these tests are. And they gave us this information at the last minute. And like, it just really gets me mad. They should tell us like throughout the year. Remind us of it and give us packets throughout the year, what to study, and what is important, and what's going to be on the test during the year so that we're prepared."

Tying It All Together

Even under the most ideal conditions, childhood and adolescence can be a mixed blessing. Under the best conditions, the good side of childhood entails being well taken care of and having at least one parent or guardian who provides the basic necessities of food, clothing, love, and shelter. Of course, under ideal conditions, the good side also includes attending decent schools and having effective teachers, which should be a given for all youths, but is often not the reality for countless students in the U.S. K–12 schools, especially not for America's stepchildren. One of the negative aspects of being a child is having people who think they know what is in your best interests make decisions that may actually end up being harmful. NCLB is a prime example. It has now been a federal law for several years, and as I mentioned earlier in this chapter, President Bush promised at the beginning of his second term to expand the law to require more testing for high school students. He did this, he said, in order to reform America's high schools.

Although I believe that the President and early supporters of NCLB (of which I was one) may have had good intentions in that their main goal may have been to improve the nation's public school system and close the achievement gaps, in the end they have done the opposite. Because of NCLB's overreliance on standardized tests, which are incapable of adequately measuring what students know and have learned in school, its proponents have created a culture of widespread cheating and have given students another reason to be disillusioned and apathetic about school. The feedback from the students at American High School suggests that as long as policy-makers ignore two major constituents—teachers and students—when making decisions that affect them, even the most well-intentioned school reforms are destined to fail. The feedback from the students clearly shows that the old adage "You can lead a horse to water, but you can't make it drink" is true. When teachers are compelled to teach curricula that aren't aligned to tests they believe are meaningless, and they don't know how to provide adequate preparation for the tests, they will find ways to express their displeasure and remain disinclined to take the tests seriously themselves. Even if they pay lip service to the tests' importance, their actions can give students the opposite message.

At American High School, a high percentage of the teachers chose to blame parents (a point I will return to in Chapter Nine) and students for the school's low test scores and overall under-achievement. At the same time, many students concluded that their teachers had failed to adequately prepare them for the tests. When high school students are required to take too many tests, especially tests for which they have been inadequately prepared, tests that are unrelated to their class work and homework, and tests that have no obvious benefits except to make the school look good to the public and to policymakers, many won't take the tests seriously. In the end, the same students who have historically underperformed on standardized tests—low-income students and blacks and Latinos—will continue to be labeled as less intelligent than middle- and upper-class whites, who by nature of their socio-economic status have test-taking advantages and insider knowledge that increases their likelihood of doing well on tests that are biased in their favor. Some of the themes that surfaced in this chapter are illustrated by the following story.

In February 2005, a rumor was widely circulated among students at a local high school that has a high percentage of black and Latino students. Rumor had it that in the spring, on the first day of testing, the teachers were going on strike to protest the state-mandated test. Given what I knew about the K–12 teaching force, I doubted that the rumor would become a reality. But I did believe that it underscored what I learned from the students at American High School about school reform based on high-stakes testing: teachers and students can derail the most well-intentioned reforms if they believe the reforms are counterproductive. Even if the rumor was baseless (which it indeed turned out to be), at the very least it sent a message to every student who heard it: "Our teachers are upset about being forced to give the state test, so something must be wrong with it." This message undoubtedly increased student apathy about the test, and I wouldn't be surprised if when the testing actually began, more students decided to cheat, as many American High School students admitted to doing, or to bubble in answers randomly and sleep through the test, as I did decades ago and as did many American High School students. Clearly, true high school reform will never occur as long as policymakers believe that more testing is the answer to the myriad problems facing our nation's schools—particularly those attended by America's stepchildren.

According to Dr. James P. Comer, the celebrated Yale child psychiatrist, "The purpose of the public school is greater than preparing students to achieve high test scores. The purpose is to prepare students to be successful in school and in life. Life success requires skills that will enable individuals to be good family and group members, learners and problem solvers, workers, and citizens of their respective communities. . . . A focus on higher test scores alone cannot produce the outcomes we want and need for our children or our nation."[15] I agree wholeheartedly with Dr. Comer's views about testing, and those of Hilliard and Kohn, who argued that the testing movement has historically harmed poor students and students of color. The problem is that few policymakers, and especially the President of the United States, are taking these and similar views seriously. Neither dissatisfaction, criticism, nor resistance from the general public, from educators, or even from state officials has changed the President's high-stakes testing agenda.[16] Instead, he has forged ahead with a plan that clearly isn't going to reform the education system.

What We Can Do

Despite the widespread dissatisfaction with NCLB's overreliance on standardized tests, the fact remains that as things currently stand, students, educators, schools, and even school districts will be penalized if their test scores remain low and if they don't demonstrate "adequate yearly progress." For this reason, teachers, administrators, and parents must become aggressive in increasing the likelihood that students—especially those who have historically performed poorly on tests—will be able to do well. In the next sections, I make my own recommendations to educators, parents, and policymakers, describing what I call a four-pronged approach to improving test scores.

Administrators

School leaders are the critical first prong in this approach. Most of the research on high-achieving, high-poverty, high-minority schools emphasizes that effective school leaders can narrow the achievement gaps and improve schools. To be effective, school leaders must begin with the "right attitude" about students, parents, teachers, and their own role in improving student achievement.[17]

The "no-fault" mind-set that Comer and others have described as essential to school reform, as well as positive relationships, inclusiveness, providing support for teachers, the creation of a community of learners that is built on high expectations, and the wise use of test data to improve the curriculum and instruction are all among the key ingredients that school leaders must include in the recipe for reform that results in improving student achievement. Some administrators have used the feedback from test data to create tutoring programs. Others have offered nutrition programs during testing periods to ensure that hunger doesn't prevent any student from exerting his or her best effort. In Chapter Seven, I describe a former school principal who visited each classroom during testing week to motivate students to do well.

Administrators should also offer ongoing professional development workshops to teachers that focus specifically on test-taking strategies, test anxiety, and stereotype threat (the belief that one is expected to perform poorly because of one's race or gender). They should establish uniform test-preparation policies for the entire school and hold teachers accountable for devoting adequate time to test preparation. They should also offer parent workshops and send newsletters to parents about how they can help their children with tests.

The main point is that with a strong action plan and adequate funding and support from policymakers, administrators can improve underperforming schools. Unfortunately, to improve test scores, administrators must also be realistic and acknowledge that in a high-stakes testing environment, many teachers and students will feel that there is little room for creativity and interesting, inclusive, and engaging lesson plans. Although I believe that it is possible for teachers to learn ways to make the curriculum interesting and inclusive and still do a good job of preparing students for tests, principals must understand that many teachers don't know how to do this. They need help in these areas through modeling, mentoring, and other types of professional development.

Teachers

The second component of the four-pronged approach that I recommend concerns teachers. Whereas schoolwide improvements can occur when outstanding administrators create a culture of high expectations and provide adequate support and resources to teachers and students, what happens in each individual classroom is largely determined by teachers. As I've stated previously, teacher quality has a significant impact on student achievement. Because many teachers apparently don't know how to adequately prepare students for state-mandated tests, as indicated by the feedback from students at American High School, professional development is obviously needed in this area. This professional development should increase teacher efficacy by:

- Providing research and strategies that enable teachers to offer adequate test preparation to their students
- Providing research and strategies that help teachers connect daily lesson plans to the content of state-mandated tests
- Assisting teachers in designing creative lesson plans that are culturally inclusive yet relevant to the state-mandated tests
- Informing teachers of the specific ways in which many high-achieving, high-poverty, high-minority schools across the nation have improved students' test scores
- Providing teachers with research and strategies to help students decrease their test anxiety and, in the case of African American and Latino students, decrease the effects of stereotype threat as well

According to Aronson and to Steele, many students are impeded from doing their best work on tests by the belief that they have historically been expected to do poorly on tests.[18] As Aronson explained, "... stereotype threat makes people anxious, which in turn can depress their performance on such challenging tasks as tests."[19]

Although administrators should offer adequate professional development for teachers, teachers shouldn't rely solely on this. Instead, they should become proactive in searching for good test preparation materials in academic journals, educational magazines, and books, and on the Internet. For example, many school districts throughout the nation devote space on their websites to strategies for teachers, and some actually include related articles and lesson plans for teachers to use in order to prepare students for state-mandated tests. Duke and Ritchhart's article "No Pain, High Gain," which is available on the Internet at Scholastic's website (http://teacher.scholastic.com), contains reading strategies, math strategies, test format fundamentals, and "six ways to ease test stress."[20] This article is one option for teachers to consider. The following are some of the recurring themes in the various materials about test-taking strategies; teachers should

- Teach students about the various types of tests
- Teach students specific strategies for each type of test
- Emphasize the importance of being well rested and of eating a good breakfast before coming to school
- Stress to students the importance of reading and following the test directions carefully.

Teachers who want to go beyond the call of duty may also want to consider having snacks available for students who haven't had breakfast. This is something that one of my former colleagues did each year during the state-mandated testing period. The bottom line is that all teachers can do more to help students become better prepared for state-mandated tests.

Parents

The third component of the four-pronged approach to improving students' test scores concerns parents and guardians. Although teachers often blame them for students' poor test performance, many parents and guardians honestly don't know how to help their children improve their test scores. One way that administrators and teachers can assist them is by intensifying their efforts to increase parent involvement. Research on high-achieving, high-poverty, high-minority schools has shown that parent involvement is positively correlated to academic achievement.[21] In addition to sending home newsletters containing test-taking strategies for parents and guardians to review with their children, administrators can offer test-taking workshops consisting of strategies that parents and guardians can use at home. These workshops can also familiarize parents and guardians with important information about the high-stakes testing movement, especially the consequences of low test scores and their impact on students. Teachers can send home test preparation materials, such as packets and practice tests with which parents and guardians can assist their children. Educators should inform parents and guardians about resources in the wider community, such as church tutorial programs and educational assistance programs run by the YWCA, YMCA, and Boys and Girls Club of America.

Like teachers, parents and guardians will also find a lot of useful information on the Internet. Parents and guardians who don't have access to a computer at home can use the public library's resources. In California, the University of California system has an online tutorial program for which parents and guardians can pay $75 per semester. Students can receive help with exams, homework, and the college admission process through this service. Of course, many families can't afford this fee. These individuals can take advantage of free advice from such articles as the U.S. Department of Education's "Helping Your Child with Test-Taking: Helping Your Child Succeed in School" (available online at www.ed.gov) and Practical Parenting

Partnerships' "Test Taking Tips for Families" (available online at www.pppctr.org). Recurring themes among the test-taking strategies that parents and guardians should be aware of are that children need proper nutrition, rest, and encouragement before they take tests. Because some researchers have found that television viewing is correlated to test scores, I also recommend that parents limit the amount of time that their children spend watching television and playing video games, especially on school days.

Parents and guardians can consider additional options that are independent of the school system. In *And Still We Rise . . .* , Corwin described the great lengths that many affluent parents go to in order to ensure that their children will get high SAT scores for college. These parents pay exorbitant fees for review courses, such as the *Princeton Review,* personal tutors, and local extensive preparation courses for their children to have advantages that poor children don't have.[22] In my own case, I purchased SAT workbooks that contained background information, strategies, practice tests, and a CD-ROM, and urged my children to work on these books on a regular basis, especially over the summer and during the winter and spring breaks. Parents and guardians can do something similar for the K–12 state-mandated tests by checking out booklets from the local library or purchasing booklets containing test-taking strategies and practice tests.

Finally, one of the most important things parents can do is not to assume that their child is dumb just because he or she has earned low test scores. There are many reasons why children may earn high scores, but those scores cannot necessarily be equated with intelligence. Parents should keep in mind that high test scores may merely mean that a student has studied extensively for the test, the student's teacher devoted a lot of time to test preparation, cheating may have taken place, and so on. High test scores also don't necessarily equate to common sense, either. For example, my Weight Watchers leader recently told our class that one of her adult sons has always done well on tests and "lorded" his intelligence over others. "But he has absolutely no common sense whatsoever!" his mother exclaimed.

Parents should keep this in mind and not assume that their child is stupid, inferior, or a failure merely because she has earned low test scores. The same child who doesn't do well on pencil-and-paper or computerized tests may outperform high-scorers on tests if she is given opportunities to demonstrate what she knows through projects, essay writing, an oral quiz, or some other type of assessment.

Policymakers

At the school site, administrators and teachers can use many strategies to improve students' test scores. At home, parents can also do their part. For true reform to occur, however, policymakers must do a lot more than they are doing. In fact, some of the recommendations that I made to administrators and teachers can't be followed unless, first and most important, policymakers ensure that schools receive adequate funding for

- Testing aids, such as work booklets and practice tests
- Before- and after-school tutoring programs
- Special nutrition programs during testing week
- Professional development for school administrators and teachers
- Parent workshops
- Summer intervention programs for students
- Adequate salaries to attract qualified teachers

Second, policymakers must reexamine the whole notion of high-stakes testing to determine whether such testing actually measures skills that students can apply to other contexts or merely measures rote memorization and drilling, and results in widespread cheating.

Third, policymakers must become more inclusive when making decisions about how schools should be improved. Hosting community forums and town hall meetings in order to truly listen to the opinions of parents, educators, and students is one way of doing this.

Another is to visit schools on a regular basis to see what's really going on, observe the conditions that exist, and interact with educators and students. Policymakers shouldn't wait until election time to do this.

Finally, policymakers must become committed to systemic reform. As I've said previously and will keep saying throughout this book, social problems in the wider community and society affect the quality of schooling that America's stepchildren receive. True and lasting school reform can occur only when these conditions have been improved.

A Final Word

Although it won't solve the problem of the inherent biases in most state-mandated tests or the fact that K–12 students in the United States are required to take way too many tests, I believe that the four-pronged approach to improving students' test scores that I just described can help administrators, teachers, parents, and policymakers increase the likelihood that the students who have historically underperformed on standardized tests will have a better chance of doing well on them. However, I continue to believe that as long as adults base their assumptions about students on one type of assessment—standardized tests—they will continue to misjudge, mislabel, and harm some of the best and brightest students. This is an important issue for policymakers to examine and for educators and parents to keep in mind. To illustrate this point, I'll conclude with a related personal story.

I once had a very brilliant younger sister named Tammie. At an early age, she was labeled as gifted, and she spent her life living up to this label. Throughout her K–12 education, Tammie excelled academically at school, always earning top grades. Her reward was a full scholarship to a prestigious four-year university—a great accomplishment for a low-income child from a single-parent household in one of the worst neighborhoods of the city. Later, after earning a bachelor's degree, she excelled at law school. But even though she was an exemplary law student and even succeeded in earning her doctorate of jurisprudence, the one thing that kept her from attaining her dream of becoming an attorney was her inability to pass California's State Bar Exam, one of the nation's toughest. Before she took the exam, Tammie would become reclusive, holing herself up in her apartment and limiting her contact with the world so that she could study nonstop every day. Nevertheless, both times when she went to take the exam, the same thing happened: as she stared at the test, her mind went blank. She'd forget almost every single thing she'd studied.

The first time she failed, her confidence decreased somewhat, yet Tammie was still certain that she would pass on her second try. The next time she failed, however, there was a noticeable effect on her self-esteem. As she prepared to take the exam a third time, she became extremely secretive. She was too embarrassed for people to know that she'd failed twice. Unfortunately, we will never know if the third try would've been the "charm," for in 1995, Tammie died unexpectedly before she took the exam again.

I too had to take numerous state-mandated tests in order to attain my professional goals. For graduate school, I had to take the Graduate Record Exam. To become a teacher, I had to take the California Basic Educational Skills Test (CBEST) and the National Teachers Exam, two tests that were, undoubtedly, much easier to pass than the state bar exam that tormented my sister. To prepare myself for each test, I did exactly what Tammie had done. I sequestered myself in a room every evening and devoted hours to studying. I took practice tests that helped me identify the areas that I needed to work harder on, and did extra work in those areas. In spite of my lifelong test anxiety and aversion to taking tests, through a lot of prayer and hard work I passed both tests on my first attempts. But this doesn't mean that I am smart, any more than Tammie's failure to pass the bar exam meant that she wasn't capable of becoming a great attorney. In fact, her brilliance, competitiveness, determination to succeed, and impressive oratorical skills convinced all who knew her that—regardless of her bar exam score—she would've been an outstanding lawyer. After her death, the unforgettable impact she had on her professors prompted them to name a scholarship in her memory.

Tammie's experience and my own illustrate what can happen when a society places too much emphasis on one way of assessing what people know and are capable of. This story also illustrates how stereotype threat and test anxiety can prevent some individuals from demonstrating what they know. I'm convinced that if in addition to the written test, Tammie had also been given an oral test covering the same information, she would have passed with flying colors. Sadly, her situation isn't unusual. Countless students—especially America's stepchildren—at all levels of the U.S. education system will have their brilliance overlooked and their potential misunderstood as long as society continues to judge them solely by test scores and as long as schools fail to provide them with strategies to help them manage test anxiety and with adequate exposure to the subject matter covered on the required tests. This is the downside of high-stakes testing.

4

"They Just Think We're Loud"

How Discipline Policies and Practices Can Affect Students' Attitudes About School

During spring 2005, many Americans were appalled to see news footage of a five-year-old Florida child being handcuffed by police officers after her teacher and school administrators claimed that she was out of control. The girl was "arrested, cuffed, and put in the back of a police cruiser after an outburst at school where she threw books and boxes, kicked a teacher in the shins, smashed a candy dish, hit an assistant principal in the stomach and drew on the wall."[1] The fact that the child was misbehaving at school is indisputable, thanks to videotaped evidence. But the way in which her misbehavior was ultimately handled is another matter altogether.

This story was so shocking that news media throughout the United States as well as abroad covered the story. On the *Today Show*, co-host Katie Couric interviewed a school official and a lawyer representing the five-year-old's family. Among other questions, Couric asked whether or not school officials and police had overreacted. Many other observers of the videotape asked the same question. On Teachers.Net, a chatboard for Florida teachers, reactions were mixed. One kindergarten teacher wrote, "This little 5 year old is in kindergarten. If you have ever taught kinder you know that some of them still have bathroom accidents. Now the idea of arresting and wrapping up her wrists etc. and bringing in a police officer sounds a bit police state to me. Only in Florida could this happen."[2]

Another chatboard respondent strongly disagreed. According to this individual, "These are the type of children, who if allowed to get off scot free, end up leading a criminal life. Kudos to any school who has the "COURAGE" to have made and [sic] arrest. Obviously, the parent is in denial—until when, some other child or teacher gets killed—it won't be the first time. More action like this needs to occur to send the message "LOUD" & "CLEAR"—that assault (verbal or physical) will not be tolerated at any level."[3]

And so the debate went, with many individuals arguing that it was inappropriate to handcuff and arrest a five-year-old, and others arguing that authorities acted appropriately. For me, the incident raised several questions. As an African American, I wondered whether or not a white five-year-old who'd been behaving in exactly the same manner would have been treated like a criminal. I'm almost certain that a white child would not. After all, researchers have found that in both the pubic school system and the juvenile "justice" system, black and Latino youths are treated a lot more harshly than whites who engage in exactly the same or even worse behaviors. It is also well known that many educators engage in "adultification" when it comes to black students, especially black boys. Instead of viewing their actions as normal, childish behavior, educators view these students in the same manner that they view adults.[4] A story I wrote about in *Through Ebony Eyes* . . . illustrates this point. A black second grader kicked a chair one day. Instead of choosing one of the more rational options available to her, his teacher chose the most drastic one: she called the police and said that she feared her life was in danger. It was clear to me and to the white vice principal who shared this story with me that instead of seeing a *second grader* who was crying out for help, the teacher saw a predatory black *man* instead. All her subconscious fears and the negative messages she had been socialized to believe about black males surfaced when that child kicked the chair, and she acted accordingly.

A second question that came to my mind about the Florida incident was "How could the situation get to that point in the first place?" To be effective, good teachers are able to manage their classroom well. Starting on the first day of school, they make their expectations and rules clear to students and parents. They use appropriate consequences for misbehavior and are fair and consistent, and, when it comes to discipline, they treat students respectfully. These teachers spend the bulk of their class time on instruction, and they don't let any student prevent them from teaching or other students from learning. The opposite is true in classrooms where teachers have weak management skills. The teacher is usually timid and nonassertive, which means that students with strong personalities and natural leadership skills will assume the position of authority figure in the class. Students are permitted to treat each other and the teacher disrespectfully; the teacher is often accused of being biased, unfair, and inconsistent in enforcing rules; valuable instructional time is lost.

Regarding the Florida handcuffing case, I also wondered whether or not the child had been set up. Why was the teacher videotaping this particular child's behavior in the first place unless she had a hidden agenda? Most teachers don't have video cameras in their classrooms, and most don't videotape their students without permission from parents. If the teacher had already experienced problems with this particular child, she may have exacerbated or even orchestrated the situation in order to show that this child was so incorrigible that she needed to be permanently banned from the classroom. What the videotape that was aired nationwide and internationally didn't show was what happened *before* the child got out of control on that particular day. Had the teacher provoked her bad behavior, for example? The videotape also doesn't show how this child behaved in class on other days. Did she misbehave to this extreme every single day, and if so, why had she been permitted to remain in the classroom without intervention for so long? As I'm writing this paragraph, I'm thinking of all the teachers who may be offended by what I've said. But as an African American educator and parent, I know for a fact that it is possible for teachers to set up kids that they don't like. Teachers are human, and every teacher has students with whom she gets along better than others and whom she likes more than others. Sometimes—either consciously or unconsciously—a teacher's own attitude and behavior can create discipline problems. Let me share two related examples.

The first example pertains to one of my favorite former students. (Yes, like all teachers, I had favorite and not-so-favorite students, for when I became a teacher, I didn't lose my humanity or the characteristics that are common to all humans.) This African American girl had been in my tenth-grade class, and during that year, I learned a lot about her home life and childhood. Like myself, she'd come from an abusive background and had grown up with low self-esteem. So one of the things I tried to do was to build her self-confidence and help her focus on her potential to rise above her painful childhood experiences. We formed a strong bond, and she seemed to appreciate my efforts to be a positive role model to her. During her junior and senior years, she often visited my classroom to give me updates about her progress and the details of her life. She was serious about graduating, but like many adolescents, personal problems sometimes interfered with her doing her best work in her classes. In spite of this, I was shocked when she came to me in tears at the end of her senior year to inform me that she wouldn't be graduating after all. She had gotten into an argument with one of her teachers—a woman who had a reputation among her colleagues and students for having extremely low standards, doing very little teaching, and for being very lazy. According to my former student, when she and this teacher were arguing, the student said, "You don't teach nothing anyway." Because the argument occurred in front of other students, the teacher became embarrassed and vowed that she would prevent the girl from graduating. She kept her word. She found the ammunition she needed: during the final quarter, the student had been absent from her class for thirteen days, and despite the actual passing grade she'd earned in the class, the teacher used the absences as justification to fail her. When I went to talk to the teacher about what I'd heard, she smugly told me that the thirteen absences justified her decision to fail this student. But she and I both knew the real reason for her actions: she was retaliating because the student had publicly humiliated her.

The other story that illustrates that teachers are not only human, but also can use their dislike of a particular student as an excuse to retaliate against the student or set the student up, is a story I included in *Through Ebony Eyes*. My third grade teacher, Ms. Root, was a white woman who clearly hated black children, even though she taught at a predominantly black school. Ms. Root used extreme forms of punishment, which included making me stand in front of the class with a wedge of cardboard in my mouth for excessive talking, permitting a father literally to whip his daughter in class after Ms. Root had complained to him about the daughter's excessive talking, not allowing children to go to the restroom when they needed to do so, and making us watch the terrifying and racist film *Birth of a Nation*. Although she was mean to all her black students (not only during the year that I was in her class, but in previous years as well), she was particularly sadistic toward certain black students. One was a sensitive little girl who often cried in class because she said she was hungry. I'll never forget the one morning when this girl didn't cry in class. Instead of being happy about it, Ms. Root walked over to the child and asked her why she wasn't crying that day. She then proceeded to goad her into crying and actually said repeatedly, "Go on and squeeze those tears out; squeeze them out" until the girl began to cry.[5]

The bottom line is what a retired white teacher from Minnesota once told me: "Everybody has baggage, and baggage counts."[6] Teachers are no exception. However, many teachers aren't aware of the connection between their teaching efficacy and "baggage" that consists of deficit-oriented beliefs about various individual students or groups of students—especially America's stepchildren. This baggage can cause teachers to engage in unfair or biased behavior of which they aren't even aware but that students notice. Discipline problems can surface as a result. Because student misbehavior and discipline problems are linked to teacher morale, satisfaction, and retention rates, and also linked to the amount and quality of instruction that students receive, discipline is a very important topic. In the next section, we hear what the students and teachers at American High School said about discipline and classroom management at the school.

What the Students Said

In the first phase of the study, the overwhelming majority of the teachers at American High School said that most of their students were well behaved during class, and that they spent the majority of most class sessions on instruction rather than discipline. On these points, there appeared to be consensus among the students and teachers, for the majority of the students who completed the questionnaire said they were well behaved in most of their classes. However, white students were more likely than Latinos and African Americans to say they were well behaved, and females were more likely than males to say so.

Despite these questionnaire results, many of the student focus group participants complained about teachers who had no class control. For example, one student said, "Most of the classes I've had are out of control. Teachers don't know how to handle the class, and it's really noisy and hard to concentrate." Another student said, "If you're going to be a teacher, you should be able to control your classroom." A third focus group participant made a similar point: "It doesn't matter how many classes you have or how many students you have, you're still supposed to be able to take control of each and every class and each and every student in your classroom. I don't care: you can be the youngest teacher here, but you should have some control over your classroom. The students will look down on you like you're a kid yourself and wonder what you're doing here."

Several students who lost respect for teachers with weak classroom management skills spoke about specific teachers or classes that were out of control, and the effect these classes had on them. An African American girl said that she failed the math portion of the HSEE for this very reason. According to this student, "Last year, I tried to get out of a math class that was out of control, and they wouldn't let me get out of the class. I didn't learn anything. It was a waste of my whole entire year, [and I] didn't pass my exit exam because I didn't get enough help with it." In complaining about her own math class, an African American girl stated, "In my fourth period algebra class, those kids are outrageous. They are horrible. I'm a 'kick back' person, but if [the teacher] is going to teach something, I'm going to do my work. Lately, he hasn't been teaching nothing because the class is outrageously horrible. He has no control over the class. Most of the kids in there are black. The white kids just separate themselves, and I don't blame them. I'll go sit with them too."

Another student said that during the previous year, her algebra class was even worse than that of the aforementioned student's: "They should be aware of the teachers that they pick. Last year, I didn't learn anything in my Algebra 1 class. The class was totally out of control. People used to smoke in that class. People threw things at the teacher. Kids were so out of control, he called security a lot. But sometimes, they wouldn't even come because they knew how it was. It was just ridiculous, and I didn't like that class at all."

According to a Latina, "Another thing is that the teachers need to keep control of their classes. I have a teacher and we all get in trouble and everybody ditches that class. Everybody's talking and you can't learn in an environment like that. Last year, I had a teacher that the students would curse out. They would just stand up; they'd leave the class. Other people from the P.E. area would come into the class, and we couldn't learn nothing and the teacher's laughing."

Discipline Referrals, Suspensions, and Fights

Three questionnaire items provided more information about student behavior, specifically the percentage of students who had received discipline referrals, had been suspended, or who had been in fights at school. Most of the students said they'd never been in a fight or physical altercation at school, but once again, race and gender differences were apparent. Males, especially African Americans, were more likely than females to have been in a fight or physical altercation. Whereas there was little difference between the percentage of white (65 percent) and Latino (64 percent) males who'd never been in a fight at school, the percentage of black males (51 percent) was noticeably lower. Among the female questionnaire respondents, white females were more likely than African Americans and Latinas to say they'd never been in a fight at American High School.

Nearly 40 percent of the students who completed the questionnaire said they had received one or more discipline referrals to the school office. In this case, a higher percentage of white students than African Americans and Latinos said they had received at least one discipline referral at American High School. In fact, more than half the white males said they had.

Regarding suspension from school, although the majority of students said they'd never been suspended, a higher percentage of African Americans than Latinos and whites had been suspended from American High School. African American and Latino males were more likely than all other subgroups to have been suspended, and Latinas and white males were less likely than all groups, including white females, to have been suspended.

During the focus group discussions, many students complained about the suspension policy at school, which they appeared to believe was ineffective and unwise. (Evidently there were two forms of suspension: in-school suspension and the traditional form of suspension prohibiting the student from returning to school for a specific amount of time.) One student said, "I think we get in trouble for the stupidest reasons. You can do something little and you get suspended. When it's something major, people don't get in trouble. But for the smallest things, you get a phone call home, or in-school suspension." Another student added, "I got suspended for fighting, but it wasn't my fault. I got suspended for five days, and it made my grades drop because during that week, I had something really important to do. I couldn't do it, because I was suspended. They say you're supposed to go up to the school to get your work, but at the same time, the principal was telling me that I was not allowed on campus. That's wasting my time. Now I have to transfer from this school to another school, because if I'm here, my grade is not going to go nowhere."

Regarding the policy of suspending students for fighting, another focus group participant explained, "If you get in a fight, you get suspended. Say, you're standing there, and a girl socks you in your face. You're not going to just stand there. I think that's a form of self-defense. Somebody hits you, you're going to hit them back. If somebody comes up to you and starts a fight, then that person should get suspended, because it's their fault."

Some students also believed that it was illogical to suspend students for violating the school's dress code. According to one focus group participant, "We're supposed to come to school to learn. What are we learning in in-school suspension? You send me there for three days for wearing flip-flops, but what am I learning? During ninth grade, they tried to make me pick up trash. My mother came up to this school and said, 'That's what the janitors get paid to do.' That's like scraping gum off the desk; you can get sick from that, and they don't even give you gloves! I'm not going to pick up nobody's trash!"

A student who believed that the length of off-campus suspension time was counterproductive and could actually lead to worse behavior stated, "I feel that when students get suspended, five days is too long for a dress code violation, for getting into a fight, or for throwing water at somebody, because you can do a lot in five days. I can think of something off the wall for five days just sitting at home."

Discipline Policies and Practices

Two questionnaire statements gave students an opportunity to express their opinions about their teachers' discipline practices and about school discipline policies in general. When it came to overall school discipline policies, less than half the student survey respondents agreed that the discipline policies at American High School were used fairly. Although a slightly higher percentage of Latino students than African Americans and whites believed the policies were used fairly, white females and Latino males were least likely to believe this.

Nearly 60 percent of the students said that most of their teachers were fair about discipline. However, whites were more likely than Latinos and African Americans to agree that this was true. More specifically, white males were more inclined to believe that this was true, and African American females were the least likely.

Some of these differences surfaced during the focus group discussions, particularly among the African American and Latino students. Many students in these groups believed they had been subjected to unfair treatment by teachers who had double standards about discipline practices. For example, an African American girl said, "We were taking a test, and this girl was talking to the teacher. They were just having a conversation. But when I asked the teacher a question, he said, 'Be quiet. Don't be talking during the test.'"

According to another African American focus group participant, "I don't like how some of the teachers talk to the students. Some students won't be doing anything, and they'll just be discussing something with the teacher. I've had teachers say to students, 'Oh, you're insecure and you're just a jerk.' Also, students have walked in late, and instead of changing it to a tardy, the teacher will mark the student absent, so it can go on that student's record. They just do it to some students."

Several African American students shared similar stories about teachers who singled out certain students. For example, three focus group participants described English teachers who were guilty of doing this. One of these students remarked, "There's one particular English teacher who likes to do that and it's only because I am the only black student in that class. So, she picks on me at a constant pace: 'Oh, you're talking. Well, I saw *you*.' I'm like, 'But she's talking to me. I'm commenting on what she said.' The teacher says, 'Well, I saw *you* talking, so you're going to get the disciplinary action.' If I don't back off, she's going to yell at me and pinpoint me, but I haven't done anything wrong."

As other students noted, the problem was not just restricted to English teachers. Another focus group participant said:

> The other day, I was in my eleventh grade history class. My history teacher constantly picks on me. We finished class five minutes before the bell rings. So, I'm sitting on the table and everybody else is out of their seats. He told me that I need to sit in my seat, and I'm looking around at every single student. Nobody's sitting in their seats; everybody's talking. And he's like, "Why aren't you sitting in your seat?" I said, "Wait a minute. Do you see any other student sitting in their seat? Do you see any other student being quiet?" He said that I was going to in-school suspension and I said, "Well, send me, because I'm about to go to lunch anyway." So, he told me that I would have to be in there the next day too. I said, "I don't care, because I feel that you shouldn't pick on me, because I'm not the only one sitting on the desk; everybody else is too." He always picks on me.

A student who said she had been treated differently by an economics teacher recounted:

> This year, I had economics with one teacher for the first few weeks of school, and then they transferred us to another teacher, because they said the class was overcrowded. The second teacher didn't know what he was talking about. My mom called many times complaining, because he treated me differently from all the other students. He always had a problem with me. He didn't know what he was talking about and couldn't control the classroom. People would walk in thirty minutes after the bell rang and he wouldn't say nothing. But let *me* walk in thirty minutes late, and he would make sure that *I* went to in-school suspension.

Right before we were about to switch to civics, he got fired. Obviously, they knew he wasn't a good teacher. That jacked up my grade for the class, because it was bad enough they transferred me in there in the first place. Then they had to transfer me out. That's playing with my grade and that's a class that I have to have to graduate.

One of the most common complaints from African American students was that teachers penalized them for being outspoken and accused them of being loud while ignoring similar behaviors from other students. As one focus group participant stated, "It seems like we just get more attention, just because we're black: 'Oh, she's loud.' The person next to me is talking too, just as loud as I am."

Another student added, "I know white people that get loud. . . . Anybody could be loud. . . . They probably say we're louder, because we're black. So, everybody always says, 'Why are you yelling?' We're not yelling." Another girl remarked, "We want to be heard."

One of the African American male focus group participants insisted, "They got it twisted. It's like everybody's loud. Everybody is like that, but they look at black people and they start pointing it out." Another African American male agreed, stating, "The classes are mostly white and Latino around here anyway. You have two or three black people and you see them talking, but everybody else is talking, but they blend into the crowd. But black people stand out."

An African American student who was suspended from class for voicing her displeasure to a teacher explained,

Last week, I got in trouble. I got kicked out because my teacher was taking class time to help students who are failing the class to help them graduate when, obviously, they don't want to graduate. This girl has not passed the Writing Proficiency Test, she hasn't passed the Math Proficiency Test, and these are things she has to pass to graduate. Three weeks before graduation, if she hasn't done it, then, obviously, she doesn't want it to be done. . . . So, I let the teacher know that's not fair to us. We're sitting [there] not doing nothing but being bored, just sitting there not doing nothing. To a lot of students that might be okay, but to me, that's not fair. I got in-school suspension for saying so. On my referral, [the teacher] wrote that I wouldn't back down and that I had an attitude. It wasn't that I had an attitude, but she wasn't understanding what I was saying, and it wasn't fair. She said, "Well, I'm trying to help a student." If a student doesn't want to help herself, then you can't help her that much. And this girl didn't even come to school today!

An African American male said that even when African American students' talkativeness was focused on class work, they were penalized by some teachers. According to this student, "We like to express ourselves. Even though we louder and stuff, doesn't mean that we ain't talking about the assignment. Sometimes, we louder but not all the time. But . . . we could still be talking about the assignment and we'll still get in trouble, because the teacher thinks that we're always loud."

An African American male who believed that teachers singled out black kids as a strategic move said, "We're outnumbered, because there is a lot of Latinos and whites out here. But the teachers look at us and they see us all huddled together. . . . They look right at us and they figure that if they can get us to shut up, then they [white and Latino students] gon' follow us. If they can get the black kids in that class to sit there and be quiet, then they figure that the rest of the kids are gon' sit there and be quiet too."

Although the African American focus group participants were more vocal than other groups in complaining about unfair discipline practices by teachers, several Latino students also complained. For example, a Latina remarked, "I'm Hispanic, and if it's a group of my Hispanic friends, and we're sitting in the back, talking whatever, and there's a couple of white girls in the front talking, the teacher will yell at us and tell us to shut up. But the two girls up in the front don't get told anything."

Another Latina stated: "That happens to us in my sixth period class. My Hispanic friends and I are talking and then, there's African Americans who come in the classroom talking, and the teacher doesn't say nothing. In my fourth period class, there's an African American student who's my friend. He didn't have his passbook and the teacher didn't let him go to the bathroom. But this white cheerleader didn't have her passbook and the teacher let her go to the bathroom."

Another Latina said,

Whenever I talk to my African American friend in class when the teacher gives us time to talk, the history teacher gets mad at us for no reason, just gets crazy all of a sudden. There'll be like somebody right in front of us talking and he won't say nothing. I'm not racist or nothing, but it'll be like two white girls, and he won't say nothing to them. But I really don't like it that he's always singling us out. It's always us; we're always getting into trouble. He's always looking at us, always checking us out, looking at us to make sure that we're not talking together. That really bugs me.

Another Latina believed that her English teacher showed favoritism toward male athletes and said that this teacher's unprofessional behavior almost provoked the student to violence:

I'm in the army and I have a teacher who happened to say that if my parents got a letter saying that I was dead, she'd laugh in their face. I felt like getting up and slapping her. She was totally serious [and said that] I joined the army to die. I think she's like Communist or something. I don't know. She says she is. I believe that if you're going to teach English, teach English. I don't care what your feelings are. She brings in her feelings. If I say something, she always has to contradict it. She always has to say something, so we're always bumping heads. She's supposed to be the teacher. She's supposed to stay on her level and let me be on my level. I let her know that it was making me feel uncomfortable, and she changed it, but she still always brings her personal feelings to the class. She does that a lot and she's in love with all of the guys and jocks. . . . She's always hugging on them, taking pictures with them, always the males. She's just always preferring the males. If you're a jock, if you're a guy, in general, if you give her a hug, then she's cool with you. One of my friends didn't have a class and didn't have nowhere to go . . . and I asked the teacher if she could stay in our class. The teacher said, "No." Later, two football players walked in and she let them chill in there. She just has a preference for the guys. She tells them, "You guys are so cute. Let me take a picture."

School Security

Nearly 30 percent of the student questionnaire respondents said that school security had treated them unfairly. White students, especially males, were more likely than blacks and Latinos to say this. Black males and Latinas were more likely than all groups to say that most security treated them fairly.

The focus group participants were extremely vocal about their experiences with school security. Recurring complaints were that (1) security often condoned fighting; (2) security practiced gender bias in favor of female students; (3) security was inconsistent about penalizing students for dress code violations; and (4) according to some African American students, security permitted white students to get away with dress code violations for which African Americans were penalized. (We'll hear more about school security in the next two chapters.) In response to the last point, some white female focus group participants pointed out that white students who dressed in black or in "goth" clothing were sometimes singled out. For example, a white student remarked:

It's not necessarily just me. It is the people that I hang out with, you know. The things they do, like, are wrong. For example, if you are walking and you look different from somebody else. You know, if you're just walking around, whatever, this is who you are. They single you out like you have something in your backpack. Like, you have a lighter in your backpack or something like that, you know, and it's just 'cause we look like this, that we have all of this crap in our backpack. You can't do that to somebody. Unless you know the facts, then don't come up to me. Because I don't like that, because, like, they do come up to you, like "Do you have something?" and, like, no you don't. They search you and they find nothing. Don't they feel stupid now that they didn't find anything? It's just like, "okay whatever."

In explaining her views about security, another white student stated:

Security's priorities are out of order. They're concerned more about what people are wearing than how they are acting. Like, if they see someone—like this actually happened to me: one of my friends was talking to another friend and, like, using a lot of foul language and the friend that was listening had a hat on. He was just sitting there. This guy was loud 'cause he was cussing loud. Security says, "Hey," and points to the guy with the hat and says, "Take that hat off and come with me." The other guy didn't get into trouble and he's like, "Wow!"

Tying It All Together

The feedback from the teachers and students at American High School about classroom management and discipline practices and policies showed that although most teachers appeared to have good classroom management skills and to be fair in enforcing discipline policies, there were some problems that needed to be addressed. Too many teachers were perceived by students as engaging in practices based on sexism, racism, or other personal biases. African Americans and Latinos were less likely than whites to believe that most teachers enforced discipline policies fairly, and less than half the students who completed the questionnaire believed that schoolwide discipline policies were used fairly. In fact, according to the students, some classes appeared to be totally out of control. In these classrooms, students felt that they were being shortchanged academically and not being prepared for the HSEE.

What We Can Do

The following sections describe my recommendations of ways to alleviate some of the problems the students described.

Administrators

There are several ways that administrators can ensure that school discipline policies and practices are effectively implemented and used fairly. Creating an advisory board that consists of students, parents, teachers, and community leaders is a good way to start. The advisory board can examine all school and district discipline policies to see if they are logical and effective, and make suggestions to the school principal.

Administrators must also do their own personal growth work. They must examine any negative, racist, and sexist beliefs they hold that can cause them to promote or tolerate unfair discipline practices and policies. For example, I've heard of several cases in which school officials created policies that prohibited students from wearing clothing that was associated with black gangs or hip-hop culture, while at the same time ignoring and thereby condoning the wearing of clothing associated with white supremacist groups. At one local high school for instance, black students complained to me that white students were allowed to write "KKK" and "white power" on their tennis shoes, but black students were disciplined for wearing so-called gang colors. At another local school in an affluent white community, a white student who wore clothing associated with a white supremacist group was attacked by a group of Arab American students after making racist statements. In another case, a school administrator unknowingly engaged in blatantly racist behavior in my presence. I was visiting his school to collect data from students for a study I was conducting. The only time he visited was when I was about to work with black male students. Before I could even begin to explain anything to the students, the principal warned them that they had better treat me with respect and had better behave. He came into that room with the expectation that this group of students would be problematic, yet he never did this for any other group of students who participated in my study. Although this principal believed that he had a good rapport with students, he wasn't aware of some of his own racist baggage—anti-black baggage that also surfaced in my presence on another occasion.

Principals should also offer professional development opportunities for teachers and become familiar with the most current research about effective schoolwide discipline. One of the most ridiculous cases I've heard regarding white teachers who were in drastic need of immediate professional development to deal with their racist baggage was shared with me by an African American principal in the Omaha Public Schools. According to this principal, teachers often sent black students to her office for sneezing and coughing in class! They wanted the principal to suspend the students for disrupting their class. Although it is possible that some students might use coughing and sneezing to disrupt class, the principal got the impression that these teachers were merely looking for any excuse to complain about African American students, and they automatically assumed that when the students sneezed and coughed in class, they had bad intentions, instead of possibly having a cold or allergy. Teachers who can't think of alternatives to suspension for sneezing and coughing need immediate classroom management assistance, or even a different type of job—one that doesn't involve African American kids.

Teachers should also have access to an on-site professional development library that includes books about effective classroom management, and they should be encouraged to attend related workshops. Administrators should provide additional assistance to teachers who continue to struggle in this area. Through classroom observation and mentoring, administrators should offer practical strategies to these teachers. The classroom management exercises in Appendixes F and G can be useful. Furthermore, giving struggling teachers opportunities to visit the classrooms of veteran teachers who have good classroom management skills is another option.

Administrators should also be receptive to what parents and students have to say. When parents and students complain about teachers' behaviors, school administrators should listen at the very least and give them the benefit of the doubt. Telling a parent or student who is complaining about a teacher, "This is the first time I've heard *that*" or "You're the first person who has told me *that*" isn't necessarily the best response to complaints. As the old saying goes, "There's a first time for everything." Just because a principal is hearing a certain complaint for the first time doesn't mean that the problem hasn't happened before or that the parent or student is lying. A wise principal will listen objectively, examine the evidence, talk to the teacher, and then decide how to proceed.

A related story that comes to mind involves a school administrator who used the ineffective approach of discounting students' complaints by saying, "You're the first person who has told me that" even if it wasn't true. At this particular school, it was well-known that a certain teacher made racist remarks to students on a regular basis. However, no one intervened. One day, the teacher pushed a student over the edge by making one racist remark too many. A Latino student rushed over to the teacher, picked him up, and slammed him to the floor. Of course, the student was punished by school officials, but finally, the teacher was removed from the classroom. Because of the strong teachers' union, he wasn't fired but merely allowed to sit at the school district office and collect a paycheck.

Finally, administrators should do what research has shown that effective leaders of high-performing, high-minority, high-poverty schools do: they should use data wisely. In an effort to learn valuable lessons about schoolwide and classroom discipline policies and prac-tices, administrators should examine patterns in teacher referrals, security referrals, in-school suspensions, out-of-school suspensions, and expulsions. If a high school student is repeatedly being sent to the office only by a math teacher but never by any of his other teachers, the principal and staff should identify the reasons. Why is the stu-dent behaving well in other teachers' classes but not in this one? If 70 percent of the referrals and complaints from a security guard pertain to African American females, the principal should figure out why this is so. As the national trend suggests, if black and Latino males at the school are more likely than all other groups to be suspended and expelled from school, the principal should figure out why this is so and use his or her advisory team (which should include black and Latino males, as well as other groups) to develop solutions.

Teachers

Teachers having good teaching skills, knowing their subject matter well, and designing outstanding lesson plans are of course critical to creating a classroom environment in which optimum learn-ing occurs. With regard to discipline, there are many additional ways teachers can promote and maintain such an environment. First, teachers must be willing to act like a leader—the person in charge of the classroom. Teachers who are weak, cowardly, and nonassertive will give students the impression that they aren't worthy of respect.[7] Time and time again, I've heard of cases where assertive students controlled the classroom of a timid teacher. As I said previously in this chapter and in some of my other work, teachers who have been socialized to be unassuming, passive, and nonassertive must work on this area of their personal growth in order to develop good classroom management skills. The following books may be helpful to these teachers:

- *Through Ebony Eyes: What Teachers Need to Know but Are Afraid to Ask About African American Students* (Gail L. Thompson)

- *The Dreamkeepers: Successful Teachers of African American Children* (Gloria Ladson-Billings)
- *The Disease to Please: Curing the People Pleasing Syndrome* (Harriet Braiker)
- *Black Students/Middle Class Teachers* (Jawanza Kunjufu)
- *Emotional Blackmail* (Susan Forward)

Second, teachers must examine their mind-set and any negative beliefs that may cause them to knowingly or unknowingly target certain students or groups for unfair discipline practices. The three-part, long-term professional development plan for educators that I described at the end of *Through Ebony Eyes . . .* can help teachers begin the process of examining their beliefs about African Americans. The exercises at the end of each chapter in Wing Sue's *Overcoming Our Racism: The Journey to Liberation* can help teachers uncover negative beliefs they may have about African Americans, Asian Americans, Latinos, and even whites.

Third, teachers should look for the messages that are hidden in students' misbehavior. A misbehaving student may be trying to hide an academic weakness, such as that he is too embarrassed to read orally because he knows he doesn't read well, has been laughed at in the past by other students, and doesn't want the teacher or his classmates to know that he can't decode words well. The student might therefore create a distraction in order to be kicked out of class or to keep the teacher from calling on him to read.

A misbehaving student might also be suffering from family problems and crying out for help in the only way that he knows how. For example, an elementary school teacher recently told me that one of the African American boys in his class was about to be expelled from school. The child had experienced a lot of personal problems at home and had been transferred from another school. At his new school, he acted out in class by cursing and through other disruptive behaviors. According to the teacher, the boy's mother had been very supportive in trying to work with the teacher to resolve the problems. After six months, however, the teacher was so frustrated with the child's behavior that he felt that expulsion was the only solution. "I did my best," he told me. But the look on his face and the tone of his voice gave me the impression that he wasn't entirely convinced that he'd made the right decision. I also sensed that he needed my reassurance and approval. Because I didn't know this teacher and had never observed his teaching and classroom management practices, I had no way of knowing what his "best" entailed. Maybe advice about additional strategies to use with the problematic boy might have changed the outcome of the situation. Maybe not. I do know that some teachers have been able to serve as positive role models and "turnaround" teachers to children with whom other teachers have failed.[8] But sometimes even the most well-meaning teachers aren't able to turn around a child who is on a path of failure. This is a reality in schools throughout the nation.

Fourth, teachers should look for patterns that emerge in their classroom. If the same individuals or groups of students are constantly off task or engaging in disruptive behaviors, and the teacher has ruled out academic weaknesses and personal problems, the teacher should look for other causes. Sometimes, for example, certain students or groups misbehave in order to let the teacher know that they don't respect him or her. During presentations that I gave in Los Angeles County in late 2005 and early 2006, two white teachers shared related stories with me. Both of the teachers were in their first or second year of teaching; one of the teachers was quite young and the other, judging from her appearance, was middle-aged or older.

The middle-aged teacher told me she needed help with classroom management because she has a "mellow" personality and had started the school year off being quite lax about discipline. Now the school year was almost over, and many of her high school students, especially the black ones, were frequently "loud" and having "side conversations" while she was trying to teach.

After hearing her complaint, I reminded this teacher of what I had said earlier during my presentation on classroom management: the way you start out the year will largely determine the type of school year you'll have. I went on to repeat that it is important for teachers to start setting the appropriate tone on the first day of school by making their rules and expectations clear and explicit, both verbally and in writing, and by having students and their parents sign a form indicating that they understand the teacher's rules and expectations.

By behaving in a "mellow" way at the beginning of the school year and being lax about discipline, this teacher had unknowingly given students permission to misbehave in her class by failing to make her rules and expectations explicit, to be consistent in enforcing rules, and to assume the role of authority figure. A teacher can't let students engage in side conversations, talk loudly in class, and remain off task from September until March and then expect them to change in April after she's tolerated this inappropriate behavior for six months out of a nine-month school year. By then it is too late.

In the second case, a young white teacher interrupted me at the beginning of one of my presentations in late 2005. "I wasn't racist when I started teaching this year, but now I'm becoming racist because I'm having problems with all of my black students." When I heard these remarks, I wondered what message *all* the black students in her class had inferred from her through her actions and the hidden curriculum that caused *every single one of them* to misbehave in her classroom. Moreover, in saying that she was "becoming racist," I believe the teacher was deceiving herself. In my opinion, her negative experiences with her black students merely brought out what was already lying dormant inside of her or what was hidden in her subconscious. In other words, I believe that she was racist when she walked into her classroom on the first day of school, but like countless teachers, she may have been ignorant or in denial about her racism—a "color-blind racist" wearing the façade of liberalism and tolerance.

In my more than twenty years of work as an educator, I've never had, never seen, and never heard of a classroom in which *all* the white, Latino, Asian American, or black students misbehaved.

Either this teacher was exaggerating when she shared her problem with me and lumping all the black kids together as an indistinguishable group, or she had given the black kids the impression that they needed to misbehave in order to send her a message. That message could have been "We think you're racist," "We think you pick on us," "We don't think you deserve our respect because we can tell that you don't like us and are scared of us," "We know you really think that black people are dumb," or "We don't think you're qualified to be our teacher, because you don't know how to teach, you don't know your subject matter, and your expectations are so low that you don't even bother to create lesson plans ahead of time." The bottom line is that in the extremely unusual case where *all* the students of one racial or ethnic group are misbehaving in a certain teacher's classroom, this should be a bright red flag to that teacher, and he or she needs to identify the reason for the misbehavior and find appropriate solutions.

Two of the "homework assignments" that I've created for teachers who participate in some of my classroom management workshops can help teachers improve their skills by identifying patterns that surface in their classroom, uncovering hidden messages that students may be trying to send, and facing their own baggage that might be creating problems in their classroom. These assignments are included in their entirety in Appendixes F and G.

Parents

It is well known that parents and guardians are children's first teachers and that children learn many lessons about life from their primary caregivers. Parents who rear their children in a home in which love and appropriate discipline are balanced are more likely than weak or abusive parents to produce emotionally healthy children. We've all heard nightmare stories about what can happen when children are abused. In worst-case scenarios, they can grow into Hitlers and Stalins. Both of these men were abused by their fathers during childhood, and when they became adults, the rest of the world had to suffer the consequences. Good parents don't take advantage of the power they wield over their children, but they do teach them to be respectful, especially of individuals who are in positions of authority.

Unfortunately, like many teachers who are nonassertive, some parents don't set the right tone with regard to respect. One woman whom I know quite well learned this lesson the hard way. Because her father had given her brutal beatings during her childhood, she went to the opposite extreme when she became a single parent. In an effort to treat her own daughter more humanely than her father had treated her, she decided that all forms of discipline were bad, especially corporal punishment. Therefore, before the child was out of diapers or could walk, she was slapping her mom in the face and pulling her mom's pierced earrings out of her ears without any consequences. Beyond saying "Stop," the mom didn't know what else to do. So, to the child's obvious delight, Mom would throw up her hands in frustration whenever the girl misbehaved. Because the mother didn't discipline her child, the girl got the impression that it was okay to slap Mom whenever the urge arose. But her treatment of her maternal grandmother was entirely different. She never slapped Grandma, because early on, Grandma had made it clear that she wouldn't tolerate this behavior. Predictably, by the time the child was in fifth or sixth grade, she was totally out of control at home, and her mother didn't know what to do. Mom couldn't even go on dates because the child would let any prospective suitor know that she was in charge of the household and didn't want her mom dating anyone. Moreover, by this time, the girl had also become verbally abusive toward her mother.

When a child is permitted to misbehave at home and allowed to verbally or physically abuse a parent, it's unlikely that such a child will be well behaved at school. Ironically, however, it isn't impossible. In the case of the mother-slapping, earring-pulling baby whose disrespect for her mother grew over time, she was a different child at school. In fact, she earned good grades and was considered to be a model student. By the time she was in ninth grade, she'd made up her mind to eventually apply to Yale, Stanford, and several other prestigious schools. In my opinion, the difference between her behavior at home and her behavior at school stemmed from explicit expectations, consistency, and consequences. At home, her mother started out by giving the child mixed messages about who was in charge and by letting her have her way, even when she behaved inappropriately. The mother failed to clearly articulate and demonstrate her expectations about how her daughter should behave, and when the child misbehaved, the mother was inconsistent in applying consequences or used ineffective ones. Evidently, school was different. The girl who was a "monster" at home was an "angel" at school. I believe that her teachers made all the difference. I remember, for example, that the girl once told me about her favorite teacher at the time. The only thing I recall from that conversation is that the teacher was a strict, no-nonsense African American woman who had very high expectations of her students, even though they were enrolled in one of the nation's worst school districts.

Although this story had a somewhat happy ending regarding the girl's behavior at school, many similar stories don't. Numerous teachers have complained to me about contacting the parents of kids who misbehaved at school and finding that the parents didn't know what to do, often even asking the teachers for suggestions on how to rear their children. Just as teachers who aren't assertive must work specifically on this problem, the same is true of weak parents. There are lots of books that can help parents in this area. The bottom line is that parents shouldn't condone their children's bad behavior *at home or at school.*

A second way in which parents can increase the likelihood that their children will behave at school is to explicitly discuss school rules and how the parents expect their children to behave. In the case where a teacher doesn't send home a form on the first day of school that explains his or her rules and expectations, parents can discuss them with the teacher during Back to School Night or by telephone.

Third, parents should listen to their children and know them well enough to determine when complaints about teachers are warranted. For instance, the parent of a lazy student or a procrastinator should know whether or not her child has had a history of complaining about teachers who have high expectations and who give a lot of homework. But the parent of a child who doesn't have a history of complaining about teachers should listen carefully and take complaints seriously when they arise. One mother whom I know became concerned when her son, an African American elementary school student, started dreading school. In the past, he had earned good grades and had loved school. In second grade, however, he began to complain that his teacher didn't like him and was always picking on him. The mother eventually transferred her son to another school, and lo and behold, everything changed. The new teacher had a positive attitude toward the boy, recognized that he was smart and wanted to do well, and treated him fairly. From that point on, he stopped complaining about going to school.

Policymakers

Some of the problems associated with unfair school discipline policies and practices are related to systemic problems, institutional racism, gender bias, and media bias. In the larger society, law enforcement and the juvenile "justice" system have had a history of engaging in unfair, biased, and racist treatment, especially of black and Latino males. Corruption is rampant in these organizations. It's difficult—if not impossible—for America's stepchildren, especially those from low-income backgrounds, to get a fair trial in America, even for minor offenses. The media have also historically provided negative and biased coverage of America's stepchildren and have thereby promoted the widespread belief that these individuals are prone to criminality. So by the time students of color arrive at school, there is little wonder that administrators, teachers, and school security may look for problems and overreact to behaviors among these children that they may ignore in whites. After all, that's the American Way.

Policymakers need to pay more attention to the widespread inequities that are fostered by law enforcement agencies and the so-called justice system. Every child who lives in a low-income neighborhood, an inner city, or any other place where America's stepchildren are forced to reside because of a limited income, residential segregation, and racist bank lending practices learns at an early age that he doesn't necessarily have the same rights and probably won't receive the same treatment as middle- and upper-class whites in America. In other words, he learns about his second-class citizenship and stepchild status early. Unfortunately, too many policymakers don't care about these problems—at least not enough to change the status quo. As long as policymakers remain unconcerned about these and other problems plaguing underper-forming schools and the communities where America's stepchildren reside, badly functioning schools will never be completely reformed.

A Final Word

When I was a high school teacher, I had an opportunity one summer to serve as a scorer for the essay component of what was then the state-mandated test. Of all the teachers who had been accepted to serve as scorers, only two of us were African American. Practically all the other teachers were white, and all the trainers and officials in charge were white. The scoring session lasted for several days. For the most part, it went smoothly for me, but on the last day, an inci-dent occurred that pertains to some of the lessons I've learned about educators, discipline practices, and negative beliefs about America's stepchildren that are common in U.S. society.

The way the scoring session worked was that all the teachers traveled to a designated site in northern California and received background information and training on the first day. The objective was for the teachers to learn to use the same criteria for scoring each essay, so that when another scorer read an essay that had already been scored by another teacher, the scores would match or be similar enough not to warrant the input of a third scorer. During the next two days, we read and scored thousands of student writing samples. Short breaks were designated, and one hour was set aside for lunch each day. Scorers were aware, however, that they were free throughout the day to get snacks from the snack table or take a restroom break when needed, even during nondesignated break times. This had been the pattern for the first two days, and there hadn't been any problem.

About three-fourths of the way through the last scoring day, a problem arose, and the rules changed. After reading numerous essays, eye strain and fatigue convinced me that I needed to get up and move a little. So I went over to the snack table, as I'd seen others doing not only on that very day but also on the previous two days as well, and proceeded to get a snack. All of a sudden, one of the officials in charge—a middle-aged white woman—approached me and whispered, "Please go back to your seat and wait for the next break. We want everybody to take breaks at the same time." My mouth dropped open in shock. When I regained my composure, I asked, "Didn't you see that teacher who just left this table, or all the other people who have come over here in the last few minutes? Why didn't you say anything to *them?*" At this point, the woman did what many teachers do when African American and Latino students accuse them of engaging in racist discipline practices: "I didn't see *them,*" she claimed. "I only saw *you.*"

I don't recall what I said to her at this point, but I do know that she ended up apologizing for her behavior. I also remember that even after she apologized, I was still quite offended, and when the formal break time was announced, I mentioned what had happened to another teacher whom I had befriended during the scoring session.

Perhaps because of her guilt or because she knew that I was still upset after she apologized, the official watched me carefully throughout the formal break and moved close enough to hear me relay to the other teacher what had happened. Then she went and told another official, a white man who had been kind to me during the previous days. Although neither said anything to me about discussing the incident with another teacher, they soon retaliated.

After the break ended, they announced that we only had a certain number of essays left to read and that because we had done such a good job all day, we would be allowed to go home earlier than planned. We were overjoyed to hear this, for the three days had been tiring, and we looked forward to going home. We all began to work quickly. I read essay after essay, and after a while I noticed that there were only a few essay booklets left at my table, meaning that my tablemates and I were almost finished. But my joy was short lived.

When the pile of booklets at our table had dwindled to just a few, the male official whose colleague had told him that I was discussing the "break" incident with another teacher walked over to our table with a large stack of essay booklets. Instead of placing them in the center of the table for any teacher at the table who had finished reading to select from (as had been the practice up to that point), the man put the booklets directly in front of me. Although my tablemates and I looked surprised, it was clear that I, and I alone, was being given extra work. This was my punishment for being an "uppity Negro" who spoke truth not only *to* power but also *about* power, when I described the incident to another teacher.

Now I had a dilemma. I could try to read all the extra booklets that the man had placed directly in front of me and accept my punishment in silence; I could ask my tablemates who no longer had booklets to read to divide them evenly with me; or I could do something else. I chose the third option. Instead of confronting this man about his obviously biased and differential treatment of me, I chose to send him a message through passive-aggressive means. After I finished reading the essay that I'd been reading before he put the stack in front of me, I simply crossed my arms in front of me and stared at him. I wanted him to know that I would not allow him to treat me as if I were an errant child, and that if he wanted to make all the scorers sit in that room until those booklets had been scored, then I was more than willing to let him.

What happened next was somewhat comical. After realizing that I wasn't going to be forced to read the extra booklets and that they couldn't make me do so without creating a public scene and attracting the attention of the other teachers in the room, the same woman who had singled me out in the first place eventually marched over to my table. She was clearly exasperated when she snatched the stack of booklets from in front of me and started to dole them out to other tables at which the teachers who had finished reading were sitting empty handed.

This story contains several messages about discipline policies and classroom management. First, as I've stated repeatedly in this and other chapters, it would behoove educators to be aware of their own baggage. Negative baggage in the form of deficit-oriented mind-sets about certain individuals and certain groups can lead people to engage in unfair and differential practices. *They* may not be aware of what they are doing, but the recipient of the unfair treatment can detect it quickly. For some reason, the middle-aged white female training official didn't see any of the white teachers who went to the snack table before I did, but she certainly saw *me*—one of the two black teachers in the whole room—even though I was quiet and unassuming when I approached the table. By the same token, many teachers, school administrators, and staff don't hear noisy white students, notice white students who are violating dress code policies, or notice when white students are misbehaving, but they certainly see almost any and every thing that a black student does.

A second message is that educators who look for trouble from certain students will often get what they're looking for. That official treated me as if I were problematic when she first approached me at the snack table, even though she had failed to approach any of the whites who did so. When she overheard me telling another teacher about what had happened, she called in the "big gun," the white man who was supposed to protect her from the "evil" and "uppity" black woman. Minor incidents in classrooms and at schools often escalate in a similar manner when teachers call security or kick kids out of class because they don't know how to handle situations appropriately.

A third message is that educators can't change the rules arbitrarily. In the case of the trainer, she decided to single me out only *after* she had allowed other teachers to do the same thing over a two-and-a-half-day period. Of course, her actions confused me and led me quickly to conclude that she only noticed me because I'm African American. In a sea of white faces, I stood out, and all of a sudden, it became necessary to change the rules. As I've said before, school rules must be explicit and enforced fairly. A teacher, administrator, or school security officer who tries to change the rules midstream is asking for trouble.

A final message contained in the story is that when people believe they are being treated unfairly, they can find ways to get even. When the male official placed that large stack of extra booklets in front of me, he knew and I knew that he was merely retaliating against me to make his colleague feel better. Although he was in a position of power over me that day, he failed to realize that I wasn't totally helpless. Instead of allowing myself to be forced to do something that I fundamentally believed was unfair, I chose not to make a scene but at the same time not to let this man get away with mistreating me either. Many students do the same thing at school. They find passive-aggressive or outright aggressive ways to voice their displeasure to teachers who are unfair, who have singled them out, or who have poor classroom management skills. These are lessons that all educators, parents, and policymakers should keep in mind. When rules are unfair and people feel that they aren't treated fairly, they can find ways to get even—at home, at school, and with society.

PART TWO

On the Schoolyard

5

"We Just Can't Seem to Get Along"

Race Relations on Campus

More than two decades ago, when I was a single parent, I rented an apartment in a low-income neighborhood in Los Angeles County. On the day I moved in, I realized that I didn't have a broom, so I knocked on a neighbor's door to introduce myself and ask if I could borrow her broom. The "thirty-something"-looking white woman who opened the door didn't seem at all pleased to see me. Was it because I was a stranger? Was it because I had disturbed a nap or some important task that preoccupied her? Or was it because I'm an African American? At the time, I didn't know for sure exactly what caused the unpleasant look on her face. All I knew was that even after I said, "Hi! I'm Gail, and I just moved in next door," her look didn't soften. When I asked if I could borrow a broom, she replied, "I don't have a broom," and closed the door.

Soon I was very surprised, however, when one night *she* came knocking at *my* door, asking if she could borrow my telephone. When I said yes, she appeared to be grateful, went into the bedroom to use the telephone, and then thanked me and left. Unfortunately, this wasn't an isolated incident. Before long, it became a predictable pattern. At night, after consuming alcohol (which I could smell on her breath), the woman would often get into an altercation (which was loud enough for her neighbors to hear) with the man with whom she lived. Then she'd knock on my door and ask to borrow my telephone. Although it was usually an inconvenience that disrupted my own nightly routine, I always complied with her request. This pattern had gone on for quite some time, when one night, after using the telephone, instead of leaving she sat down and began to weep. "You've always been so nice to me," she cried, "and I don't even like black people!"

In spite of my shock, she didn't stop there. Instead she proceeded to tell me that one day on her way to junior high school, a group of black girls followed her from a bus stop. In the process of trying to take her watch, one of the girls cut her arm with a sharp object. From that point on, the frightened white girl had developed a strong hatred for *all* black people. She blamed the entire race—millions of people—for what a few thugs had done to her. As I listened to her story, my heart went out to her. I imagined how terrified she must have been. This was a horrible tragedy that no individual—especially a child—should ever have to experience.

Since then, I've often wondered why she and others like her choose to hate whole groups, when others who have been wronged choose not to do this. I, for example, have experienced much racism from various white people throughout my life, but have made a conscious choice—and often it is a struggle—not to blame all whites for what some have done. But I must admit that whenever I get on my own self-righteous high horse, I'm reminded of the times when I felt exactly as she did. One of those times occurred many years ago, during my undergraduate years. While working as an intern reporter one summer in Oregon, I experienced quite a bit of blatant racism, subtle racism, and cultural insensitivity. After that, I went through a period of intense hatred for whites as a group, while excluding from that group the individual whites whom I personally liked. This hatred gave me a strong desire to leave the United States, even if only temporarily, because its intensity made me fear that I would eventually lash out in violence. I'd always wanted to go to Africa, and this hatred made me long for Africa even more. At the time, the Peace Corps, which offered a free two-year trip to Africa, became my salvation.

In many ways, Africa was the perfect solution to my problem. In the land of my ancestors, it felt great not being a "minority" for a change, because my dark skin allowed me to blend in with the masses. Unless I opened my mouth, revealing that I had an American accent, most people assumed that I was an indigenous African. I also saw many aspects of Africa that most Americans never see or hear about, both physical beauty and beauty in the close-knit family structure of many of the people whom I met. But Africa also taught me two important lessons that I would remember for the rest of my life. An obvious one was that I was blessed to be an American because of the opportunities for economic advancement that awaited me when I returned home, for in spite of my race and stepchild status, my college education would undoubtedly open doors for me. The second lesson was about racism. I had left America in a huff, angry at whites as a group. I returned to America with the strong belief in the importance of viewing and judging people on an individual basis. This lesson came about because one of the dearest friends I made in Africa is a white American woman who is married to an African. Together, they have five biracial children. Not only did this woman become a close friend, but she and her family welcomed me to their home for meals and especially during the holidays. The other reason I learned this lesson was that in Africa, I was deeply troubled by often witnessing "man's inhumanity to man." On several occasions, for example, I saw wealthy Africans mistreating the poor. Because of my own impoverished childhood, I've always identified with poor people, and witnessing their exploitation and mistreatment left a negative image of *some* Africans in my mind.

Nearly two years later, when I returned to the United States, I found that racism continues to be prevalent in all sectors of U.S. society, including churches, the judicial system, the real estate industry, bank lending practices, and the workforce, despite the fact that many Americans deny its existence. According to the FBI, in 2003, more than seven thousand hate crimes occurred in the United States, and more than half were based on racial bias.[1] Although hate crimes are more likely to occur "in or near residences or homes, . . ." schools are no exception; the FBI reported that nearly 12 percent of hate crimes occurred at schools or colleges.[2] In fact, racism is prevalent not only in higher education[3] but also in K–12 schools, through tracking, which places blacks and Latinos disproportionately in non-college-preparatory courses;[4] low teacher expectations for students of color;[5] unfair discipline practices, resulting in blacks' and Latinos' being disproportionately suspended and expelled from school;[6] the use of standardized tests whose inherent biases disfavor low-income students and students of color;[7] and educators' deficit-oriented mind-sets about students of color.[8] Negative stereotypes about blacks and Latinos are widespread not only in the larger U.S. society but in K–12 schools as well.[9]

Adults aren't the only perpetrators of racial prejudice. In recent years, interethnic tensions at schools has led to violence among students, particularly in California, where in some cases, schools have been temporarily closed until order could be restored.[10] In other cases, the "threat of race-related gang violence . . . kept hundreds of kids out of dozens of schools."[11]

Although the number of hate crimes in California decreased in 2004, those against blacks, Latinos, and Asians actually increased,[12] and a disproportionately high number of hate crimes continue to occur in California. In 2003, for example, more hate crimes were reported in California than in any other state.[13] In fact, more than twice as many hate crimes were reported in California than in New Jersey, which had the second highest number, and New York, where the third highest number occurred.

When racial prejudice results in violence at school, safety becomes a related issue, and both, undoubtedly, affect student achievement, for in order to work at their maximum capacity, students must feel safe at school. If students are preoccupied with safety issues, they aren't likely to be able to fully concentrate on academics.[14] Because of this relationship between student achievement and racial tension that erupts into violence, there is a need to explore what students themselves say about their experiences with racial prejudice at school. This is all the more true at schools that have been designated as "underperforming," because NCLB was established on the promise of closing achievement gaps. Researchers have suggested many theories to explain the gaps,[15] yet few have asked students about their experiences with racial prejudice at an underperforming high school. So, in the next section, we hear what the students at American High School said about their race-related experiences at school.

What the Students Said

There was only one item on the teacher questionnaire that gave the teachers at American High School an opportunity to share their views about race. That questionnaire item stated, "I believe that students' race/ethnicity has some bearing on their aptitude." Of the teachers responding, 17 percent agreed with this statement, indicating that they believed that race and a student's ability to learn are related.

In the student phase of the study, the questionnaire contained four items about students' experiences with racism, permitting them to state whether or not they had experienced racial prejudice from students, teachers, administrators, and school security. The results revealed that a considerable percentage of students had experienced racial prejudice at school, but they were more likely to experience it from other students than from adults.

Student-to-Student Racial Prejudice

Regarding racial prejudice from other students, more than half the students who completed the questionnaire said they had been subjected to racial prejudice from other students at American High School. There were obvious differences among the three main racial and ethnic groups that participated in the study. More than half the African Americans, nearly half the Latinos, and a majority (68 percent) of whites said they had experienced racial prejudice from other students. White males were more likely than all others to say they had been subjected to student-to-student racial prejudice, and Latino males were less likely than all others to say so.

During the focus group discussions, many students spoke about racial prejudice among students at American High School. One of the recurring themes was that there were ongoing conflicts between African Americans and Latinos that often led to fights and riots. A white male focus group participant said, "This school has a race war every year between the blacks and the Mexicans. . . . I don't know what starts it. One fight, then, somebody jumps in." A Latina recounted: "There was like a whole feud going on between the Hispanics and the blacks for a couple of days. It was like all the Mexicans would come out and bring their straps or whatever, and all the blacks, straps or when they carry guns or weapons, or whatever."

Although the interracial and interethnic conflicts usually started at school they often spilled over to the outside community and involved individuals who didn't attend American High School. For example, a Latina stated, "Sometimes, they bring people from somewhere else to come and back them up. They bring kids from other schools, and there's like a whole bunch of Mexicans waiting at the restaurants nearby to beat up the black people, and a whole bunch of black people. Sometimes, security hears about it, and sometimes they don't do nothing about it. They bring people from other schools, and it's been going on all year long."

In explaining the causes of the ongoing conflict between African Americans and Latinos at the school, students gave several explanations, including "stupid things, just stupid activities," "looks," "hostile stares," and interracial dating, flirting, or friend-ships. Some students claimed that they felt pressured to interact solely with members of their own race. For example, according to a Latina, who said she felt harassed by other Latinos, "It's by my own race, because I hang out with a whole bunch of white people, and they're like 'Oh, what? You're whitewashed now?' And I'm like, 'Yeah. I just don't hang out with a lot of Mexican people; that doesn't mean that I'm whitewashed.' It comes from my own race." Describing similar peer pressure, another Latina remarked, "You're not gonna put yourself in a situation where you could be in danger. I'm Mexican and there's this feud going on between Mexicans and blacks. I'm not about to go and stand where all the black people are, you know? You just don't do that. You stay away from all that."

An African American male said that the black-Latino conflicts usually started "in groups over little stupid things and people are scared. Then, they feel they have to bring their friends into it, which [leads] to these big ole situations." One of the "little things" was when African American males spoke to or befriended Latinas. As one African American male focus group participant explained, "All it takes is for somebody to holla at [speak to] a Mexican dude's girl or just be her friend. The dude says, 'Yo, homes! What you talkin' to my girl for?' Then, right then and there, you got a problem because you his girl's friend, and he wants to fight you because of that. And that's not even no reason to fight somebody."

In addition to creating a sense of uneasiness that caused some students to feel unsafe at American High School, the black-Latino conflict had prompted school administrators to divide students into two separate lunch groups that ate at different times. Although some students felt that having the separate lunch periods had decreased the number of fights between African Americans and Latinos, others felt that the practice was ineffective; it also separated friends from each other. Several students recommended that the practice of having separate lunches be eliminated.

Students also complained of frequent conflicts between African Americans and whites and between whites and Latinos. During the focus group discussions, several white females said they felt that black students, particularly males, often harassed them. Several white students agreed with a white female who said she felt unsafe at American High School because she was subjected to racial prejudice. According to this student,

> If I'm walking down the hall alone, like I'll be picked on or something by black people or Mexican, Latino people. They call you names, push you. Okay, for example, yesterday, I was walking by myself, and I thought I was just walking. I wasn't doing anything bad. I was walking to class and some guy was like "Stupid white girl," and like I looked. And he said, "Yeah, I'm talking to you, little bitch." He's like, "I'm talking to you,

you stupid white girl." I'm like, "What?" And he's like, "Yeah. Shut up, you little white girl; walk away." I didn't do anything, and I just like walk to class and it gets me so mad.

In explaining how her own experiences with racial prejudice at American High School had caused her to retaliate, a light-skinned Lebanese student who most students perceived to be white said:

People hang out with their own little groups. . . . I really don't care. I am not racist or anything but people are racist towards me because of who I am. You call me, "Stupid, white bitch," I'm gonna call you "stupid" whatever. I'm white, but I'm not white. You know what I'm saying. I don't know. I'm white, but my attitude. . . . I look white, but I am not. When people find out what I am, they start making fun of me. I'm Lebanese. Yeah, and because of my religion another thing happened. I was put on a hit list and everything. People found out about it, and they started harassing [me]. It's like, don't think I'm not going to do anything. And people would just harass you about whatever you are. You'll be in the classroom. They walk in [and say,] "Oh, you look stupid, so we're going to start talking crap about you." It's like, there's so much crap in this school. The reason why people are like that to other people in this school is because they are sick of other people making fun of them. They are sick of other people, like totally harassing them, bumping them. Like, have common courtesy! Don't bump into somebody and not say "Excuse me" and not expect a person to do anything about it. It's common courtesy, and if you are going to be rude to me, then I am going to be rude to you. People are rude in high school. It may be just high school. I don't know, but that's just how it is.

A white female summarized what several other white focus group participants believed:

The black kids in our school, they're really saying "Oh [whites are] really racist, we're put down, we're discriminated [against,]" but they are the ones that are being racist to white people in general. And we're scared of even saying "That black girl over there with the dark hair." When we say something . . . they're sitting up, saying "Oh, you're just a white girl, you know." I just don't know what to say. . . . I find it interesting that African Americans do not really enjoy being called "black," which is a color, but "white" is also. So, technically, wouldn't we just be Americans?

When asked whether or not African American students specifically targeted white students in order to subject them to racial prejudice, the black focus group participants disagreed that conflicts between black and white students stemmed from prejudice. For example, most African American focus group participants agreed with a black female who said, "It may be true that sometimes black students harass white students, but black students harass black students. So, it's not like we just pick on a specific race. It's mutual. It's everyone. They pick on their own race. I've seen more black kids fighting each other than I've seen them fighting white people."

Regarding whether or not black male students harassed white female students on campus as several of the white female focus group participants had claimed, all the African American male focus group participants disagreed that this was true. However, some said that often misunderstandings occurred. When black males flirted with white females, the females may have misunderstood their intentions. All the African American males who participated in focus groups agreed with the black male who maintained, "All it takes is that a black dude could be interested in a white girl. And he'll try to holla, say he's interested, or try to get at her, and right there, she'll feel harassed, just because he's interested in her. That could be a big thing. I'll bet you that probably a lot of black dudes here would date some white girls here, but don't wanna holla because they feel intimidated. A white girl can get a black dude in trouble like that. But if it were vice versa, naw."

This same student continued by describing a related incident involving a white woman and black security guard at American High

School, who was also a minister. The incident occurred off campus, but the student felt that it illustrated the point he was trying to make about how white females' fear of black males could lead to trouble: "That happened to one of our security guards. He supposedly was ministering to some lady in a trailer park and she just said that he raped her. All of a sudden, he's not at school; he's in jail. He was innocent, but his fingerprints were on the doorknob. So he's not at this school anymore. It's just that they're intimidated. That's all that I can say."

Despite the administration's attempt to decrease racial conflicts between students at American High School by implementing separate lunch periods, some students felt hopeless about race relations among students at the school. Many believed that there wasn't anything that administration could do. As one African American girl stated, "You can't make somebody like somebody else." But an African American girl who disagreed countered, "At one of my old schools, they sat people of different races down, had them introduce themselves and talk about their ethnic backgrounds, where they were coming from, and perspectives. When they left, they saw things differently. Maybe, if we sat down and had a group discussion with different ethnicities, and let people realize that black people are not so bad, or Latinos are not so bad, or whites are not so bad, even though things have happened in the past, we could all get along."

Adult-to-Student Racial Prejudice

The student questionnaire also gave the respondents a chance to say whether or not they'd experienced racial prejudice from three groups of adults on campus: administrators, teachers, and school security. Although student-to-student racism was more common than racial prejudice from adults, numerous students indicated that they'd been subjected to prejudice by adults at school. Furthermore, students were more likely to say they'd experienced racial prejudice from teachers and security than from administrators, which makes sense, considering that students undoubtedly have less contact with school administrators.

Racial Prejudice from Administrators. Nearly 30 percent of the students who completed the questionnaire said they'd experienced racial prejudice from administrators. Although there was little difference among the three major racial and ethnic subgroups, white students were slightly less likely to say they'd experienced racial prejudice from administrators than were African Americans and Latinos. However, there were some noticeable gender differences in that a higher percentage of males, especially Latinos, said they'd experienced racial prejudice from administrators.

Racial Prejudice from Teachers. Nearly 40 percent of the students said they'd experienced racial prejudice from teachers, and a higher percentage of African Americans and Latinos did than whites. African Americans were almost twice as likely as whites to say they had. In the focus groups, several themes emerged from students who said they'd been subjected to racial prejudice from teachers. One of the most common complaints, which we looked at in Chapter Four, was that teachers engaged in unfair discipline practices and were more likely to punish African Americans and Latinos than white students who were engaging in the same behaviors. Another complaint was that teachers actually permitted segregation within the classroom. According to an African American student, "In my ninth-grade English honors class, there's a separation of the whites and all the other groups. It's like a line. We can sit anywhere, and the whites sit on one side and blacks on another side. The students sit like that, but the teacher shows more respect to the white students than the minorities. She's always like down-talking the minorities."

Another focus group participant complained about her English teacher: "My ninth grade English teacher, she sits all the black people up in the front and then, the Hispanic and white people, they be sitting in the back, and they talk. As soon as we try to turn around or say something to the person on the side of us, and we're all black sitting in the front, my teacher says something to me. Then, she gonna put me in the middle, directly in front of her, so she can watch me, and I don't like that. I asked, 'Why you put me in the middle?'"

A Latino student reported that a substitute made an offensive comment to him: "One substitute in math came up to us because we were talking [during] free time, and asked us why we weren't doing our work. We said, 'Because we didn't feel like it right now, but we were still going to do it.' And he said, 'Well, most Mexicans are stupid, and that is why you have to challenge [them] more,' and some dumb crap."

Racial Prejudice from School Security. Slightly more than 30 percent of the students who completed the questionnaire said they'd been subjected to racial prejudice from school security. Whites and Latinos were more likely than African Americans to say this. Although males in general were more likely than females to say they'd been targeted by school security, Latino males and white males were more likely than African American males to say they'd encountered racist security.

During the focus group discussions, however, females, especially black females, were the most vocal in their complaints about school security. According to these participants, school security routinely engaged in biased behavior based on alleged dress code violations, and showed favoritism toward various groups, especially white girls. An African American female said, "Not to be racist, but half the time you see the little white girls going around with flip-flops and little shorts on, but they don't say anything to them. They don't even look at them." Another African American student remarked, "Last week, I was trying to wear my sandals, because it was hot. There was a girl who walked right by me with the same shoes, just a different color, and this white female security didn't say anything. When I pointed it out to her, she said, 'Well, I'll get her later.' It was a little white girl. And she [the security officer] has looked at my shoes ever since then."

An African American girl maintained, "I get called by white and black security all of the time for stuff. White girls with no butts don't get in trouble for wearing skirts that are shorter than mine, but because I have a butt, I get in trouble."

According to another African American student:

I was walking with my friends and all of a sudden, this guy comes up to me and says, "Is it correct that you have improper footwear on?" And I said, "Yeah, I have flip-flops on; my tennis shoes are wet," and he said that I was going to in-school suspension. A whole group of white girls passed me. They all had flip-flops on. I said, "Why don't you say something to them?" He said, "I'll get them later." I said, "No, I'm not going to [in-school suspension] until you say something to them too." He said, "Well, you're getting an attitude too, so we're going to send you for defiance." He was white.

Tying It All Together

Since September 11, 2001, Americans—people who had once been insulated from terrorism on American soil—have been bombarded with reports about the likelihood of future attacks. Attacks in Egypt, England, and Spain and the ongoing conflict in the Middle East have underscored the message that when hatred leads to violence, the world can be a dangerous place. Whether the hatred stems from religious differences, ethnic rivalries, or other factors, the outcome can be the same: a sense of anxiety and fear. If living with constant anxiety stemming from the fear of imminent danger is difficult for adults to handle, how much more difficult must it be for youths whose emotional reserves and coping strategies are less developed?

Although I didn't set out to determine whether or not there was a direct link between the students' experiences with racial prejudice at school and their academic performance, the results that I presented in this chapter from my study at American High School contain some important messages for educators, policymakers, parents, and society as a whole. One message is that race continues to "matter" in our nation.[16] More than half the students had experienced student-to-student racial prejudice and a substantial percentage had experienced adult-to-student racial prejudice. A second message is that when racial tension permeates the school environment, no group is immune; students in each racial and ethnic group had experienced racism. A third message, and one of the clearest, is that although many adults claim to be color-blind and therefore incapable of being racist,[17] students are quite aware that the converse is true, for student-to-student racial prejudice and adult-to-student racial prejudice were quite prevalent at their school.

What We Can Do

Educators, parents, and policymakers can use the feedback presented in this chapter as a springboard for beginning the difficult task of improving race relations in schools and thereby possibly increasing student achievement by creating a less hostile school environment. In the following sections, I describe specific ways in which administrators, teachers, parents, and policymakers can do this.

Administrators

Society as a whole must do its part to eradicate racism, and educators can do a lot to ease racial tensions in schools. Administrators can set a "zero tolerance for racism and racial prejudice" policy and enforce it swiftly and continuously. For example, in *Exposing the Culture of Arrogance in the Academy*, my coauthor and I described a preschool director who did this. When the director learned that students were ostracizing and picking on the two lone black preschool students in the school, she summoned all parents to a meeting. The director explained the problem and told parents that this behavior wouldn't be tolerated. She also promised that the school would develop lesson plans to help students understand that they should be respectful of their classmates who were racially "different," and asked parents to work with their children at home to address the problem.[18] That preschool director effectively and professionally handled a situation that could have escalated; another story illustrates how administrators can unwittingly foster racism and prejudice at school.

A white middle school teacher in South Carolina told me that she wanted to improve race relations at her school but didn't know how to do so, especially because school administrators didn't seem to know what to do either. One of the incidents that she described occurred on a day when some of the students were going on an overnight school-sponsored field trip. Right before the bus was about to leave the school, a white parent drove up with her child. When she saw that her child had been seated next to a black student, the mother became visibly upset and "yanked her child off the bus," the teacher told me. At this point, school administrators had several options:

1. They could have told the mother that her behavior was inappropriate. After all, we're living in the twenty-first century, and it's high time that Americans learned to get along with each other, including those from different racial backgrounds.

2. They could have suggested that the parent drive her own child to the field trip site.

3. They could have asked the parent to keep her child at home if her child couldn't sit in his assigned seat.

4. They could have given in to the parent's demand.

The administrators chose option 4. Instead of conveying the message that this parent's behavior was totally inappropriate and, undoubtedly, extremely hurtful to the black student, the administrators found another seat for her child.

As I listened to the teacher recount this story, I wondered how that black child must have felt during that field trip when the entire busload of students and teachers witnessed his humiliation. I also wondered what that child must have thought about the administrators and teachers who were too spineless to do the right thing when they were in a position of leadership.

When school administrators create explicit guidelines about racist behavior at school and enforce those guidelines, these ugly scenarios aren't likely to occur repeatedly. Once parents and students get the message that "Racism won't be tolerated at this school," they aren't likely to behave in such offensive ways. School leaders can also organize schoolwide assemblies for students, and professional development in-services for parents and teachers about strategies to combat racial prejudice. But first they must face their own baggage related to racism. Until they examine their own beliefs and behaviors that are rooted in racial prejudice and stereotypes, administrators aren't likely to succeed in doing this on a schoolwide basis.

Teachers

I'm a strong believer in the idea that the blind can't lead the blind. Just as school administrators can't create a school free of racial prejudice until they've faced their own mind-sets and behaviors through personal and professional growth work specifically in this area, teachers who are racist cannot create classrooms free of racial prejudice. Another story I recently heard emphasizes this point.

A veteran teacher, an African American woman, told me that many years ago, her principal hired a young white woman, a first-year teacher, to work at the predominantly black middle school where she taught. This new teacher had recently graduated from a conservative Christian college that has repeatedly been accused of fostering racist beliefs. One day, the young white teacher announced to some of her colleagues that she always kept her purse locked in her car when she came to work. When asked why, she replied, "My boyfriend said that black parents teach their kids to steal, and they reward them for stealing from teachers. That's why I keep my purse in the car. I don't want these kids stealing from me." Upon hearing this, the black teacher told me, "We were incensed, absolutely incensed!" This white teacher clearly had baggage that she needed to address before she could help her students face any racial prejudice that they might have. I'm certain that her failure to face her own racist beliefs eventually surfaced in other ways that impeded her ability to be an effective teacher of black students.

A white teacher who taught at a South Carolina middle school that was 50 percent black and 50 percent white told me,

> My colleagues would be mortified to hear me say this, but racism is alive and well at my school. Their perception is "that's the way it's always been." I just want to know how to jump-start a change. . . . The races are totally separated at our schools, and we've just learned that the black males aren't learning to read and write well. From what I've learned, [the students] get it at home, at church, and from the Bible—that there should be "no mixing." It's the good ole boys' club. It's rural South Carolina. I've gone from anger to accepting that that's the way these people are, and how can *I* change *them*?

A related story that this teacher shared was about one of her students. The teacher had started a pen pal exchange program with another teacher and class in New York. However, "one of the sweetest little white kids said, 'I can't have this pen pal because she's a different race than me.'"

In the classroom, teachers can teach directly about racism through current events, literature, writing assignments, projects, mock trials, debates, and guest speakers. Using culturally relevant teaching methods that emphasize *exposure* to and *respect* for other cultures and expand students' sociopolitical consciousness is also crucial.[19] Further, teachers should incorporate conflict resolution skills and lessons in the curriculum, in order to teach students non-violent ways of dealing with problems.[20] Finally, to address their own racial prejudice and denial, adults must receive ongoing professional development training at school and be willing to work on their personal growth away from school.

Parents

Like educators, parents and guardians are in a unique position to help children and teenagers learn to behave in nonracist ways. Because children get their earliest messages about tolerance, race relations, and how to treat people who are "different" from their primary caregivers, parents and other adult relatives are often the very individuals who create "little bigots."

For example, my sister Tracy told me a story about her son, Armande, and a former playmate who was the grandson of one of Tracy's Latino neighbors. Armande and the grandson would often play together whenever the boy visited his grandparents. One day, they were playing together at Tracy's house when the boy said he had to leave in order to go to the restroom. Tracy said, "You don't have to go all the way home; you can use one of ours." To her surprise, the boy replied, "I can't. My grandma will get mad, because she doesn't like black people."

After the boy left, Tracy began to remember other little incidents—ones she had previously ignored. Now they made sense to her and confirmed that what the child had revealed was probably true: His grandmother didn't like black people. Although for some reason they "tolerated" letting their grandson play with Armande—the only other boy in close proximity to their house in his age group—if they had their way, they wouldn't have any interactions at all with blacks, including their black neighbors. Once Tracy realized this, her opinion of these neighbors changed. "They probably threw away that sweet potato pie I gave them for Christmas," she told me. Since that day when the grandson refused to use her restroom, Tracy and her neighbors have been estranged. They don't speak to each other, and their grandchild no longer interacts with Armande. Of course, Tracy doesn't bother to give them homemade pies or anything else during the holiday season either.

One of the most ridiculous yet saddest stories that I heard about parents imposing their racist beliefs on children was shared with me by one of my cousins. She told me that although she had permitted her three daughters to play with anyone regardless of race when they were children, she also taught them that they probably wouldn't experience "real racism" until they got to high school, when peer pressure would become powerful, and that's what actually happened. In high school, the girls' former white friends wouldn't even speak to them. But in some cases it started long before high school, and instead of coming from peers, the pressure came from parents. For example, during elementary school, one of her daughters was good friends with a white classmate. But the white girl was never allowed to invite the black child over to her house. "I really like you," she constantly told her African American friend. "I'm not like that, but my mama is. I don't know why my mama doesn't like black people. She won't even let us drink iced tea because she said it'll make my skin turn dark!"

These stories are classic examples of how adults in the home can foster racial prejudice and intolerance, and this behavior is common. Moreover, too many parents are in denial or are hypocritical about their own views and actions toward people who are "different."

The late Senator Strom Thurmond illustrated this hypocrisy well. Many whites considered Thurmond to be an arch conservative because he made it clear that he supported racial segregation. Many blacks considered him to be a blatant racist. But like many racist southern whites, Thurmond's words were different from his private deeds. He went to his grave without ever publicly acknowledging that he'd fathered a half-black daughter, Essie Mae Washington-Williams.

A parent's hypocrisy about race relations can be confusing to children. I've learned that some of the most liberal and seemingly tolerant adults are often bigots underneath it all. In fact, this very issue caused a huge controversy among evangelical Christians many years ago. The uproar started after it became public knowledge that a prominent liberal white pastor had warned white parents to stop their children—particularly their daughters—from associating with blacks. The pastor allegedly went on to warn the white parents that if they didn't act quickly, their daughters might end up dating and eventually marrying black men. Ironically, at the time that he made these statements, this pastor was supposed to be the close friend of a black man—another prominent minister who was outraged to learn how his "friend" really felt about race relations.

One of my favorite authors, Gavin De Becker, said, "Children learn most from modeling."[21] Although he was referring to children who witness domestic violence between their parents, I believe that his statement also applies to race relations. For this reason, I strongly urge parents to deal with their own racial prejudice, examine their own views, and address any unacknowledged racism and hypocritical behavior of their own before they attempt to teach their children to treat others—regardless of race and ethnicity—humanely.

Policymakers

Like most white Americans, many policymakers are in denial about the prevalence of racism in the United States and how policies they have created promote institutional racism at *every* level of society. Because many policymakers come from privileged backgrounds and have benefited from institutional racism, they aren't in a hurry to face the truth or to change the status quo. Their denial and lack of commitment to improving race relations are quite obvious. History has shown that when national leaders and politicians condone and promote inequality, racism, and sexism, they give their subordinates "permission" to behave badly. Throughout this book, I'll continue to underscore the fact that policymakers impede reform when they lack commitment and aren't willing to improve the social conditions that prevent many of America's stepchildren from having a fair chance to compete in ways that can improve the quality of their lives. The first step in making this commitment is for policymakers to address all levels of institutional racism in American society. First, however, they must face their beliefs and attitudes about America's stepchildren that prevent them from progressing. The next section underscores these points.

A Final Word

In November 2005, a series of riots erupted in numerous French cities. Hundreds of cars were burned, police officers and ordinary citizens were injured, and, after several days of rioting, the French government issued a curfew. The riots were sparked by the deaths of two youths who were accidentally electrocuted while fleeing from police. What soon became clear, however, was that these tragic deaths were merely the "last straw" for Muslim and North African immigrants who felt marginalized from mainstream French society. During media interviews, some of the immigrants complained that they were angry about a number of issues, including police brutality and high unemployment rates in their communities. Some complained that business owners refused to hire immigrants who lived in the very communities in which the businesses were located. The result was that many immigrants felt hopeless and that they had no future. Some had coped and found a sense of belonging and an income through gang affiliation. Others had just seethed with anger until the deaths of the two youths sent them over the edge.

During the period when the riots occurred, I read numerous related articles and listened to many radio and television news briefs about the situation in France. Some reporters drew parallels between the French riots and the Los Angeles uprising in 1992 that occurred after the police officers who beat Rodney King, an African American, were acquitted. In the Los Angeles case, the acquittals became the catalyst for long-simmering anger to erupt over unemployment and routine police brutality in South Central Los Angeles.[22]

Although most news reporters and radio and television commentators appeared to be objective in assessing the situation in France, at least two U.S. radio hosts used it as an opportunity to promote their own racist beliefs and thereby reveal their ignorance about human nature and race relations. These two "angry white men" who have built their radio careers on an anti–illegal immigration platform said that the true cause of the French riots was that you can't mix people from different racial or ethnic backgrounds and expect them to get along. These men totally ignored all the underlying social conditions and the well-known fact that Muslims and Africans are treated like stepchildren in France.

As I've repeatedly stated in this chapter, racism is common in the United States at every level of society, including in schools, churches, businesses, banking, real estate, the judicial system, and even in government—something that America's stepchildren know very well. For instance, as I was working on this book, two race-related controversies received a lot of national attention. The first concerned the widespread criticism that President George W. Bush and the Federal Emergency Management Association (FEMA) received for their slow response to assist the victims of Hurricane Katrina. Most of these victims were poor blacks. The second controversy pertained to statements that William Bennett made on his radio show. According to numerous reports, Bennett said that if all black babies were aborted, the national crime rate would decrease. Although he claimed that his comments were taken out of context,[23] what is most interesting to me about Bennett's statement is that he is the former secretary of education—an individual who was paid to reform schools, including schools attended by black children, the very population that he said should be aborted. If his remark is truly reflective of how a lot of whites feel about blacks—and I believe that it is—it's no wonder that the achievement gaps persist and that predominantly black schools continue to fare poorly. Policymakers who are in key positions to change the status quo won't make reforming these schools a priority if they believe that these schools are populated by individuals who shouldn't be alive in the first place, who deserve second-class citizenship, and who deserve to be treated like stepchildren.

Until schools and the wider society adequately address racism, neither NCLB nor any other education reform will succeed in closing achievement gaps. As long as the "sins of the fathers"—unaddressed racism, hatred, corrupt policies and practices, and fear of the "other"—are passed on to youths, schools will never reach the ideal, never become places where all students can feel safe, be treated fairly by adults, coexist peacefully regardless of race or ethnicity, and, most important, reach their maximum academic potential.

Each year, countless Americans travel to foreign lands in search of exotic locales, rich cuisines, and a chance to experience different cultures. Ironically, in so doing they leave behind a land that is geographically and culturally rich. The United States is one of the most fascinating nations on earth, partly because it is perhaps the most ethnically and culturally diverse country in existence. With all of its wonders and attractions, however, America continues to wrestle with a demon that has haunted it for more than four hundred years. That demon is racism, the ugly stain on the nation's history and current era that refuses to disappear.

In *Quitting America*, Randall Robinson, an African American, wrote about the factors that compelled him to permanently leave the United States for St. Kitts, where he currently resides. Unlike Robinson, most people who become frustrated with America's racism can't afford to leave the country permanently, and many don't even desire to do so. We are therefore stuck together, for better or for worse, and we must learn to coexist for the sake of the nation's children. The American High School students have made it clear that the sins of the fathers are truly being passed on to subsequent generations. Our children don't get along with each other because we adults don't get along with each other. We have been bad role models, and we haven't taught our children how not to follow our example.

6

"You Don't Know If They're Gonna . . . Bust a Columbine on Everybody"

Why Schools Won't Ever Be Entirely Safe

On December 14, 2004, I received a frantic telephone call from my son, Stephen, a sophomore at a brand-new local high school: "Mom, can you come and get me? There's another riot going on." He was calling me from a classroom, using the cell phone that I'd loaned him. Because of the riot, the second that had erupted between Latino and black students at the end of lunchtime in less than a week, the entire school was on "lockdown." Lockdown meant that the students who had obeyed school authorities and gone straight to class were required to remain in their classrooms until further notice. Later I learned that students who hadn't complied with the request to go to class were pepper-sprayed, and some of the ringleaders were arrested.

I quickly telephoned the school's main office to see if officials were allowing parents to pick up their children. No one answered. Evidently, all administrators and personnel were too busy getting the situation under control to answer the telephone. So, like numerous other parents, I hurried to the school. When I arrived, a security guard let me pass through the gates that led onto campus. The administration building was full of other parents, but an eerie calm hung in the air. After a short time, my son came into the office, and we went home. On the way home, Stephen filled me in on many of the details: during lunchtime, a few kids had started fighting. Before long, two groups separated along racial lines, and what started as a simple fight quickly became a riot between Latino and black students.

Because two riots had occurred in such a short time span, school officials decided to shut down the school completely. It was almost time for winter break anyway, so they told students to remain at home until January. Although many students were undoubtedly overjoyed to be given an unexpected longer winter break, they didn't know at the time that they would have to pay for it later: the school year was extended to account for the missed days. That meant that when the school year ended for all other students in the district, the students at the rioting school would still be attending classes until later in June. Students who hadn't participated in the riots, such as my son, had to suffer the consequences of the behavior of those who did.

After school officials announced that the school would be closed until January, they scheduled a series of meetings with parents and students. At the parent meeting that my husband and I attended, news reporters were present, and hundreds of parents showed up. What impressed me the most was the number of officials who came. In addition to the principal and his staff, the school superintendent, the mayor, the city council, and the police chief all showed up. Throughout the meeting, every official conveyed the same message: "Rioting and racially motivated violence will not be tolerated at this school!" The principal also explained what had precipitated the two riots. We learned that both fights had been started by a few troublemakers, and other students soon jumped in and aligned themselves by race. The principal made it clear that parents needed to emphasize to their children that they shouldn't be followers, and should tell their children that they were not "upholding their race," as many of the rioters later claimed, by participating in the violence. The principal urged parents to eradicate the silly belief that students were upholding their race by fighting strangers merely because of their race.

After the principal explained what had caused the riots, and how school officials and police had responded, he described his action plan. Among other things, his multifaceted plan included a series of student assemblies and other meetings with students, as well as the formation of numerous committees that would give parents, local clergy, and other community leaders opportunities to become involved beyond the traditional PTA. He also told us that he had already started the process of having the riot instigators expelled from the school. According to the principal, the instigators had gang ties and weren't interested in the academic side of school.

When the principal and other officials finished describing their thoughts about what had happened and their plan for resolving the conflict, they permitted parents to speak. As I sat there listening and taking notes, I kept hearing the same basic message, regardless of the race of the parent: "We want our kids to get along with each other," and, "This is a shameful and intolerable situation." Everyone— including the Spanish speakers who relied on the school-provided translators to share their concerns—emphasized that they wanted their children to get a good education. Not once did any parent indulge in the blame game. The black parents didn't blame Latinos for the problem, and the Latino parents didn't blame African Americans.

Unfortunately, the two riots at my son's school weren't unusual. As I mentioned in Chapter Five, the students at American High School told me that the ongoing tension between Latino and black students often led to violence on campus. Also, during the last few years, there have been riots and race-related fights at other high schools throughout southern California. Most of the fighting has been between Latinos and blacks. This ongoing racial conflict isn't isolated to schools, however. In 2006, for example, a series of jail riots in southern California resulted in numerous deaths and injuries among Latino and black inmates. As in the case of the interracial school riots, gang members played a key role in instigating the conflicts. In jails throughout California, inmates may be segregated by gang affiliation, and those who are not in gangs are pressured to join and not to associate with inmates from other racial backgrounds. In the past, media reports have indicated that sometimes the fighting is instigated by prison guards.

In addition to racial conflicts that sometime result in violence, there are other well-known safety issues that can surface at schools. One is bullying, an age-old problem plaguing schools. Bullying often starts in elementary school and can continue all the way through high school. As a result, the K–12 schooling experiences of the victims can be nightmarish. One of the most unforgettable stories that I've ever heard (and one that I used to share with my junior high and high school students) illustrates this point. I heard this story on a late-night radio talk show more than twenty years ago. The host, the late Bill Balance (who has been described as one of the best talk show hosts in U.S. history), asked listeners to call in and describe any interesting stories that they knew about the topic of "retribution." Although numerous callers telephoned his show that night, the only story that I've always remembered was the one that an elderly woman shared about being bullied during her childhood.

When she was in elementary school, this woman had contracted polio. After she had missed a lot of school due to the illness, the time eventually came when her mother couldn't let her remain at home any longer. The child was terrified about returning to school as a "cripple," but despite her pleas, she was forced to go back. As she expected, a group of kids began to torment her. They called her names and made fun of the way she walked. Day after day, the tormenting continued, and the little girl began to hate school. Over time, however, things changed. Gradually, most of the bullies stopped picking on her. Maybe they just got tired of teasing her, or perhaps they eventually felt guilty for making her cry each day. A more likely explanation is that they may have found a new, more vulnerable victim to attack. Although most of the kids stopped teasing the girl, one bully refused to stop. Unlike the others in the group who stopped picking on the polio victim during elementary school, the meanest girl in the group continued to make fun of her all the way through high school. For this reason, the polio victim couldn't wait to move far away from the town in which she grew up.

Ten years after she graduated from high school, she received an invitation to her class reunion. At first, she thought about throwing it away. After all, she had few positive memories of the town, and even fewer of the high school. But as she gave the situation more thought, she decided, "Why not attend the reunion?" After all, her mother still lived in the town, and the woman had made a success of herself. She had nothing to be ashamed of, so why shouldn't she go back with her head held high?

I don't remember what the caller said about the actual class reunion. What I do remember is that during her visit to her hometown, she was in a grocery store one day, when she ran into her former tormentor—the girl who had bullied her from elementary school all the way through high school. The fact that the ten years since graduation hadn't been kind to the former bully showed on her face. But something else caught the visiting woman's attention: her former classmate was carrying a baby, and this baby appeared to be severely disabled. Instead of gloating over her enemy's misfortune, the caller said that she treated her kindly. From that point on, she was able to let go of the anger and pain that she'd held on to since childhood.

In some ways, this woman's story is unusual, but unfortunately, in other ways it's not so unusual, for research has shown that bullying is all too common in schools. According to the U.S. Department of Education's "Student Reports of Bullying,"[1]

- Among twelve- to eighteen-year-olds, 14 percent reported being the victims of bullying in 2001.

- Gender differences weren't detected in most types of bullying.

- Whites were more likely than black and Latino students to say they had been bullied at school.

- Younger students were more likely than older students to report being bullied.

- There were no measurable differences between the percentages of public school and private school students who reported being bullied.

- Victims of bullying were more likely to avoid certain areas of the school and certain activities out of fear of an attack.

- Victims of bullying were more likely to report that they carried weapons to school and were engaged in physical fights.

- Victims of bullying were more likely to report receiving D's and F's than their nonbullied counterparts.

- Fewer students reported bullying in schools with supervision by police officers, security officers, or staff hallway monitors.

Sex crimes are another school safety issue. A few weeks before I began writing this chapter, for example, students at three separate southern California schools reported that they were raped in school restrooms. During media interviews, many students at these schools said they were fearful of using school restrooms and fearful about being at school, period.

Another sex-related school safety issue pertains to the number of teachers who have been accused, arrested, and convicted of molesting students. Most of these cases involve male teachers who abused male or female students, but in the last decade, there has been an increasing number of female teachers who have been accused of sexually abusing students. Of course, Mary Kay Letourneau, the teacher who sexually abused one of her sixth-grade students, bore two of his children, and later married him, is the most notorious of the female teachers who are child sexual predators. A more recent case was exposed in April 2006 when Rachel Holt, a Delaware elementary school teacher, was arrested for having sex with a thirteen-year-old student, permitting the boy's twelve-year-old friend to watch, and giving the children alcohol. During the last week of March 2006 alone, thirty-four-year-old Holt allegedly raped the child 28 times.[2] Another teacher, Sharon Rutherford, was arrested in 2006 for not only allegedly having sex with her students but also trying to coerce them into killing her husband.[3]

School safety is clearly an important issue, one that can affect students' learning, grades, and sense of well-being at school. Safety is a significant component in Maslow's Hierarchy of Needs, which consists of two types: deficiency needs and growth needs. If basic deficiency needs, which include food, shelter, and safety, haven't been met, growth needs, which include intellectual development, aren't likely to be met.[4] In other words, a student who sits in class with an empty stomach is going to have difficulty concentrating on academic work; the same is true of a student who sits in class wondering if he's going to be assaulted at lunchtime, on the way to another class, or after school, or a student who has to wonder whether or not the teacher is going to make inappropriate sexual advances.

Because school safety and student achievement are so clearly linked, during my study at American High School I wanted to know how safe the students felt. In the following section, we hear what the students said about school safety.

What the Students Said

Although the teacher questionnaire didn't contain any items pertaining specifically to school safety, three questionnaire items may have been indirectly related. The fact that nearly 30 percent of the teachers didn't consider American High School to be one of the best schools in the district, most didn't consider it to be one of the best schools in the state, and nearly 30 percent said they wouldn't want their own children to attend the school might indicate that teachers were concerned about school safety, but of course, these results might be related to other issues as well.

The student questionnaire did contain an item that pertained specifically to school safety: "I often feel unsafe at this school." Nearly 40 percent of the students said they often felt unsafe at American High School, and several noteworthy findings surfaced among the subgroups. In general, females were more likely to feel unsafe than males, and a higher percentage of white females felt unsafe at school in comparison to African Americans and Latinos. In fact, nearly 60 percent of the white females said they often felt unsafe at school. Latino males were more likely than African American and white males to feel unsafe at school; black males were the least likely to say they felt unsafe.

During the focus group discussions, many students spoke about why they did or didn't feel safe at American High School. Several said they felt unsafe because they knew of instances when students had brought weapons to school. As one girl explained, "One guy got expelled because he had a knife. That's what made me feel unsafe. I'm in the same class with him. That just kind of scared me that he had a knife at school." In describing an incident with a gun, a girl remarked:

> I know somebody who just had a gun on campus and got suspended for it, but it was *on campus*, and [the gun] made it on campus. That shows how easy it was for him to bring a gun on campus. I see people, like the Columbine shooting, kids walk around in trench coats and could have guns in their trench coats and nobody knows. But they get girls for flip-flops and for skirts and for spaghetti straps, but they don't get somebody for wearing a trench coat. What am I going to hide in my spaghetti strap shirt where you can see almost everything? But this boy has on a trench coat. He could have knives and guns and sharp things in his pocket.

Some students also felt unsafe at American High School because they didn't believe that they could count on school security officers to protect them. One focus group participant stated: "I see kids fighting and it takes like twenty minutes for security to get there. Say, some girl is beating me up, I'm bleeding and she's stomping my head to the floor and security's not even there. We have security guards all around campus who get us for dress code but are not around when somebody's fighting. It takes them like ten minutes to get there when somebody's fighting."

Numerous students agreed with the focus group participant who remarked, "One time, there was a fight going on and the security guards let them fight for awhile, and then they separated them when everybody started coming and crowded [around]. They let them fight for a while and when it gets really crowded, and when the principal has to come out and everything, that's when the security stops them."

Citing two personal stories to illustrate why she didn't believe school security officers were reliable, a student recounted:

My friend had an altercation with another student, and you could tell it was going to escalate into a possible fight. And security walked by, and we said "Security, you know it's possible there's a fight over here." He looked at me, laughed, and drove away. I had almost the same experience, except I went to the security office and told them that there was going to be a fight [that day]. I wrote a report, a statement, and so did a couple of my other friends. We told them several times that there was going to be a fight [that day]. Some girls were threatening us for no reason. . . . So, [the girls] came up to us . . . at lunchtime. On the same day we told security. . . . they came up to us and it did take security like five minutes after those girls were yelling at us to come out there and do something, when we told them that they should be waiting outside . . . because we didn't want to get beat up. . . .

In explaining why she too felt unsafe at American High School, another girl added:

There's some crazy kids here. . . . [T]here's just some kids that you don't know what they got hidden. You don't know if they're gonna spaz out and bust a Columbine on everybody, seriously. There's some weird kids that go to this school. You don't know if you're sitting there and they just decide to shoot you or something. That's why I feel unsafe.

A third reason some students felt unsafe at American High School was that they believed that certain students were looking for trouble. According to one focus group participant, "Some kids are just troublemakers; they love looking for trouble and just try to start something with you, even if they don't know you or they've never seen you. You could be like innocent and they could act crazy."

As I noted in Chapter Five, many focus group participants mentioned that each year, race riots and fights between African American and Latino students erupted at American High School. This also caused some students to feel unsafe. As I also mentioned previously, some of the white female focus group participants said they often felt that African American males were harassing them. When asked specifically about this charge, however, the African American male focus group participants disagreed, and insisted that the white females had equated flirting with harassment.

Tying It All Together

School safety is one of the most important issues tied to student achievement. In an unsafe school or classroom, teachers aren't able to teach, and students can't learn.[5] Although researchers have reported that students are more likely to be subjected to violence away from school, many students across the nation not only feel unsafe at school but have actually been subjected to violence, harassment, and bullying at school. Few of the American High School students who participated in the study mentioned specific acts of violence that occurred at school. However, the fact that nearly 40 percent of the student questionnaire respondents often felt unsafe at school indicates that school safety was a great concern to a substantial number of them. Moreover, nearly 60 percent of the white female students often felt unsafe at American High School. Bullying and actual physical altercations at school weren't necessarily race specific, but the feedback from the students at American High School indicated that the sense of unease many students felt was connected to ongoing racial and ethnic tension.

What We Can Do

As the feedback from the students suggested, particularly with regard to security staff, adults clearly could do more to improve school safety. In the next sections, I make specific recommendations to administrators, teachers, parents, and policymakers.

Administrators

I began this chapter by describing how school administrators at my son's high school handled the two race riots that occurred in late 2004. The action plan that school leaders created to eradicate the problem can be useful to other administrators. Among other things, the administrators and city officials

- Cancelled school temporarily in order to strategize
- Required students to make up the lost class time at the end of the year
- Held meetings with parents and students
- Made it clear that rioting and disruptive behavior wouldn't be tolerated
- Identified and punished the ringleaders swiftly
- Listened to feedback from students and parents
- Shared their plans with both groups
- Found creative ways to increase parent and community involvement

The way that administrators handled the race riots at my son's high school underscores the truth that in any organization, the tone leaders set will affect people's behavior.[6] For example, I recently met an African American principal who was hired at an underperforming high school near the end of the 2006 school year. When she arrived, she learned that students had been gambling and using drugs on campus and disrespecting teachers, and that there were ongoing conflicts between Latino and black students. In fact, a few years earlier, the high school had been on the television news because of race riots that had occurred there.

Shortly after her arrival, the principal began to take swift action. She sent a letter to students and teachers that explicitly explained her expectations regarding how everyone should behave on campus. She also made it clear that negative conduct that had been tolerated in the past would no longer be permitted. One of the most innovative strategies she used was summoning Latino and black student leaders together for a forum in which they discussed the ongoing racial tension and brainstormed solutions. From what I heard from other educators, the students who participated in the forum were extremely grateful that the principal gave them an opportunity not only to express their views but also to help her develop solutions. Even the educators who had been skeptical of the wisdom of putting two "warring" groups together to discuss a controversial issue were impressed at the outcome and at how well the students had behaved.

Pedro Noguera, a professor at New York University and an expert on school reform, stresses the importance of listening to feedback from students, particularly about the topic of school violence. According to Noguera, "Consulting with students increases the likelihood that the policies enacted to insure safety actually address their fears and concerns about violence."[7]

School administrators can also host ongoing assemblies in which students learn conflict resolution skills from guest speakers, role playing, and films. Administrators should also ensure that school security officers are well trained, well supervised, and held accountable.

One of the most important things that school administrators can do is to believe students who complain about bullying and harassment. Time and time again, in the cases of school shootings that have occurred, administrators, teachers, and parents missed or ignored warning signs that a bullying victim was about to retaliate. When a student complains to a school administrator that another student is bullying him or that a teacher is harassing him, it would behoove the administrator to listen, investigate, and take appropriate action.

Finally, district officials and school administrators can make schools safer by doing thorough background checks on all personnel before hiring new teachers and staff. In the city in which I live, in the past few years, teachers, school security, and coaches have been arrested for sexually abusing students. For example, a local AP science teacher was recently put on leave pending an investigation of her alleged sexual relationship with a female student. A year earlier, a local middle school teacher was arrested for downloading child pornography on his computer at work; in a neighboring city, a middle school principal was fired after child pornography was found on his work computer. Unfortunately, I could go on and on, telling related stories that involve schools throughout the nation. Child abuse, especially sexual abuse of children, has reached epidemic proportions in the United States, and schools are one of the best places for predators to gain access to victims. The need to conduct thorough background checks is especially crucial in underperforming, high-poverty, and high-minority schools, where teacher attrition rates are high and administrators are often desperate to hire teachers.

Teachers

Because of their sustained time with students, teachers have multiple opportunities throughout the school day and the academic year to teach students conflict resolution skills and to convey important messages about bullying, violence, and racism. Teachers can do this through the curriculum, storytelling, and lectures, and by inviting guest speakers to discuss these topics. During the fourteen years that I taught junior high school and high school, I used all of these strategies to teach about these topics, but current events, storytelling, and literature were the three that I used most frequently.

When I taught ninth grade, for example, *The Friends*, a novel by Rosa Guy, was one of the books I most enjoyed reading and discussing with my students. The book tells parallel stories. The main plot centers around Philisia, a West Indian immigrant who has recently moved to New York. Philisia's father, Calvin, is an arrogant owner of a small restaurant. Although he is struggling to make ends meet, the fact that he is West Indian and a business owner causes him to look down on American-born blacks. Therefore, he encourages Philisia and her sister, Ruby, to view themselves as superior to African Americans and dissuades them from associating with them.

The subplot focuses on Edith, a U.S.-born African American from an extremely poor family. Because her mother died when she was young, Edith has to help her father take care of her younger sisters. Consequently, she often misses school, arrives at school late, or arrives unprepared to concentrate on academic work. Because she and Philisia are in the same class, their paths cross.

In some ways, their classroom and school are stereotypical, but in others, they're typical. Their teacher, Miss Lass, an angry white woman who hates most of her black students, especially the gum-chewing, back-talking Edith, spends much of the school day trying to get her unruly class under control. Many of the students are rude, defiant, and uncooperative. Philisia is one of the few exceptions. She's always on time, always does her class work and homework, and, unlike her classmates, she's cooperative and eager to answer Miss Lass's questions. As expected, some of her classmates begin to resent her. Not only does she act like the teacher's pet and a "Miss Goody Two-Shoes," but her arrogance is unmistakable. She has adopted her father's disdain for American-born blacks, and her classmates detect her sense of superiority.

Once Miss Lass becomes aware of the students' growing animosity toward Philisia, she decides to use it to her advantage. In an effort to turn the students' wrath brought about by her racism, weak classroom management skills, and boring curriculum away from herself, the teacher actually creates a classroom climate that leads to violence. Predictably, after school one day, Philisia is physically attacked by one of the school's most notorious bullies.

As I was thinking about the lessons that I've learned about school violence, and particularly the interracial tensions that are common among Latinos and African Americans, the book *The Friends* and the way in which I used it and other strategies to teach my students about tolerance, conflict resolution, and racism came to mind. I believe that many teachers, school administrators, and other adults are as guilty as Miss Lass in creating a hostile classroom environment. For example, when educators ignore racist and culturally insensitive comments between students or ignore other signs of racial tension in and outside the classroom, they allow these situations to escalate. Incorporating conflict resolution skills into the curriculum and allowing students to read about, write about, and discuss related current and historical events are simple strategies that teachers can use to diffuse tensions and teach problem-solving skills instead of ignoring the obvious.[8] The Community Problem Solving project that I describe in *Through Ebony Eyes* is another useful strategy. Teachers can have students conduct research and create projects that are designed to alleviate interracial conflicts in their communities. The Cultural Awareness project (also described in *Through Ebony Eyes*) can help teachers create an inclusive classroom environment in which all students are respected. This activity should be used at the beginning of the school year, and the teacher should start by presenting her own Cultural Awareness Project first.

It is important to note that if assignments that focus on race and culture are used incorrectly, they can be counterproductive. A good example is the story of a new teacher at a predominantly black and Latino underperforming high school, who approached me after one of my professional development workshops. According to this young white woman, she had tried to teach a unit on Mexican American history and was upset because the black students were resistant. "That cultural awareness stuff doesn't work!" she exclaimed. "The black kids hate it." Because of a time constraint, I could spend only a few minutes sharing my thoughts with her, but I wanted to emphasize two important lessons that I'd learned from my own teaching experiences.

The first point that I stressed to her was the importance of starting to create a community of learners in the classroom on the very first day of school. The teacher can do this by emphasizing that every student is important, every student will be treated respectfully and will be expected to treat the teacher and classmates respectfully, every student will have multiple opportunities to share his or her views during discussions and to contribute to class projects, and students will frequently collaborate through partnerships and group work throughout the school year. As a high school teacher, I also used the Time Line project and the All About Me project (described in *Through Ebony Eyes*) early in the school year as icebreakers that allowed me to share details about myself, allowed students to share important information about themselves, and encouraged students to get to know each other better. My decorating the classroom walls with students' time lines brought two additional benefits: the students, especially those who had never had any of their work displayed in class, felt that the classroom belonged to them, and it gave students an incentive to urge their parents to attend Back to School Night. They were proud of their time lines and wanted their parents to see their work.

The second point that I explained to the new teacher regarded the importance of giving students choices and using creativity in presenting lessons. For example, if she had required *all* students to do a Cultural Awareness project in which they researched a culture that *interested them*, wrote a related paper, created a related project, and presented it to the class, then *all* students would have benefited from learning about multiple cultures and would have been less likely to be resistant.

When I returned home after my brief conversation with this young teacher, I told my husband what she'd said. Like me, he has worked as an educator for more than twenty years. He is also a lot more perceptive than I am about some things, for when I finished telling him the story, he said, "Duh! It's Black History Month! The black students were probably wondering why this white woman was teaching Mexican American history in February." When I was reminded of this, the students' resistance made even more sense to me. For some reason, a white teacher who was teaching at a predominantly black and Latino underperforming high school that has had a history of racial conflict between Latinos and blacks had decided to teach about Mexican American history during the one

month of the year designated for educators to focus on the contributions that blacks have made to American society, yet she couldn't
understand why the black students were resistant.

This story illustrates two points. First, teachers must not be
naïve about race relations. If they refuse to address their own racial
baggage, they can unknowingly demonstrate cultural insensitivity
and even exacerbate racial conflicts among students. Second,
teachers who haven't done community-building work in their classroom, starting at the very beginning of the school year, may find
that their best efforts are thwarted and met with resistance.

A related example was described to me by an educator who told
me about another new teacher at the same underperforming high
school I just mentioned, who assigned students to do group work.
The students not only were uncooperative with each other but
spent much of the group time calling each other derogatory names
and insulting each other in other ways. This situation reinforces
what I have said elsewhere: it is critical that teachers have good
classroom management skills, that on the first day of school they
explicitly state their expectations about student conduct (including
a policy of zero tolerance for name-calling or other insulting behavior), and that they begin developing a sense of community at the
very beginning of the school year.

The bottom line is that there are many strategies teachers can
use to make schools safer. Teaching conflict resolution skills
through the curriculum, storytelling, and discussing current events;
inviting guest speakers; and taking advantage of teachable moments
are just a few that I found to be effective during my own junior high
and high school teaching years.

Parents

Parents must also do their part to make schools and communities
safer. If parents are bad role models to their children, whether by
encouraging them to be violent (unless it involves self-defense),
rewarding bad behavior, or permitting them to misbehave at school,

they are doing a great disservice to their children, to educators, and to society. Good parents model appropriate behavior, and they teach their children explicitly about acceptable behavior and the consequences of bad behavior.

Like teachers, parents can use storytelling as a great way to convey important messages about violence and to teach conflict resolution skills. They can share stories about nonviolent ways in which they handled bullying during their own childhood, and also use stories from literature and current events. I did this when my own three children were growing up. One of the easiest ways to do it was to share stories with them as I was driving them to and from school.

Parents should also be proactive about being advocates for their children when they complain about bullying, by contacting school officials and ensuring that their children can get to and from school safely. If a student tells her parent that a teacher permits derogatory name-calling, bullying, or any other threat to safety and psychological well-being to occur in the classroom, the parent should notify school administrators and, if necessary, request that the student be transferred to another classroom.

As I write this section for parents, I'm aware that in inner cities, many of the problems that students and parents face are quite different from those faced by the middle and upper classes. Community violence and extensive gang activity are two problems that are directly tied to school safety. When kids grow up in neighborhoods where violence is common, many parents believe that it is unwise and even naïve to teach their children to "turn the other cheek."[9] I grew up in such a home and community.

One of my most vivid memories from childhood involves a related incident. One day, when I was still in elementary school, I was hiding out in our small apartment. Because it was a beautiful day and unusual for me to be hanging around inside instead of playing outdoors like my siblings, my mother eventually noticed my presence. When she asked why I wasn't outside playing, I admitted that I was scared. Terrified would've been more accurate. A girl who had recently moved into our apartment complex and whom I'd befriended had turned against me and wanted to beat me up. I was hiding from her because I knew she could fight. She had once socked me in the arm, and I still remembered the pain from that powerful blow. Although I was a "hood rat" (a kid from a rough neighborhood) at heart, I didn't want to tangle with her, for whereas I had a big mouth, she had an even bigger punch!

Upon hearing my explanation, my mother wasn't sympathetic at all. In fact, instead of sympathy, I got anger, and she quickly made two things clear to me. The first was that I should never let anyone chase me home; her second and scarier point was that she was going to make me go outside and face my enemy. Like the mother of Richard Wright, the author of *Black Boy* (a book that I enjoyed reading and discussing with my tenth graders), and undoubtedly countless other black parents, my mother believed that the only way to keep me from being victimized in a hostile society was to teach me to defend myself. So, with her following close at my heels, I left the apartment to face my enemy. It wasn't my decision; I had no choice.

When my friend-turned-enemy saw me approaching, she wasn't even phased by my mother's presence. Her face lit up with glee, and the fight began. A crowd quickly formed. As I'd expected, I was no match for this opponent who had honed her skills over time. After the girl had punched me, scratched me, and pulled out enough of my hair to prove to the spectators that she was the true victor, her mother, who had watched the entire fight from her apartment window, yelled for her to stop. Her daughter obeyed, and the fight, which had seemed to last forever, was finally over. My "reward" for clearly losing the fight was having to hear my older sister taunt repeatedly, "You got your butt kicked!"—as if I didn't already know. But that wasn't all. My mother, who had undoubtedly been humiliated by my loss, put me on restriction. Now I couldn't leave the apartment if I wanted to.

For many years, I judged my mother harshly for making me fight that day. I thought her actions were cruel. However, when I became a parent, my attitude changed. When my own daughter Nafissa came running home one morning, yelling that Roland (not his real name), the little white boy who lived down the street and who had once been her friend, was going to beat her up, I felt just as indignant as my mother had after learning why I was hiding in the apartment long ago. "If you let him chase you home today," I said, "he'll be chasing you home for the rest of your life. Go back outside and defend yourself!"

When Roland and Nafissa began to fight, Roland's father, who had been working under the hood of his car, looked up and told her to go home. "My mother told me to defend myself!" she bellowed. At this point, Roland's father noticed me standing on the sidewalk in front of my house. Because it was early morning, I was still wearing my pajamas and hadn't combed my hair yet. The combination of my appearance and the expression on my face must have spoken volumes to him, for he took one look at me and put his head back under the hood of that car! The "fight" lasted only a few minutes and consisted mostly of pushing and a few punches. From that point on, however, Roland and Nafissa were able to play outside whenever they wanted, without further problems with each other.

Today, nearly two decades after that incident occurred, I'm not proud to tell others that like my mother, I too once forced my child to engage in a physical fight. But if I had to do it all over again, I'm almost certain that I would do the same thing. As an African American woman—one of America's stepchildren—I belong to a racial group that has historically been oppressed. Because I'm a female, I also belong to a gender group that is more likely to be subjected to abuse than males are. Because of racism, sexism, and the violence that was prevalent in my home and community during my childhood, I had to learn to be tough in order to survive in this society without constantly allowing myself to be victimized—not only physically but verbally, emotionally, and psychologically as well—at home, in the community, in churches, and especially in the workplace. These are lessons that I've had to pass on to my three children. In an ideal world—one where there are no societal stepchildren—I would've been able to rely on words and mental strategies to protect myself and to teach my children how to survive. But the world is not ideal, especially for black people and other oppressed and marginalized groups. So I'm grateful that my mother taught me the importance of protecting myself. She made it clear that I should never start a fight, but if someone started one with me, I needed to be willing to defend myself. This was the same message that I instilled in my children.

At this point, I realize that some readers may be appalled and may even be shaking their heads in dismay that a veteran educator, author, and parent would condone violence for self-preservation. To these readers, I will merely say what my friend the late Margaret Goss, a veteran educator, often said: "Get real!" or try being black or Latino for a year in America, or try living in an inner city. As I said previously, the world is not always a nice place, and researchers and others have found that people—particularly women—who choose to be naïve are a predator's delight. Anna Salter, an author who has done extensive interviews with every type of sexual predator imaginable, and Gavin De Becker, an expert on serial killers and other types of violent individuals, repeat this message throughout their work: being naïve and wearing blinders about reality are often the precursors to tragedy.[10] According to Salter, sexual predators find that two of the easiest groups to prey on are religious people and single mothers in search of male companionship, because both tend to be naïve and tend to look for the "good" in people. In her popular radio broadcast, Laura Schlessinger emphasizes that it is wise for women to take self-defense classes. Salter, De Becker, and Schlessinger are aware of how dangerous the world can be. It would behoove parents to keep this in mind as they teach their children about safety issues.

Although it is extremely naïve and foolish for parents to fail to arm their children with self-protective strategies before they leave for school, the path that each parent chooses to take is an individual choice, and every parent must live with the consequences of his or her actions. Each parent must do his or her part to make schools safer places, but at the same time ensure that she is not unwittingly increasing her child's chances of being victimized through poor parenting practices. A recurring message about children who are victimized by adults and other children is that the predator detects a sense of vulnerability and an unwillingness to be self-protective in the potential victim. Bullies and predators are less likely to try to take advantage of a child who appears to be assertive and who will use any means necessary to defend herself. This is something that parents should keep in mind as they decide which strategies to use with their children.

My final recommendation to parents regarding school safety is probably even more controversial than what I said about telling my child to defend herself, for it pertains to a very sensitive subject: mental illness in children. I think that it's safe for me to say that most parents want their children to be perfect or as close to perfect as possible. We want our children to look good, to be smart, not to embarrass us, and not to appear to be defective. The fact remains, however, that children are usually just as imperfect as their parents. Because no child is perfect, most children will misbehave periodically; that's human nature. As I stated previously, one of the ways that parents can make schools safer is to hold their children accountable and enact consequences for inappropriate behavior. Another thing that parents can do is to be honest with themselves about their children, for although all children will misbehave from time to time, some children display behaviors that suggest that something is seriously wrong with them. When patterns of destructive and antisocial behavior emerge, parents who pretend that all is well and that the behavior is normal are asking for trouble in the long run. Some of these parents will be visiting their kids in juvenile hall or jail one day.

At the extreme end of the continuum of mental disorders that often are manifested through inappropriate and destructive behavior is sociopathy. According to Martha Stout, a clinical psychologist who worked at the Harvard Medical School for twenty-five years, one out of every twenty-five people is a sociopath. I believe the number is actually much higher. These individuals have no conscience, are unable to feel empathy, are incurable, and thrive on bullying and manipulating others.[11] If a child gets a thrill from hurting animals or other children, or laughs at another person's pain, he might be showing signs that he is incapable of feeling empathy and perhaps even has other sociopathic tendencies. Therefore, one of the best ways that the parents of such children can make schools safer is to face the truth about their child and seek assistance from a trained medical professional.

Policymakers

The popular O'Jays song which repeatedly says, "Money, money, money, money. Money!" captures in a nutshell one of the main ways that policymakers can make schools safer. More money needs to be earmarked for schools, especially urban and high-poverty schools, for adequate and well-trained security, metal detectors, and metal-detecting wands, and for professional development to educate teachers and administrators about better ways to teach conflict-resolution skills, share strategies with students, and learn ways to eliminate unsafe behavior. The old sayings "Money talks" and "Actions speak louder than words" definitely apply to the ways in which policymakers can improve schools.

A second related point is that policymakers must become committed to addressing social problems. In the case of many underperforming and urban schools, excessive fighting and gang activity usually stem from problems in the communities that surround schools. There is a strong correlation between poverty and community violence, and gangs tend to be more prevalent in marginalized and low-income neighborhoods.

Unfortunately, I've become convinced that most national and state policymakers don't really care about the problems plaguing inner cities and high-minority and high-poverty underperforming schools. Sometimes politicians and others talk about revitalizing these communities and improving underperforming schools in high-poverty communities, but as another saying goes, "talk is cheap." Most policymakers aren't willing to invest enough money and time into using a holistic and long-term comprehensive approach. Of course, if their own children were attending under-performing schools in neighborhoods that were plagued by violence, it would be a different story. However, history has shown that most people with money and power wouldn't permit their children to attend such schools, and they don't want kids from these communities attending schools with their children.

Another lesson that I've learned over time regards the role that hypocrisy plays in keeping many schools and communities unsafe. Most policymakers want their children, grandchildren, and other school-age relatives to attend great schools, but they don't care about America's stepchildren nearly as much as they should. They often get elected to office by promising members of minority groups that they will revitalize their communities, bring in more jobs, get tough on crime, and improve the schools, but in the end, as time has shown, these are usually lies. So until more policymakers become truly committed to improving inner cities and underper-forming schools, countless students in America will continue to perform poorly as a result of being required to attend unsafe, poorly funded, inferior schools.

A Final Word

Of all the chapters in this book, this one on school safety was the hardest for me to write because of what I've learned about school reform and most policymakers' lack of commitment to improving underperforming schools and the surrounding communities. But writing this chapter was also difficult for me because of the related lessons that I've learned from studying history—one of my favorite subjects. For this reason, I feel like a hypocrite—a charge I just made against policymakers.

History has taught me that it is somewhat hypocritical for adults to tell children to be nonviolent and for us to expect them to be pacifists. As I've already stated, the world is not always a nice place.

Some people commit heinous acts, often against women and children. History has also shown that warfare and the use of force have been the ways that many leaders, especially some of the most famous, have handled disputes. In fact, the list of political leaders who used force to expand their empires and to subjugate other nations and groups is endless. Even my favorite biblical person, King David, was known as a bloody man.

History also emphasizes that one of the main reasons leaders are able to use force to attain their goals is that most people are followers and cowards. Most individuals don't think for themselves, and most will not speak truth to power, even if they disagree with the leader's approach. Stanley Milgram, a social psychologist who created the famous Obedience Studies and the Six Degrees of Separation Studies, proved this point well.

In his Obedience Studies, Milgram sought to understand why so many so-called law-abiding and decent German citizens could not only permit the Holocaust to happen but also actively participate in one man's plan to eradicate an entire group of people. What Milgram discovered was that most people are indeed followers and "would readily inflict pain on innocent victims at the behest of an authority figure."[12] This same message surfaced during the Nuremberg trials, when time and time again, high-ranking German officials justified their actions by saying, "I was merely following orders."[13]

With these lessons from history in mind, policymakers, teachers, administrators, and parents shouldn't be so shocked when school violence erupts, nor should they be so quick to snub their noses at youths who join gangs. After all, these youths have realized what Milgram learned: "Membership in authority-dominated social groups provides enormous advantage in coping with a hostile environment."[14] So as we search for solutions to improving student achievement by making schools safer, we must remember the lessons of history; we must understand that: without commitment and money to improve social problems in neighborhoods, schools will never become totally safe; and we must acknowledge that children are aware of our hypocrisy.

7

"Everybody's Intimidated by Us"

A Candid Conversation with African American Males

One day during fall 2004, I had lunch with an assistant super-intendent of a large school district in southern California. Although we discussed many topics related to the public school system and education reform, two stories that he shared were a lot more inter-esting to me than the other topics. Both stories were about boys, both were about standardized tests, and both had taken place years earlier when this man, an African American, had been an elemen-tary school principal.

The first story was about a white student at the elementary school where the man had served as principal. During his years as principal, white parents often voiced their dissatisfaction to him if their chil-dren weren't placed in the Gifted and Talented Education (GATE) program. GATE students are generally perceived to be the best and the brightest students, those who are college bound and who as adults are destined to end up in the highest-paying professions. In general, GATE students receive a more rigorous curriculum, and their teach-ers have higher expectations. At an early age, these students have been given the prerequisites that they need for academic success. They gain reinforcement by receiving frequent homework assign-ments. They strengthen their study skills and knowledge base by devoting more hours to homework than other students.

Because African American and Latino students are underrepre-sented in GATE classes, critics of GATE abound, and some see it as an elitist feature of the public school system that favors white students. In *African American Teens Discuss Their Schooling Experiences,* I described the K–12 schooling experiences of nearly three hundred African American seniors at seven high schools. One of my conclusions was that being placed in GATE can be both advantageous and disadvantageous for black students. Among the negative experiences was a sense of loneliness and isolation that some students felt because of the low number of African Americans in GATE, a factor that prompted several teens who participated in the study to voluntarily leave the program. However, positive benefits included the fact that GATE students "receive a better quality of instruction and they tend to express more satisfaction with their homework and the overall quality of instruction they receive."[1]

In spite of GATE's critics, many parents are extremely assertive in attempting to get their children into the program because it is equated with a better education. In fact, when my own three children transferred from private to public schools, I successfully advocated for them to get into GATE and for my high school–age daughter to get into AP courses.

So when the African American assistant superintendent told me that he'd been bombarded with requests from white parents to have their children placed in GATE, I wasn't surprised. Like most parents, they wanted the best for their children and assumed that GATE was the best the public school system had to offer. The problem was that the principal wasn't able to grant some of the requests because the school district relied on students' standardized test scores to determine which students were "GATE material."

When the principal told white parents that their children's test scores weren't high enough for them to qualify for GATE, many were shocked. Others were outraged. Most assumed that he'd made a mistake. Therefore, he always had to provide evidence—the actual test score printouts—that their children hadn't scored high enough.

The anger wasn't isolated to unhappy parents either. At least one student who wasn't accepted into GATE because of low test

scores voiced his displeasure. According to the assistant superintendent, one day a white third grader approached him and
complained, "My mother said that *I* should be in GATE and *you*
won't let me in." The principal showed the child his test scores and
explained that he didn't qualify because he'd only scored in the
70th percentile. Instead of accepting the principal's explanation,
the boy exclaimed, "Then *something is wrong with that test!*" The
assistant superintendent concluded this story by saying that the
white third grader believed so much in his ability that he felt that
the *test* was at fault, instead of *his performance* on the test.

The second story concerned an African American student at the
same elementary school where he'd once been a principal. He
couldn't remember if the boy was a third grader or fourth grader when
the incident took place, but he had vivid memories of the child, and
most of his recollections were negative. Even though many years had
passed, he still remembered the boy's name, LeVelle.

Because LeVelle was perceived as a discipline problem by his
teacher, he and the principal had frequent contact with each other.
This was during the time when corporal punishment was still
permitted in California public schools. So one day, after the teacher
sent LeVelle to the principal's office, given the seriousness of his
misbehavior and the frequency of his visits for disciplinary purposes,
the principal decided that he had two options: to send him home or
to "discipline" him with the same type of wooden paddle that many
school administrators used at that time. (During the 1980s when I
was a junior high school teacher, at a white vice principal's request,
I served as a witness to one of these infamous paddlings. It seemed
to me that this frail man used every ounce of strength within his
body to apply force to the paddle that repeatedly struck a black
student's bottom. Afterward, I was so traumatized that I never again
agreed to serve as "witness to a paddling," and I became a staunch
opponent of corporal punishment in schools.)

In continuing the story, the assistant superintendent said, "So, I
telephoned LeVelle's mother, who was at work at the time, and
explained the situation. I told her, 'You can either come and pick

him up from school, or I can paddle him.'" As expected, the indignant African American mother replied, "I don't want anyone hitting my son." "Then you'll have to come and get him," the principal answered. "But I can't leave work," the mother said, thereby sealing her son's fate. After the telephone call ended, feeling that he had no other choice, the principal administered corporal punishment to LeVelle. Whether or not he achieved his desired goal is doubtful, as the next part of the story reveals.

In the spring of that same year, the annual time arrived for teachers in the school district to administer the Comprehensive Test of Basic Skills (CTBS). Back then, the CTBS was the state-mandated standardized test in California. In order to set the serious tone about testing that he wanted to permeate the school environment during testing week, the assistant superintendent told me that as principal of the elementary school, he visited every classroom on the first day of testing. His goal was to give students a motivational speech about the importance of the test and urge them to take it seriously.

At first, his plan seemed to go well, for in each classroom that he visited, the students appeared to be receptive to his comments and eager to do their best on the test. Then he visited LeVelle's classroom. In the other classrooms the principal had visited, after his speech ended, the teacher would read the test directions, and the students would begin to work. In LeVelle's classroom, however, after the principal's pep talk, the teacher read the directions, and all but one student began to work. As his classmates worked earnestly on the test, LeVelle was the only student who hadn't even picked up his pencil. And the look on his face and his demeanor suggested that he didn't plan to do so at all.

The principal walked over to him and began to whisper that the test was very important and that the boy needed to get started right away. LeVelle then said something the principal never forgot: "I ain't giving that white woman one more reason to say I'm dumb," he announced matter-of-factly. The principal was so taken aback that he was at a loss for words. Realizing the deeper ramifications of the child's statement, he left the classroom without further attempts to change LeVelle's mind. As he recounted the story to me, he concluded that unlike the white third grader who strongly believed that something was wrong with the test when his scores didn't qualify him for GATE, LeVelle "had created the perception that what tests were for was to show what was *wrong with him*"—a little black boy. LeVelle had also inferred that his teacher would add his test scores to her arsenal of weapons to prove that he was deficient.

I don't know whether or not the story about the white third grader is unusual, but I know for certain that the story about LeVelle, the African American boy, is typical in several ways. Although many, and I would even venture to say most, black children start school with as much excitement, eagerness, and optimism as their nonblack peers, they are more likely than other children to have negative labels applied to them early in their schooling. In my opinion, this labeling is part of what I refer to as the culture of arrogance that is deeply entrenched in American society. The culture of arrogance "is characterized by four beliefs: (1) Whites are smarter than Blacks; (2) Blacks do not have the aptitude to do outstanding work; (3) Whites know what is best for Black students; and (4) The research of Black scholars is inferior to the work of Whites."[2] Because of this "culture of arrogance," most Americans, including K–12 teachers and administrators, have a very negative perception of blacks. This negative perception often affects educators' attitudes, behaviors, and expectations of black students and becomes a self-fulfilling prophecy. Most African American students are aware that they are presumed by many nonblacks to be intellectually inferior. That LeVelle, a young African American boy, already believed that his test scores would be used against him is very telling, and it speaks volumes about student underachievement on standardized tests.

In *Young, Gifted, and Black*, Perry discusses what she refers to as the ideology of black intellectual inferiority. Although this ideology is less overt than in previous eras ("few respectable people will publicly assert that black people are intellectually inferior"[3]), Perry believes it has a stronger impact on students today than it did during the pre–civil rights era. Most African American students have experienced instances when they were "automatically assumed to be intellectually incompetent."[4]

Assumptions about African American males are even more insidious. Research has repeatedly shown that black males are demonized in American society as predators, criminals, and thugs, and are even referred to in animalistic terms, such as "endangered species."[5] African American males are aware of their precarious place in American society. As early as second grade, according to Foster and Peele, they know that negative stereotypes about them exist.[6] Seemingly paradoxically, although the media have portrayed African American males in ways that create fear among the general public,[7] the heavy burden of being demonized at such a young age also engenders fear in African American boys. In *Bad Boys*, Ferguson wrote, "The very boys who were being constituted in school and in the media as demonic, terrifying, and unsalvageable were themselves fearful."[8]

Ferguson provided ample evidence of this demonization. In her study of an elementary school in northern California, she described how adults at the school engaged in "adultification" when it came to black boys. Instead of viewing black students' behavior as that of children, they viewed the boys as if they were adults. One of Ferguson's main conclusions was that the adults were unknowingly preparing some of the black fourth- and fifth-grade boys for the prison system, through detrimental discipline practices that could have long-term consequences.

In *What African American Parents Want Educators to Know*, my own study of a diverse group of black parents, I learned that several of the parents and guardians felt pressured by educators to have their sons placed on medication for Attention Deficit Disorder (ADD), even when doctors found no evidence of ADD. Some of these boys had been high achievers who earned outstanding standardized test scores in elementary school, but then became labeled as discipline problems. Their parents concluded that their children were bored with an unchallenging curriculum, and, finishing their class work early, had idle time on their hands that led to misbehavior in the classroom, which their teachers decided was evidence of ADD.[9]

At the same time that many black students, particularly males, are receiving negative messages from the media, educators, and the wider society about their aptitude, behavior, and way of speaking, they are also receiving messages from home and from their peers. Even when parents stress the value of education, the students' peers may be planting anti-education messages in their ears and making "street life" seem more appealing. Some students conclude that because the school system has rejected them with negative messages about their aptitude and through the denigration of their culture, way of speaking, and behavior, they will reject the formal education system for the "lure of the streets."

One consequence is that in urban communities throughout the United States, thousands of African American, Latino, Southeast Asian, and even white youth join gangs. According to Noguera, "Black males learn at an early age that by presenting a tough exterior it is easier to avoid threats or attacks."[10] During a conversation I had several years ago with a white detective working in one of the Los Angeles Police Department's gang units, I learned more about this national problem.

One of the specific examples that he shared with me was the story of an African American teenager whom he'd gotten to know well. This teen grew up in a two-parent middle-class home; his parents stressed traditional values, including the importance of getting a good education. Nevertheless, the young man eventually joined a gang. When his parents found out, they were shocked. Later, their son ended up in a wheelchair after being shot multiple times in gang-related violence. After he was no longer able to "gang bang," he and the detective developed a rapport with each other. In fact, the detective often invited him to share his story with youngsters who were considering joining a gang or who had already gotten into trouble with the police. According to the detective, the young man would speak openly to the youths about the pitfalls of gang life.

However, in private conversations with the detective, the former gang member always made it clear that he had no regrets: if he could relive his youth, he would make the same choices, for the thrill of gang life had been worth it all—even if it meant that he would never walk again.

This detective told me that in urban communities, boys are under a tremendous amount of pressure to join gangs, pressure almost impossible to resist. He said that in his experience, only two groups of boys in inner cities are not constantly pressured to join gangs: those who are extremely involved in the church and those who are heavily involved in sports. In his opinion, there was an unspoken rule that "church boys" and jocks were exempted.

Miles Corwin, a former *Los Angeles Times* reporter, also described many of the difficulties that youths in inner cities face. In *And Still We Rise*, Corwin chronicled the lives of a small group of AP students at Crenshaw High School in South Central Los Angeles. During the year that he observed and interacted with the students (as well as with administrators and two of their teachers), most of them experienced personal and economic hardships that made focusing on school more difficult than it should have been. In addition, the gang violence that is prevalent in South Central Los Angeles often spilled over into the school, making school safety a big issue. According to Corwin, because of poor funding, overcrowding, gang activity, low test scores, and the fact that armed police patrol the school, Crenshaw has one of the worst reputations among schools in Los Angeles.[11]

Regarding the particular plight of boys at the school, Corwin wrote, "Given the distractions and disadvantages, it is difficult for all inner-city students to succeed academically. But boys have an added burden," exacerbated by an environment in which "teenage machismo is venerated . . . [and] athletes and gangbangers gain the most attention in the school hallways." Consequently, ". . . the serious student often is regarded as effete, as a sellout, as someone who has disdained his culture."[12]

Two of the male African American AP students whom Corwin profiled illustrate these points. Although he had been identified as gifted during elementary school and won debates and oratorical contests, Sadi had eventually joined a gang. However, after he was nearly killed in a gang-related shooting, he changed his ways and applied himself to his schooling. Curt, one of the few students who came from a middle-class family, like Sadi had been identified as gifted during elementary school. Despite the fact that he remained a high achiever throughout his schooling and hadn't surrendered to the "lure of the street," Curt had often been harassed and criticized by his peers. During elementary school, although he fit in with his peers in "gifted classes[,] . . . in the mainstream courses . . . he was called a 'punk' and a 'fag.' He was accused of 'acting white.' In class, Curt was teased constantly. In the schoolyard he was goaded into fights."[13] He attended a predominantly white junior high school, where peer pressure and racism from teachers compounded his problems; for a while, the teen gave into the peer pressure by refusing to raise his hand in class and choosing to work below his potential. But in the gifted program at Crenshaw High School, Curt once again began to excel. Nevertheless, while walking home from school one day, he was almost shot by gang members for wearing the "wrong" color shirt to school.

It's obvious that attending school can be a difficult experience for any student from a challenging background, regardless of race, ethnicity, or gender. However, the stories and research that I've presented in this chapter thus far underscore the fact that African American males occupy a unique place in U.S. society, and, according to researchers, their schooling experiences are more likely than those of other groups to be negative. As Noguera states, "Given the range and extent of the hardships that beset this segment of the population, there is no doubt that there are some legitimate reasons for young Black males to be angry."[14] For these reasons, I was excited about having a frank discussion with some of the African American male students at American High School. In the remainder of this chapter, I describe the schooling experiences of the forty-five African American male students at American High School who completed the questionnaire, and present many of the comments that twenty of these students shared during a focus group discussion.

Nearly 60 percent of the black males who completed the questionnaire were ninth or tenth graders at the time. Most were involved in school sports, and 6 percent participated in other extracurricular school activities. One-fifth were employed. Taken together, their comments can give educators ideas about how they can increase their efficacy with black males in schools, and the feedback can provide parents, policymakers, and the wider community with insights into the unique challenges and issues that many black males experience in school and society. These voices deserve to be heard. Also, because the black-white achievement gap has concerned educators, researchers, and policymakers for decades, and the original goal of the student study was for me to collect feedback solely from black students, a chapter devoted to capturing the voices of black students makes sense.

What the Students Said

Although the purpose of the focus groups was for students to elaborate on topics that were covered in the questionnaire, when I began to talk with the black male students, the conversation turned almost immediately to stereotypes and societal beliefs about black males. This happened because contrary to popular opinion about black males, most of the focus group participants said that they actually liked school, even though most believed that school was boring. In fact, among the larger sample of black males who completed the questionnaire, 76 percent said that they liked school, but most focus group participants said the main reason was that it gave them a chance to socialize with their friends.

Because this reply surprised me, I asked the students what statistics say about black males. The students said that according to statistics and stereotypes, most Americans believe that black males "don't like school; they're dumb; they're gangbangers; they're dropouts; they're gangstas; and they stay on the street and hustle." One of the focus group participants said that some of the negative statistics about black males come from biased sampling procedures, because "They survey areas where black males don't want to do nothing with their lives. If they take the surveys [in communities] where black males want to do something, then they'll get a different statistic."

It was clear to me that these students were very aware of the prevalence of negative stereotypes about black males, so I asked them how it felt to grow up always hearing negative information about themselves. More than half the focus group students said that they refused to let the stereotypes bother them, and more than half said that being constantly bombarded with this negativity made them want to work hard to dispel the stereotypes. All the focus group participants agreed with a student who said that believing the negative stereotypes about black males would be extremely harmful. According to this student, "You got to look at it like this: the people who do trip on the statistics, those are the same people who are in the streets right now. Those are the people who are saying, 'People already look at me like this, so I might as well be like that.' But, I'm like 'whatever': I'm gon' go on regardless of what anybody thinks."

Many of the participants also said that it is important for black males to counter stereotypes by focusing on positive role models. For example, one participant said, "There is a group of black males that are doing something with their lives. You see them every day in the NBA and NFL." However, another participant accused him of engaging in stereotyping himself, saying, "That is a stereotype: that the only way that you can get out of the hood is through sports. We got businessmen. We got a group that got an education, that wants to do something positive. There is probably more of them than gangstas and hustlers."

Their Teachers

Although most of the focus group participants insisted that they refused to let the negative stereotypes about black males harm them, many complained that they'd been subjected to unfair discipline practices, mostly by teachers, because of stereotypes about black students. The questionnaire data from the black males indicated that they had a mixed view of their teachers. Despite the fact that most said their teachers were good teachers who treated them fairly, were willing to give extra help and to answer questions, were patient, were fair with discipline, liked them, and cared about them, black males were the least likely of any group to rate their teachers as good teachers. Furthermore, a lower percentage of black males than other students believed that their teachers treated them fairly, and like Latino males, black males were more likely than females and white males to say that most of their teachers viewed them as troublemakers.

Additionally, even though most of the black males who completed the questionnaire said they got along with most of their teachers, most of the black males who participated in the focus groups believed that their teachers held negative stereotypes and misconceptions about black males in general that were rooted in fear. The students believed that this fear was exacerbated by clothing styles that people equate with "rappers" and "gangstas" when in reality the clothing reflected a hip-hop style of dress. Most agreed with the focus group participant who said, "People are intimidated by black people. Every black kid that is walking around with his pants sagging and an earring in his ear, they think he is carrying a gun. They come into class intimidated by this person. So, if the person is loud, they try to be defensive and they send him out of class." Another student made a similar comment: "It don't matter: all it takes is for that person to walk around looking like a thug or a gangsta or a rapper or something. That's what they really call it. That's what they think—that we really want to be like a rapper. Just because a rapper dresses a certain way, they think we're dressing like that. But naw, it ain't really like that. It is just the new fashion." Another student added, "Hip-hop culture and gang culture are different. Hip-hop culture is into fashion, but the gang culture, they be wearing the same color, or something like that. Not everybody into the hip-hop culture [gang] bangs."

One focus group participant attributed the widespread fear of black males in society to ignorance. According to this student, "I believe that people are intimidated by things they don't understand. They see one thing, they try to figure us out, and we do a totally different thing. So, that is when the fear starts coming out. The stereotypes have made it where [society believes] that most black males are thugs, gangstas, you know this or that or whatever. So, then, obviously, they make it look like all of us are, and that is what they see in us."

Most of the focus group participants believed that, like the larger U.S. society, many nonblack students and teachers are intimidated by black males. This fear on the teachers' part often resulted in unfair discipline practices. As one student explained,

> Teachers follow the stereotypes, like the students. They see a black male on TV. All the roles he has on TV is that of a gangsta. He has a gun and he shoots people. So, they see a dude come into class with his pants sagging, all loud and stuff, talking to his friends, and they're intimidated by him. So, what's the first thing you do when you're intimidated? Try to get rid of the problem. That is fear. So, they try to get rid of the student. They discriminate against the student because he is black and they're intimidated by him. The way they try to get rid of the problem is that as soon as that student messes up—the first thing—bam! He's outta there. A student could talk outta turn or something and get in trouble.

However, one participant admitted that in his English class, he did behave in stereotypical ways. He explained:

> This one teacher gon' try to tell me one day what my grade was and she didn't even know me. She just came into class, and I said, "I got a B in here," and she said, "Oh, no you don't." I was like, "Well do you know me?" It's like the stereotypes. It was in English class. I guess you can say that I'm disrespectful in class. I ain't gon' lie to you. You know, I like to be loud, talk, and have fun in class, because it's boring. I like to entertain people I guess. I be doing my work, most of it. I don't be doing homework though.

The Curriculum, Homework, Effort, and Achievement

Just as a mixed portrait of their teachers emerged from the questionnaire data and focus group feedback from the black males at American High School, the same was true about their attitudes and effort toward their schoolwork. For example, less than half the black males who completed the questionnaire said their schoolwork was very important to them. Although this percentage was low, in actuality it was higher than the percentage of white males (44 percent) and Latino males (39 percent) who said their schoolwork was very important to them.

The same pattern emerged regarding effort. A dismally low 36 percent of the black males said they always did their best to get good grades, yet this percentage was higher than that for white males (35 percent) and Latino males (33 percent). Despite the lack of value that many of the black males placed on their schoolwork, grades were an entirely different matter. In comparison to 57 percent of white males and 56 percent of Latino males, 73 percent of black males said that getting good grades was very important to them. An obvious explanation is that many of the black males were athletes. To remain eligible to play school sports, they had to maintain a certain grade-point average.

Besides Latinas, black males were more likely than all other groups to say that most of their homework wasn't useful. They were also the least likely to say they always completed their homework on time, and most likely to say they spent one hour or less nightly on homework. In spite of this, 80 percent said they were doing their best in most of their classes. This was a much higher percentage than the percentage of white males (70 percent), equal to the percentage of Latino males, but lower than the percentage of females in all three racial or ethnic groups.

The students' reading skills may or may not have been related to the effort and time they devoted to schoolwork and homework. Although 91 percent of the African American males said they had good reading skills, they were the least likely of any group (84 percent) to say they could read and understand most of their textbooks, compared to 85 percent of Latino males and 87 percent of white males.

Testing

Nearly 60 percent of the African American males who completed the questionnaire said they were serious about doing well on standardized tests; white males (52 percent) were the least likely of all groups to say this. At the same time, black males (56 percent) were also more likely than all groups to say that in the past, they hadn't done their best on standardized tests because the tests were a waste of time, even though black and Latino males were more likely than all others to say that most of their teachers had done a good job of preparing them for standardized tests.

Discipline, Suspension, and Fighting

Although nearly 60 percent of the African American males had never been suspended from American High School, this percentage was lower than that of all other groups. Black males were less likely than all other groups to say they had received one or more discipline referrals, but along with Latino males, they were less likely than all other groups to say they were well behaved in most of their classes. They were also more likely than all other groups to say they'd been in a fight or physical altercation at American High School, and along with Latino males, they were less likely than others to say they got along with most other students.

Peer Pressure, Grades, and College

Although only 29 percent of the African American males who completed the questionnaire said that if they earned good grades, they were afraid that people might think they were nerds, this percentage was higher than for all other groups. Black males (65 percent) were also less likely than all other groups to say that most of their friends wanted them to get good grades and that most of their friends (62 percent) earned good grades. In spite of this, 71 percent of the African American males planned to attend a four-year postsecondary institution immediately after high school, and 16 percent planned to attend a two-year institution. The percentage of African American males who planned to go to a four-year institution immediately after high school was higher than for any other group.

Tying It All Together

When I first conceived of this chapter, my goal was to identify some of the unique experiences of African American males that might affect their K–12 schooling. My work with the students at American High School confirmed that the way that black males are portrayed, viewed, and treated in the larger society does have an impact on their schooling experiences. In other words, as Noguera says: "It's not surprising that there is a connection between the educational performance of African American males and the hardships they endure within the larger society."[15] The African American males at American High School who participated in the study said that they were quite aware of the negative stereotypes about them that are common in America. They also realized that as a result of these stereotypes, many individuals, including teachers, fear black males and feel intimidated by them.

As noted, some of the black males in the study chose to work hard in school in order to dispel the stereotypes. But, like LeVelle, the elementary school student who refused to take the standardized test, others chose not to exert their best effort on their schoolwork, homework, and standardized tests. Some students also chose to misbehave in class. In fact, along with Latino males, African American males were more likely to misbehave in class and more likely than all other groups to have been in a fight at school. There are many possible explanations for these findings, including the fact that black males were more likely than all groups to believe that their teachers treated them unfairly. In fact, although white males were less likely than any other group to say they treated most adults on campus respectfully, black and Latino males were less likely than all other groups to say that most adults treated them respectfully.

While it is obvious that the black males in the study appeared to be unique in some ways and doing poorly in some areas when compared to their peers, they were also doing better than their peers in several ways, such as in the high percentage who planned to go to a four-year postsecondary institution immediately after high school. Although this chapter was intended to capture the experiences of black male students at American High School, an unexpected message that surfaced was that males as a group weren't doing as well as females at American High School. The following list summarizes some of the ways in which the male participants' experiences, attitudes, and effort differed from those of their female racial or ethnic counterparts. Males were more likely than their female racial or ethnic counterparts to

- Be unsure about graduating on time
- Say they weren't doing their best in most classes
- Say they weren't well behaved in most classes
- Say teachers viewed them as a troublemaker
- Have been in a fight or physical altercation at school
- Say they did not treat most adults on campus respectfully
- Say they couldn't read and understand most of their textbooks
- Be concerned that if they earned good grades, they'd be viewed as a nerd
- Have friends who didn't want them to get good grades
- Not always complete their homework on time
- Spend one hour or less on homework each night
- Spend one hour or less nightly studying for tests
- Say their schoolwork wasn't very important to them

- Say that passing state tests wasn't that important to them
- Be employed

Although I was not deliberately seeking to compare males and females, these findings shouldn't come as a big surprise to most adults. In recent years, much attention has been given to reports indicating that females often do better in school than males. For example, in its January 30, 2006, issue, *Newsweek's* headline story was titled "The Boy Crisis: At Every Level of Education, They're Falling Behind. What to Do?" Furthermore, according to the U.S. Department of Education, for nearly thirty years, more females than males have enrolled in colleges and universities.[16] Moreover, another article in the same issue of *Newsweek* reported that high school boys are more likely to use cocaine than girls, more likely to drop out of school, and tend to have lower reading scores on standardized tests.[17]

In *Keeping Black Boys Out of Special Education,* a book that I highly recommend to educators, parents, and policymakers, Jawanza Kunjufu writes about several factors that contribute to the disproportionate placement of black boys in special education and other problems that they face in schools. Gender differences, learning styles, instructional practices, and teacher attitudes are just a few of the reasons why black males and other males may be misunderstood and mislabeled by educators and have negative schooling experiences in relation to females.[18]

This research and the information presented in this chapter make it clear that one significant facet of school reform should focus on the needs of boys and the reasons why there are so many differences between their experiences, attitudes, and efforts and those of girls.

What We Can Do

The following recommendations provide administrators, teachers, parents, and policymakers with specific solutions to address issues that are unique to black males, but also issues that males in general may experience at school.

Administrators

By high school, many boys have already dropped out, and for those who make it that far, ninth grade is a crucial year, according to researchers. The quality of students' ninth-grade year—the transition year from middle school to high school—can largely determine if boys will drop out or remain in school. For this reason, administrators should offer extensive support to all ninth graders.

During ninth grade, administrators should make strong attempts to help struggling students improve academically and socially. Students need to be able not only to earn good grades but also to acclimate to the high school culture. Some schools have created "small learning communities" that are similar to middle schools in order to help ninth graders. At the high school where I used to teach, for example, ninth graders had fewer teachers than other students, and they received more support in the form of academic interventions, motivational assemblies, awards assemblies, and the direct teaching of study skills.

Administrators can also create mentoring programs for ninth graders, and specifically for males. One school administrator whom I know formed an after-school intervention program for black males. Teachers received extra pay for tutoring, mentoring, and providing other types of support to these students through a culturally relevant curriculum. Other schools have created summer "bridge" programs for incoming ninth graders. Kunjufu emphasizes how important it is for African American males to have effective black males as teachers throughout their schooling.[19] Therefore, administrators must make the recruitment of such teachers a top priority.

As I said previously, administrators should also examine school policies and practices to determine whether or not any group, such as males, is being unfairly targeted. As researchers have repeatedly found, unfair practices tend to result in higher suspension and expulsion rates for African American and Latino males. "Changing the culture and structure of schools," Noguera maintains, "such that African American male students come to regard them as sources of support for their aspirations and identities will undoubtedly be the most important step that can be taken to make high levels of aca-demic achievement the norm, rather than the exception."[20]

To repeat a theme that I've mentioned in every chapter, admin-istrators must also face and deal with their own mental baggage. Administrators who have negative beliefs and stereotypes about black males, Latino males, or any group of students can create and condone a climate of intolerance and one in which certain groups of students are mistreated on campus.

Just as I learned a lot about the schooling experiences, attitudes, and behaviors of the students who participated in my study at American High School, administrators can use a similar approach. They can meet with groups of students periodically to hear their concerns and seek advice about how the school can be improved. Although it might be viewed as too controversial for administrators to meet with racially homogeneous gender-specific student groups, they can at least divide groups by grade level and gender without running into too much controversy. The groups should be small enough for students to feel comfortable sharing their concerns and suggestions. The principal could meet with a few student groups each month, until all students at the school have had a chance to participate. Guiding questions for male focus groups might include the following:

- What are some of the ways that we can make this school better?

- How can we make this school more interesting to male students?

- How can your teachers make your classes more interesting?

- What can we do to help you improve your grades?

- What can we do to help male students get along better with each other and with their teachers?

Administrators should also visit classrooms on a regular basis, a recommendation that I've made in other chapters. This will help them see what is actually going on in classrooms and enable them to determine if teachers are treating certain students unfairly, especially in terms of race or gender. Of course, administrators should also take complaints from parents and students seriously. In addition, administrators can offer professional development workshops that describe specific strategies to help teachers increase their efficacy with male students. Finally, as Noguera suggests, administrators should become familiar with the strategies that are used at schools where most African American male students are doing well academically.[21]

Teachers

Once again, I recommend that teachers examine and address their own mental baggage that may impede their progress with any group of students, but in this case, male students—especially African American males. A lot of white *and nonwhite* teachers have issues with black males before they even get to know them on an individual basis. As the black males at American High School said, many teachers believe negative stereotypes, are fearful of black males, and assume that any black male who wears hip-hop clothing is a gang member. When black males realize that their teachers are judging them according to stereotypes and fear, some will act out in class, others will become apathetic, and some may try to prove the teacher wrong. Dealing with teacher behavior that stems from stereotypes can be an added burden to students that detracts from their focus on academic work. Teachers should be honest with themselves and realize that their attitudes and behavior can have a negative effect on students. Until they are willing to face the truth about their beliefs, they won't be as effective as they could be with certain students. In addition to reading professional literature and autobiographies and biographies of black males, I suggest that teachers attend related workshops and presentations.

Parents

There are several ways in which parents can improve the schooling experiences of their sons. Of course, one of the main ways is to rear their children in a stable, loving, and supportive environment in which the children's basic needs are met and in which parents serve as positive role models.

Second, as early as possible, parents should teach their children the importance of getting a good education and doing well in school. This is an especially important message to convey to boys before peer pressure to be "cool" starts to drown out positive messages about doing well in school. This is a strong theme in the work of Kunjufu and other researchers.[22]

Buying books for children, taking them to libraries, listening to them read, reading to them, and modeling reading are important ways to let boys know that reading is not "just for girls." Researchers have found that many boys eventually begin to view reading as something that is not masculine, and this attitude can contribute to their lower reading scores and lack of motivation to read for recreational purposes as they get older. By constantly talking about books with their children and continuing to give boys books and magazines that interest them as they get older send an important message to them about reading. When my son, Stephen, reached high school, I realized that his interest in politics and world affairs had increased. Buying and discussing related books with him was one way that I tried to motivate him to keep reading for recreation.

Another lesson that I learned during my son's high school years may also be helpful to other parents. During his eleventh-grade year, a time when my son was overwhelmed by the amount of work assigned in his four AP classes, I noticed that his habit of being a procrastinator hit an all-time high. Procrastination is sometimes a sign of fear of failure or can be caused by feeling overwhelmed. Stephen had a hard time getting started on homework, was usually unmotivated to do his homework, and often "escaped" by spending too much time playing computer games. Sometimes my pep talks would help him, but usually not for long. Nagging, lecturing, and threatening to take away his computer and television didn't work well either. These strategies seemed to make him feel worse than he already felt. Three strategies that eventually seemed to help were (1) a behavior modification exercise, (2) a timed exercise, and (3) the "blob" exercise.

I'd learned about the behavior modification strategy from one of the many self-help books that I've read over the years. I don't remember which book described it, but the strategy was so simple that I never forgot it. I suggested that Stephen consider wearing a rubber band on his wrist for at least thirty consecutive days. Each time he started doing his homework and got the urge to play a computer game, watch TV, or give in to some other distraction—or couldn't even start his homework in the first place—he was to pop his wrist with the rubber band as a reminder to get started on his work or to keep working when he was tempted to stop too soon. For some reason, he loved this strategy and continued to use it for a while—even though I had to keep him well stocked in rubber bands.

The second strategy, the timed exercise, required him to make a deal with himself. For a specific amount of time—twenty, thirty, forty-five minutes, or an hour—Stephen was supposed to work nonstop without taking any breaks. Then, after the time period ended, he could take a short break to play a computer game, get a snack, and so on before resuming his work for another specific amount of time. This strategy was less effective for him than the rubber band method. The main reason appeared to be that once he took a break, he had a hard time motivating himself to get back to work, especially if he had started playing a computer game.

The "blob" exercise is my favorite and, in my opinion, my most creative suggestion for motivating a procrastinating male adolescent to do his homework. One day, when Stephen was complaining about how hard it was for him to get motivated to do his homework, I told him to think of his problem of procrastination as if it were an ugly, green, misshapen blob sitting on the back of his neck, whispering negative messages to him. "I'm stronger than you," the blob would hiss. "I am P, for procrastination, and I can outsmart you." Because Stephen likes science fiction and is a very competitive person who can't even stand to let his poor ole mother beat him in checkers, Mastermind, Scrabble, or any game, I knew that this strategy would get his attention. To make it even more effective, I told him that he should draw a huge green blob, post it on his bedroom wall, and throw darts at it whenever he got the urge to procrastinate. Although he didn't go so far as to draw his enemy, he did love the idea of visualizing his opponent—procrastination— and outsmarting it by continuing to do his homework when the negative messages started to tempt him.

In addition to trying to think of creative ways to help their sons stay on track academically, parents should also help them develop good conflict resolution skills as alternatives to fighting. Parents should also teach their sons the importance of being respectful to others and that a little respect can go a long way toward avoiding problems and misunderstandings. These strategies may alleviate some of the problems that many male students experience at school. Parents should also become familiar with numerous books that Kunjufu has written specifically about the plight of African American boys. His three-volume set, *Countering the Conspiracy to Destroy Black Boys*, is a good place to start.[23]

Policymakers

Again, policymakers can do their part by focusing on systemic change. In the United States, racial profiling, police harassment, police brutality, and unfair sentencing practices are some of the systemic problems that have a negative effect on many of America's stepchildren—especially black and Latino males. The corruption and racism that are rampant in law enforcement and the so-called justice system must be addressed.

Once again, funding is pertinent to the problems facing males, especially those from low-income communities and inner cities. Too many children grow up in communities where there are few, if any, positive and safe places for them to go after school and on weekends. Funding is necessary for more community-based academic intervention, mentoring, and recreation programs. I have repeatedly heard that many youths, especially males, get into trouble because they have too much idle time on their hands when they're away from school. Adolescent boys who can't find honest jobs in their community, whether because of racism or low availability of work, are often tempted to commit robberies or sell drugs to earn money. This can start the cycle leading to juvenile hall and eventually to prison. In fact, this very scenario happened to one of my own brothers. Unable to find a part-time job in our community, he started selling drugs at around age sixteen. From his teenage years onward, he became trapped in a cycle that eventually led to his demise. In July 2004, at age forty-two, he died in prison.

Mentoring programs may also serve as a deterrent to gang involvement. Many youths join gangs in search of a father figure or a sense of belonging, or for protection from bullying. These are just a few of the ways that policymakers can improve the experiences of males, but the list of systemic changes that need to occur is extensive. As Noguera states: "Poor children generally receive inferior services from schools and agencies that are located in the inner-city and . . . poor children often have so many unmet needs that it is nearly impossible to disentangle one need from another."[24]

A Final Word

Throughout his K–12 schooling, my son, Stephen, has had some good teachers, some mediocre ones, and some bad ones. Two of his best teachers taught elementary school. Mrs. Linthicum, his kindergarten teacher, loved *all* children, including America's stepchildren. Mrs. Suzuki, his second grade teacher, was the same way. Both were white women who had high expectations of *all* students and recognized their students' potential for academic and lifelong success. Unlike many teachers, they looked for the good in their students, instead of concentrating on their weaknesses. Mrs. Linthicum taught Stephen to read and to love reading. During a parent-teacher conference, Mrs. Suzuki told me that she expected my son to become America's first African American president! She told me that my child was brilliant and that she expected greatness from him.

Although he is a procrastinator who usually doesn't work up to his full potential, and thinks that most of his high school classes are extremely boring and irrelevant, Stephen *is* a brilliant child. He has an analytical mind; he is an excellent graphic artist, a great debater, and a gifted musician who plays the trumpet, guitar, and clarinet. In fact, on the Myers-Briggs personality test, Stephen's profile is the same as Einstein's. In spite of this, as he has grown older, I've seen more and more teachers treat my son the way some of the African American males at American High School were treated, and he has become more apathetic about school. Stephen's command of standard English, his extensive academic vocabulary, his directness when speaking, his intelligence, and his habit of questioning the logic behind certain requirements and class assignments—the same qualities that would be *valued* in "gifted" white students—have created problems for him with a few teachers. Two teachers, in particular, accused him of being disrespectful and cocky. In both cases, after further investigation, my husband and I learned that the teachers felt intimidated by our son. Although he didn't fit the profile of their expectations of black male students, a big part of the problem was their own unaddressed, underlying stereotypes and insecurities about black males—in other words, their negative mental baggage.

In each case, my husband and I had to force Stephen to apologize to the teachers, for we knew that because they were in a position of power over him, they could penalize him with bad grades, label him as a discipline problem, and blackball him among their colleagues. Of course, Stephen was quite upset with us. He asked me, "Mom, why did you make me apologize to that teacher? You made me tell a lie. Why did I have to say that I was sorry when the teacher was wrong?" Once again, we had to explain to him that in America, there are different rules for society's stepchildren, especially for black and Latino males, when dealing with authority figures. When authority figures who are insecure feel intimidated by members of these groups, myriad problems can ensue. In the case of run-ins with law enforcement officials, these conflicts can even lead to death.

So until educators, parents, and policymakers all do their part to improve the problems that make it hard for many males, especially male stepchildren, to concentrate on their schooling and do their best work, years from now, Stephen will undoubtedly be forcing his son (if he ever has any children) to apologize to people who have lost his respect, and decades later, his son will have to do the same thing to his son. The cycle will merely continue.

8

"This Place Is Nasty"

How the School's Physical Environment Can Contribute to Student Apathy

More than two decades ago, as a Peace Corps volunteer, I lived in a third world country for nearly two years. During the first year, I ended up residing in a motel while my long-term housing arrangements could be worked out. Because I was on a tight budget, I often ate at cheap restaurants. Unfortunately, on at least two occasions, the price I paid for selecting the wrong restaurant was food poisoning, which resulted in unpleasant consequences.

As Americans, we are used to a certain standard of sanitation in public places. As taxpayers who fund schools, many adults would be quite surprised, if not appalled, to learn about the shocking conditions in countless public schools. A *Washington Post* article, "Amid Disrepair, Students 'Just Can't Think,'" described some of these conditions, including "cancer-causing asbestos" in school walls, faulty electrical wiring, "crumbling paint, broken walls, watery floors covered with patches of growing fungus," dim lighting, and broken drinking fountains.[1]

Admittedly, most of the problems cited in the *Washington Post* article aren't common in the vast majority of U.S. schools. However, one problem that the article mentioned, bad school restrooms, is much more common. According to Tom Keating, the founder of Project CLEAN (Citizens, Learners, and Educators Against Neglect), "Dirty school bathrooms are a national disgrace."[2] This wasn't an understatement, for reporters have uncovered deplorable conditions in school restrooms in Washington, D.C., Wisconsin, California, New York, Pennsylvania, and Louisiana, among other places.[3]

On the mild end of the continuum, students complained about needing toilet seat covers, paper towels, and soap. For instance, an investigation of New York schools indicated that ". . . 90 percent of more than 1,000 schools investigated had inadequate supplies. . . ."[4] However, during an undercover investigation of fifty schools in southern California, CBS2 News found that inadequate bathroom supplies were the least of students' worries. At one high school, "the floor was wet with urine and feces. The stench was unbearable."[5] At a middle school, reporters saw that a urinal was "overflowing onto the floor. We went back a week later and the same urinal was still clogged. . . . In three visits . . . we found just one boys' and one girls' bathroom open for 2,000 students. We never found any soap."[6]

An obvious cause of these problems is that school restrooms have traditionally not been well monitored by adults on campus. Consequently, they have become havens for vandals, who write graffiti on the walls, in the stalls, and on the bathroom doors—if doors even exist. But bathrooms can also become the most dangerous places on campus. In 2000, for example, tragedies that occurred in school restrooms included the suicide of a Texas sixth grader, the stabbing of an adult who interrupted a drug sale in a Utah school restroom, and the shooting of an eleven-year-old by another student who was playing with a gun in a Chicago school restroom. Classes at three separate schools were cancelled after "threatening notes were found in restrooms."[7] In Chapter Six, I mentioned that in 2006, there were reports of students being raped in bathrooms at three different southern California schools. A year earlier, a New York reporter revealed that "At some schools, bathrooms are well-known hot spots, where troublemakers hang out and harass or even rob students."[8]

In addition to bullying, violence, sexual activity, and drug deals, one of the main safety issues involving school restrooms is an increased likelihood of health problems. Because of unsanitary conditions, some students choose to avoid school restrooms completely. This means that for several hours, students aren't taking care of normal biological needs, which can result in bladder problems, among other consequences. According to Rochelle Feldman, a pediatrician, "They hold it and hold it and hold it and what they do is they change the muscle tone in their bladder and they end up getting urinary tract infections. The kids get sick if they don't use the bathrooms and they get sick if they do. We are creating another epidemic of infection."[9] Michael E. Mitchell, another pediatrician, said he ". . . frequently sees children, especially girls, with bladder and kidney infections because they refuse to urinate in dirty school restrooms. Some develop a persistent inability to empty their bladders properly. . . ."[10]

Although some students choose to sneak off campus in search of cleaner restrooms, many who decide to use the school restrooms find them locked. This is a drastic measure that some school officials have taken to deal with vandalism and safety issues. For at least one child, public humiliation was the price she paid for a locked school restroom. The student, who attended a school in New York, ". . . wet her pants because the cafeteria lavatories hadn't been opened. All day, students laughed about her."[11]

Media attention and Tom Keating's Project CLEAN campaign to improve school restrooms have resulted in some improvements. For example, in 2003, California lawmakers passed a bill that ". . . with certain exceptions, requires every public and private school to have restroom facilities that are open as prescribed during school hours, and at all times to keep every restroom maintained and cleaned regularly, fully operational, and stocked with soap and paper supplies." School districts that refuse to comply could lose funding.[12] In 2003, after a student-led protest, school officials in Washington, D.C., promised to spend $33,000 to repair high school restrooms.[13]

Although some districts have made efforts to correct the problems associated with unsafe and unhealthy school restrooms, widespread changes haven't occurred on a national level. This is all the more sad when one thinks of the undue pressure that students are currently under to improve their standardized test scores. As one teacher asked, "How can a school be conducive to learning if we don't make the building climate inviting?"[14] An assistant principal made a similar statement: "how can good learning occur if we have facilities that are horrendous? . . . Philosophically, I think we can raise test scores by improving the bathrooms."[15] According to Tom Keating, "Dirty school restrooms signify much of what's wrong with schools, and catalyzing their cleanup not only paves the road to better achievement . . . but forges the foundation of citzenship."[16]

During my visits to American High School, I didn't specifically ask the teachers and students to share their opinions about the school's physical appearance or quality of sanitation, or about how these issues might be related to student achievement. However, the fact that nearly 30 percent of the teachers said they didn't believe that American High School was one of the best public schools in the district, nearly two-thirds said it wasn't one of the best public schools in the state, and nearly 30 percent said they wouldn't want their own children to attend the school may be a reflection of their views about the school's physical environment and sanitation.

Although I didn't specifically ask students at American High School to comment on the school's physical environment or sanitation, at the end of each focus group discussion, I asked them if they had any additional recommendations that they wanted me to share with the school's administrators. A strong theme that emerged among the groups was that the students had little pride in their school because they felt that it was poorly maintained and unsanitary. In the next section, we hear what they said.

What the Students Said

In complaining about the school's physical appearance and lack of sanitation, the focus groups tended to target the school's overall appearance and the classrooms, cafeteria, and bathrooms. Many students felt that in general, the school looked bad, especially when they compared it to a high school in a more affluent area of the city in which they lived. Many students believed that the school needed more janitors, school buildings needed to be painted, and classrooms needed to be upgraded and better maintained. A white male said, "If you look at this classroom right now, this is not a nice area to sit in for an hour and try to learn a subject." Another white student said, "Some of the classrooms are just gross. [In] my first period classroom, there is piles of dirt on the floor." For one African American student, the drinking fountains were a bigger concern: "We live in the desert and ain't got no water fountains that work, or they shoot out black water, and we don't drink that."

Some students also complained about the cafeteria and the cafeteria food, such as the white female who exclaimed, "They got cruddy shelves and eggs and termites are getting into the shelves. And the food is moldy." Several students said that at one point, the cafeteria had to be closed because of a health issue. According to a Latina, "That was disgusting with the whole cafeteria ringworm problem. The wrestlers weren't cleaning their mats, so they had to close the whole cafeteria because the cafeteria floor had ringworm and the wrestlers got it." Another student added, "It's not fair that they're not paying attention, and the wrestlers weren't cleaning their mats and the whole school gets sick." One girl summarized this situation succinctly: "Our food was heated up in there. It's nasty. It's just nasty."

Given that school restrooms are a great source of dissatisfaction for countless students throughout the nation, it isn't surprising that most of the focus group participants' recommendations about the school's physical appearance and sanitation pertained to the restrooms. As an African American male student explained, "Most people probably don't even want to use the bathrooms here. They need to clean up the bathrooms better." A white female said, "The way that this school looks, personally, I don't want to go to any of the bathrooms." Another white student agreed. Several students also complained about the lack of soap, such as the African American female who said, "You cannot find any soap to wash your hands," or another African American female who said, "Most of us get sick because if you go to the bathroom and there's no soap, and you touch your face, you get sick."

Another common complaint was that some of the school restrooms didn't give students any privacy. For example, a white student said, "Some of the stalls don't even have doors. Both the walls in the stalls open up. The sinks are all crappy too." Another white student asked, "How much is it for a little lock on the door?"

Others complained about the lack of toilet tissue, seat covers, and paper towels. One student remarked that the lack of toilet paper started early in the school day: "You can go [to the restroom] in first period and there's no toilet paper." Another girl asked, "Can this school worry about our personal hygiene? It's very disgusting in the girls' bathroom. What's up with no toilet paper or paper towels?" Another noted, "For sanitary purposes, they should have toilet seat covers in the girls' bathroom."

Students also complained about restrooms being locked when they should have been open. For example, a black male said, "Every boys' bathroom is always locked." A white male said, "There are a couple of bathrooms open, and the rest are shut up." Some students suspected that administrators used clean bathrooms as "window dressing"; an African American male stated, "I heard that they lock the good bathrooms up. So when people come to look at the school, they'll open the good bathrooms, so people can look at those bathrooms. Then they'll lock it up because they don't want it to get dirty again."

Adding to the students' dissatisfaction about the school's physical appearance and poor sanitation was the common belief that American High School was the district's stepchild, and that a high school in a more affluent section of the city was much better. For example, a male focus group participant remarked, "I went over to [the other high school in the district]. The bathrooms are clean. They have doors on the stalls and everything. The floors are clean, and then you walk in our bathrooms. You ain't even got a toilet. Toilets are ripped off of the wall. You ain't got no toilet seat." A white female said simply, "Everybody thinks this is a ghetto school."

Students believed that there were definitive steps that school administrators could take to improve the school's physical appearance and cleanliness. In addition to suggesting that the school hire more janitors, paint the school, fix broken drinking fountains, and enact stiffer consequences for students who disrespect school property, several said that the restrooms in particular should be monitored frequently. According to one focus group participant, "I heard there's people having sex in the bathrooms." Another girl replied, "There are people having sex everywhere." In describing several other problems that occurred in the school restrooms, a third focus group participant explained, "There are females in the bathroom who are tagging [writing graffiti]. There are females who are smoking. There are females who are doing all sorts of things. There needs to be security there, because females don't need to be smoking in the bathroom. Females don't need to be tagging. If you're a female, then act like a female."

Whereas most focus group participants thought that school administrators could do more to improve the school's physical appearance and sanitation, several felt that the situation was hopeless. The only student who defended school officials, an African American male, said, "I think they do a good job of cleaning up the trash. It's just that the students throw it right back. I came here at six o'clock one morning and the school was clean, and at three forty-five, it was messed up." Similarly, a focus group participant added, "If we had new restrooms, then a week later, it would be messed up. So, they just feel like 'What's the use?'" But another student countered, "I'm not talking about trash. Anybody can pick up trash. I'm talking about the buildings." An African American male remarked, "I don't see why if the campus were cleaner, the students would do better in class. I think the teachers have to improve." According to another student, the status quo at American High School would continue until school officials began to take students' concerns more seriously. This African American female said, "We have a Principal's Advisory Committee, but I don't think they really take us seriously. I think that next year, and in the years to come, they should have more student involvement, listen to students more."

Tying It All Together

More than any other chapters of this book, Chapter Six (about school safety) and this chapter on school sanitation clearly show how America's stepchildren are treated, permitted to behave, and are expected to behave by the "haves"—people with power and money. The focus group participants at American High School gave vivid descriptions of the deplorable conditions at their school. These conditions undoubtedly contributed to student apathy and a lack of school pride. As the students stated, horrible conditions were allowed to exist at American High School, the so-called ghetto school, but not at the high school in the more affluent area of the city. No wonder nearly 30 percent of the teachers at American High School said they wouldn't want their own children to attend the school, and the overwhelming majority of students who completed the questionnaire said the same thing.

What We Can Do

Administrators

As I've mentioned repeatedly throughout this book, school administrators must set the appropriate tone for how people should behave at school. This includes expectations about how the school should look and how school property should be treated. The feedback from the students at American High School revealed that when classrooms aren't cleaned properly on a daily basis, restrooms are deplorable, drinking fountains don't work, and the cafeteria is viewed as unsanitary—when a school looks dirty and unkempt—students will have little or no pride in the school.

In my opinion, every school should have adequate funding for beautiful flowers and shrubs to be planted and maintained. Graffiti should be removed quickly. Restrooms should be monitored, inspected, and cleaned throughout the school day. All restrooms should be stocked with liquid hand soap (bar soap can spread germs), toilet seat covers, and paper towels. Restroom stalls should have doors and locks. Toilets should be flushable (preferably the kind that flush automatically), and sinks should have running water (both hot and cold water would be ideal). Dilapidated buildings should be renovated, and classrooms should be cleaned daily.

In addition to setting a schoolwide tone about expectations and ensuring that classrooms, buildings, and grounds are well maintained and attractive, the principal should

- Ensure that custodians are doing their job.
- Implement a rotating schedule for various adults at school to inspect school restrooms throughout the day. (This would also make it easier for adults to identify students who destroy, deface, and find other ways to damage school property.)
- Punish students who damage and disrespect school property.
- Insist that students pick up after themselves at lunchtime and that they use trash cans throughout the campus.
- Constantly convey the message to parents, students, and adults on campus that everyone needs to treat the school respectfully.

Teachers

Teachers can also do their part to make schools cleaner. First, they can make sure that their classroom is clean, appealing, and decorated with student work and multicultural posters, and that desks are arranged in a creative manner. When students arrive, the classroom should be clean, and before they leave, their teacher should require them to pick up after themselves, so that the next group of students will enter a clean classroom. If custodians don't vacuum the classroom, empty trashcans, and clean white boards and chalkboards on a daily basis, the teacher should complain to school administrators. Teachers should also encourage students to take pride in their classroom.

Another way that teachers can improve school sanitation is by empowering students to exercise their civil rights and to put their skills to practical use. One way of doing this is to inform students that if they are dissatisfied about conditions at their school, especially classrooms and restrooms, they can use their writing skills to express their views. Students can start by writing letters to school administrators. If administrators fail to take action, the students can send letters to the school board, health department, local politicians, and state and national policymakers. They can also ask their parents to complain to officials. When I taught high school, I offered my students extra credit for writing letters to local newspapers in order to share their views about topics that concerned them. This is another option for teachers to consider. However, new teachers and those who are still considered to be "probationary" should be cautious in their use of strategies to empower students, and realize that if school administrators view them as troublemakers and radicals merely for trying to do the right thing by students, administrators may retaliate when evaluating them and recommending whether or not to grant them "permanent" teacher status.

Parents

Parents can also do a lot to make schools cleaner. Ideally, they should visit their children's school periodically so that they can be aware of any problem that might negatively affect their children's ability to learn and any conditions that might cause health problems. Like students, parents can express their views loudly and clearly. Making telephone calls and writing letters to school officials, the health department, and policymakers about unacceptable conditions in restrooms are just two strategies that parents can use. Another is contacting the media. Requesting that news reporters and television crews visit the school to see the deplorable conditions for themselves may result in swift action. Parents can also attend school board meetings to voice their complaints publicly. Another useful strategy is to organize other parents to put "the heat" on school officials and policymakers.

A final way that parents can do their part is to teach their children to be respectful of school property. They should teach their children at an early age to pick up after themselves, not to litter, and not to draw, scribble, or write on other people's property or on public property, which includes the school. Regarding personal hygiene, parents should teach their children to flush the toilet after they use it, wash their hands thoroughly, and put their trash in the trash can, and parents should model these behaviors.

Policymakers

Throughout this book, I've repeatedly said that many of the problems that are common in underperforming schools like American High School are related to social problems in the surrounding communities and to systemic problems in the wider society. There is no way that policymakers would allow their own flesh and blood to attend schools in which the awful conditions like those at American High School existed. But when it comes to "ghetto schools" like American High and countless similar schools throughout the nation that America's stepchildren attend, policymakers are willing to ignore or pretend that they aren't aware of the filthy, unhealthy conditions that these students are forced to endure. Once in a while, when media scrutiny and public pressure force them to take action, a little window dressing may go on, but that's about the extent of the reform that occurs.

I believe that on some level, many policymakers believe that poor children and children of color deserve what they get: leftovers, scraps, and substandard schools. If people believe that these groups are inferior, uneducable, lazy, and apathetic, and that they come from dysfunctional homes where parents don't care about their children's education—as many educators and policymakers believe—they won't see a need to make the schools that these students attend a high priority on their agenda. The lack of adequate funding to improve these schools reflects this attitude.

Every student should attend physically appealing schools at which clean, well-equipped, functional classrooms, cafeterias, and restrooms are the norm. After all, these are basic necessities, so why should they be absent in schools located in one of the supposedly greatest, most developed, and prosperous nations in the world? America is not a third world country, yet atrocious conditions have been allowed to exist in schools attended by students who are viewed as second-class citizens. Like their parents, they are viewed as stepchildren who deserve less than middle- and upper-class whites. Until policymakers change their view of students in underperforming schools and high-poverty communities, make a long-term commitment to holistic reform, and provide adequate funding to eradicate the inequities in the schools and surrounding communities, many students will continue to lack pride in their school and be apathetic about schoolwork.

A Final Word

Although the high school that I attended long ago had one of the city's worst reputations and, like American High School, was merely viewed as a "ghetto school" attended mostly by poor blacks and Latinos, a major difference was that we had pride in our school. Many of our school administrators and teachers created such a strong sense of family and community within the school that a lot of us became protective and very proud of our school. Yes, we knew that most whites in the city looked down on our school and that the athletic teams at schools located in middle- and upper-class white neighborhoods were scared to come to our campus. Some of us were even aware that some of the teachers at our school had low expectations of us and didn't expect us to go far in life. But this didn't stop most of us from being proud of our school. Therefore, most of us treated the school respectfully. In fact, as I reflect back on the three years that I attended this high school, I don't recall ever seeing a filthy restroom or any graffiti on the walls. The restrooms were often full of marijuana smoke, but we had running water, paper towels, flushable toilets, and locks on the bathroom stalls. How very sad for the students who attend schools where these necessities are lacking, and what a dismal statement this is about the failure of school reform throughout the decades.

My memories of the appearance of my old high school are very different from my observations of a high school that I visited recently. Like the high school that I attended during my youth, this school also has a negative reputation and is attended mostly by blacks and Latinos. When I first arrived in 2006, I noticed that the buildings looked ancient and were painted a very bland shade of tan. There was brown grass in front of the school, but not one flower or any appealing shrubbery. The inside of the school reminded me of a huge cave. The corridors were dark, and as I walked up a stairwell, I noticed that graffiti was scrawled on a wall near me. The combination of the darkness and graffiti made me feel uneasy. But I also felt indignant as I thought, "If this were Bel Air, that graffiti would've been painted over quickly."

At this point, I can hear some people say, "But the kids in Bel Air don't scrawl graffiti on school walls." Perhaps they don't. Maybe kids in the "hood" wouldn't scrawl graffiti on school walls either if they believed that conventional means of communication worked for them. They probably wouldn't join gangs either if they felt a sense of belonging in mainstream America and if many of the social conditions that are affiliated with gang membership didn't exist in their neighborhoods. The fact of the matter is that the school that I was visiting wasn't in an affluent, predominantly white community. By the way, schools in suburbia may not have graffiti on the walls, but they do have their share of other serious problems, including mental illness among students, suicide attempts, rampant hard-core drug addiction, apathy, widespread cheating, and sometimes even parent intimidation of teachers.[17] If the truth be told, the "haves" aren't really in a position to snub their noses at America's "stepchildren." The "haves" have plenty of skeletons in their own closets and in their schools, but the media tend not to report these problems. Instead, they give the public what they want to hear: more bad news about low-income kids and children of color and how they *still* can't pass the latest standardized test.

Despite the many problems that are prevalent in suburban schools, the students in these schools, their parents (which include many teachers who teach in "ghetto schools"), and policy makers will continue to believe that they are superior to poor children and children of color, and consequently, believe that they and their children deserve more than America's stepchildren. In the next chapter, I'll say more about parents and their involvement in their children's education.

PART THREE

Out in the World

Beyond the Classroom
and the Schoolyard

9

"Yes! They Do Care About My Education"

Parent Involvement in Schools

At the end of one of my Weight Watchers meetings, an African American woman whom I'd never seen before approached me. She had heard that I was an author and wanted advice about how to distribute a book that her husband had self-published. When she realized, however, that my books were mainly for educators, the conversation took a different turn, and she began to describe her little boy's schooling experiences.

Before long, a very familiar story—one that I've heard from many black parents—started to unfold. The woman's son, who attended a predominantly white elementary school in the affluent neighborhood in which he, his parents, and younger sister lived, was one of the few African American students at the school. But he'd already been labeled a "discipline problem," and school officials were trying to pressure his parents into having him medicated for what they claimed was ADD. Because the boy's parents were adamantly opposed to having their son medicated, his teacher and school administrators viewed them as problematic. In the meantime, the child had become disinterested in school. According to his mother, "He loves music and art and he's very creative, but he hates school." As the mother shared some of the options that she and her husband were considering, including homeschooling their son, tears rolled down her cheeks. I felt so sorry for her that I had to hold back my own tears.

Another African American mother who shared her story with me turned to homeschooling as the last resort. After seeing me on

Tony Brown's Journal, this woman had called to invite me to appear on a radio program in New Jersey. During the course of the conversation, she too described her children's schooling experiences. In the end, she said she became so frustrated with the constant disrespect that she experienced from school staff and teachers while trying to be an advocate for her children that she eventually withdrew them from the public school system completely.

These stories are common. One of my neighbors, a white woman, constantly reminds me that many white parents are also frustrated with the school system. She and her daughter, the mother of three little girls, are examples. It seems that from the moment my neighbor's eldest granddaughter—a half-white, half-Mexican child with a Hispanic surname—started school, teachers couldn't find anything good to say about the little girl. They complained about the quality of her work, and they complained about her behavior. Often, out of frustration, my neighbor would ask me for advice. Once, to test the teacher's fairness, the child's mother and grandmother did her homework themselves. When the little girl returned home, her homework was, as usual, marked up in red ink.

Each time my neighbor told me about one of the latest incidents that landed her grandchild in trouble at school, I reached the same conclusion: the child sounded "gifted" to me. However, because she was outspoken and questioned practices that her kindergarten classmates accepted meekly, she was viewed as uncooperative, and soon she was labeled as a discipline problem. The negative labels that were applied to her in kindergarten followed her into first grade and then to second grade. By this time, her teacher was strongly urging the girl's parents to let the school retain her, instead of promoting her to third grade. But a few months before the end of second grade, my neighbor's daughter, son-in-law, and their children moved to a predominantly white, more affluent community in a different school district. All of a sudden, the reports that the parents received about the child changed. The new teacher couldn't stop praising the child's intelligence and complimenting her! Instead of red marks, her school work and homework received gold stars and happy faces.

The child even received a certificate for good work. When my neighbor proudly told me about these developments and the good grades that her granddaughter was earning at her new school, I couldn't help but say, "I told you she was gifted."

If time and space permitted, I could go on and on, recounting similar stories that I've heard from parents and guardians. Through e-mails, telephone calls, and stories that have been shared with me face-to-face, I've heard from many families across the country. From these numerous stories and from my own research, I've concluded that most parents do care about their children's education. The majority of students in my first study gave their parents a "good" or "excellent" rating for their involvement in the students' education, but students were more likely to give their parents a high rating for their involvement in their elementary and middle school education than in their high school education. In the second study, the majority of parents and guardians gave themselves a "good" or "excellent" rating for their involvement in their children's education, and they described specific ways in which they assisted their children academically. Other researchers have reached similar conclusions about parent involvement.

During professional development workshops that I conduct in schools and during conference presentations for educators, I often encounter skepticism when I share this information about parent involvement. For example, at the end of one of my presentations in which I described the sections on parent involvement in my first two books, a disbelieving teacher asked, "But what *kind* of parents were they?" When I told her that the parents and guardians were a diverse group, including some who were on welfare, some who were single parents, some who were college educated, some who were business owners, and some whose children had had very positive experiences with the public school system, the woman—a foreign-born black teacher—clearly remained skeptical. Her facial expression and additional comments gave me the impression that she had a very low opinion of African American students and their parents, and nothing that I said was going to change her mind.

My research was met with skepticism once again when I appeared on a radio talk show. The skeptic was the white host, who'd invited me to appear on her show to discuss black students' test scores. When I mentioned the high level of parent participation that had been revealed in both of my two earlier studies, she said "But your sample size was small." Her point was that I didn't have thousands of black parents or thousands of black students in my studies, so she had trouble believing that they were representative of most black parents and their children. Undoubtedly, this same woman wouldn't have bothered to question any of Jean Piaget's research, even though some of it was conducted on his own children. Yet today Piaget is considered to be one of history's foremost experts on child development. I also doubt that this woman would have been critical or skeptical of the work of Jean Rousseau, a man who wrote the "blueprint for child development," whose work sparked the Romantic Movement, and who is considered to be the "father of developmental psychology," yet he was a hypocrite. In actuality, although Rousseau's work described how children should be educated, he never even raised—let alone educated—his own children. Instead, he abandoned all five of his children to be raised in orphanages![1]

The teacher and the radio talk show host who were skeptical about parent involvement weren't unusual. They were merely reflecting the widespread belief that too many parents, especially African Americans, Latinos, low-income parents, and other second-class citizens, don't care about their children's education, and the belief that if they did care, the problem of student under-achievement would disappear. This parent bashing fundamentally contradicts what I found in my research.

Researchers who have used larger groups than I did in my work reached similar conclusions. For example, in *Parent and Family Involvement in Education: 2002–03*, the U.S. Department of Education described the results of a study involving the parents of thousands of K–12 students throughout the nation, including more than eight thousand black students and more than eight thousand

Latino students. The report showed that, regardless of race or ethnicity, the parents of the overwhelming majority of students were very involved in their children's education, but parents of elementary school children were more likely to be involved than parents of older children.[2]

The majority of parents said they had attended a general school meeting, attended regularly scheduled parent-teacher conferences, and attended a school or class event. Smaller percentages of parents said they served on school committees, acted as volunteers, and participated in school fundraising; white parents were more likely than black, Hispanic, and Asian parents to do so. In each of these situations, the parents of students who lived above the poverty level were more likely than those whose parents lived at or below the poverty level to be involved in these school activities, even though the overwhelming majority of low-income parents reported that they attended a general school meeting and attended regularly scheduled parent-teacher conferences.

The majority of the parents, regardless of race or ethnicity, also reported that they engaged in various activities outside school to assist their children academically. For example, 95 percent of black parents, 92 percent of Asian parents, 90 percent of white parents, and 83 percent of Hispanic parents said they had a place at home that was set aside for homework. The majority of parents in each subgroup also said that an adult in the household checked to confirm that homework was completed, and parents who lived at or below the poverty level were more likely to do so. Most parents of middle school and high school students also said that they discussed time management with their children, and a higher percentage of blacks and Latinos did. When it came to taking their children to visit a library, Asian parents were more likely than any other group to say they did, black parents were second, and whites were the least likely to do so.

Another report that was issued by the U.S. Department of Education, *Efforts by Public K–8 Schools to Involve Parents in Children's Education: Do School and Parent Reports Agree?* shed some light on the reasons why so many educators criticize parents for their perceived lack of involvement and why so many parents report high involvement.[3] There were noticeable discrepancies between what school officials said and what parents said. For example, 84 percent of the parents of the K–8 public school students said they attended Back to School Night, but only 49 percent of school representatives said that most or all parents did. Eighty-one percent of the parents said they attended parent-teacher conferences; however, only 57 percent of school officials said that most parents did. For schools with high minority enrollments, the discrepancies were even greater. The authors suggested that although both school officials and parents may bear some responsibility for the discrepancies, schools should do more to increase parent involvement. According to the authors:

> [A]n important task for schools in the future may be to increase parents' awareness of school programs designed to encourage parent involvement. Schools need to work harder, or perhaps differently, than they claimed to have done to let parents know the importance of being involved in their children's education. In addition, middle schools, large schools, and schools with a high minority enrollment may need to strive especially hard to develop alternative strategies aimed at engaging parents and helping them to become involved. For example, to increase the involvement of parents of children in high-minority schools, schools may need to address cultural differences through multicultural awareness programs and develop other effective strategies to involve parents. . . . To work with parents with limited-English skills, schools need to take an active role in initiating involvement (such as visiting students' homes) and provide various services to make it easier for parents to get involved (e.g., offering translations or interpreter services for parents). . . . Finally, to reduce the barriers to communication between schools and parents, schools can make use of newly developed information

technology, such as voice mail, e-mail, and the World Wide Web, to communicate with parents.[4]

The MetLife Survey of the American Teacher, published in 2005, focused on "transitions and the role of supportive relationships." The researchers collected feedback from over eight hundred public school principals, eight hundred public school teachers, and more than one thousand public middle school and high school students about a variety of topics. One section of the report pertained to parent involvement in schools. The majority of students believed that it is important for parents to be involved in their children's education both at home and at school. Although the majority of high school students said that their parents were involved in their education, most agreed that their parents "really don't know what is going on in my school."[5] This didn't seem to bother the students, because only 15 percent said that they wanted their parents to become more involved. In evaluating the school's efforts to increase parent involvement, most high school students said that their school contacted parents only when there was a problem with the students. The students' perspectives about the school's efforts differed from that of the principals and teachers in the study. Almost all the principals and teachers agreed that at their school, "involving parents in children's education is a priority."[6]

Regardless of their differing perceptions of parent involvement, all groups—parents, school personnel, and students—agree on one point: parent involvement is important. In the research on high-performing, high-minority, high-poverty schools, a recurring message is that school leaders and teachers at these schools find effective ways to include parents and to increase their involvement.[7] Parent involvement has been linked to better grades, higher test scores, better school attendance, higher graduation rates, and several other benefits.[8] Unfortunately, however, barriers between parents and educators can prevent these groups from developing relationships that could benefit students.[9] For example, in the 2005

MetLife survey, 70 percent of the teachers agreed that "Too many parents today treat their children's school and teachers as adversaries."[10] The teachers in this study were also more likely to say that their relationships with parents were unsatisfying in comparison to their relationships with all other groups on campus (other teachers, students, administrators, staff, and the principal). Twenty percent of the teachers said that their relationships with parents were unsatisfying, and teachers who taught in schools that had 50 percent or more low-income students were the least likely to say that their relationships with parents had been very satisfying. At the same time, almost half the teachers admitted that to be effective, teachers must be able to work well with parents. Sadly, both the principals and teachers in the study agreed that the biggest challenge that teachers face is finding effective ways to involve and communicate with parents.

Because parent involvement is such an important factor affecting student achievement, and misunderstandings continue to exist, the next section presents feedback between parents and educators, from students and teachers at American High School about parent involvement.

What the Teachers and Students Said

Several items on the teacher questionnaire pertained to teachers' views of their students' parents and home life. Some of the teachers didn't appear to hold a negative perception of their students' parents and home lives, but others did. Thirty-four percent of the teachers believed that most of their students didn't have parents or guardians who cared about their education, 34 percent believed that most of their students didn't come from decent homes, and 64 percent blamed parents and guardians for students' low achievement. However, most said they wanted to interact more with students' parents.

Contrary to what the teachers believed, the overwhelming majority of the students who completed the student questionnaire said their parents or guardians were very concerned about their education. In response to a different questionnaire item, over 80 percent of the respondents said that their education was "very important" to their parents or guardians, and only 4 percent indicated that their education was "not important" or "not very important" to their parents or guardians.

Even though the overwhelming majority of students in each racial and ethnic group said that their education was very important to their parents, a slightly higher percentage of whites (88 percent) said so in comparison to Latinos (85 percent) and African Americans (84 percent).

Like race and ethnicity, gender didn't seem to matter much. However, Latinas were slightly more likely than Latino males, and white females were slightly more likely than white males, to say their education was very important to their parents.

Tying It All Together

Study after study has shown that most parents care about their children's education. This is also true of parents of adolescents, even though these parents tend to be less involved than the parents of elementary school students. And this is true of black, Latino, and low-income parents—the groups that have historically been viewed as uncaring and uninvolved in their children's education. Despite this overwhelming evidence, many educators, policymakers, and other segments of the larger U.S. society continue to hold negative views of these parents, and the blame game continues.[11] Teachers blame parents for student underachievement, and many parents blame teachers. In other words, as the MetLife survey indicated, teachers often view parents as adversaries. Many parents also view teachers negatively for various reasons.[12] And although teachers, principals, and others often complain about the lack of parent involvement and assume that parents don't care about their children's education, students themselves believe that the opposite is true.

What We Can Do

In the next sections, I offer recommendations to help educators, parents, and policymakers improve educator-parent relations so that both groups can do a better job of working together to improve student achievement and students' schooling experiences.

Administrators

To increase parent involvement and improve relations between parents and educators, administrators must first decide whether or not they truly want real and extensive parent involvement. Administrators often *say* they want more parents to be involved, but they either knowingly or unknowingly send messages that certain parents aren't really wanted on campus. They do this by creating an exclusionary climate and by condoning rude and off-putting behavior toward parents by school personnel. So, first and foremost, administrators must decide if they really want *all* parents—including African American, Latino, and low-income parents—to be visible and highly involved in school activities. This means that administrators must be honest about any negative and deficit-oriented beliefs they have about certain groups of parents. This brings us yet again to the requirement that administrators must deal with their mental baggage.

If administrators decide that they do want *all* parents to be active in the school community, then they must do what is necessary to create a welcoming and inclusive school environment. They can do this by making it clear to all adults on campus that parents should be treated respectfully. On several occasions when I have gone to schools to speak, I've witnessed the rudeness and disrespect that black and Latino parents constantly experience. At one school where I was invited to give a talk to teachers and administrators, when I walked into the front office, the secretaries looked at me, then turned their heads and proceeded to do other things. Not one secretary acknowledged my presence or asked, "May I help you?"

It was obvious to me that even though I was dressed in a business suit and was wearing an identification tag from my university of employment, they assumed that I was "merely a black parent," and their actions suggested that they didn't think that black parents were worthy of their time, attention, or respect. Of course, at the first opportunity, I not only described this incident to the principal but also, during my presentation, told all the staff, teachers, and administrators who were present, "I can see why black parents don't want to come to this school. I don't blame them!" I also know of other cases where black parents were treated rudely by school personnel and even harassed by school security.[13] These poor "customer service" practices at schools can send negative messages to parents, make them feel unwelcome and unwanted, and discourage them from coming to campus.

I also recommend that school administrators create opportunities to listen to parents' concerns and suggestions. Hosting parent forums periodically throughout the school year is one way of doing this. School administrators can also use these forums as opportunities to provide parents with updates about school-related events, information about services that are available to assist their children, and strategies to help parents assist their children academically; they can also disseminate educational newsletters and other information. These parent forums are also an opportunity to solicit suggestions from parents about creative ways to increase parent involvement. Sometimes the traditional PTA and Booster Clubs can be cliquish; school leaders should think of alternative ways to get parents involved. Some parents might even be willing to volunteer their time to start after-school clubs.

In trying to find ways to increase parent involvement, administrators need to remember that sometimes, silence is golden, but at other times, it's not. Too often, administrators avoid, ignore, and are fearful of outspoken and assertive parents, especially if they're black. By treating assertive and outspoken parents respectfully and humanely, administrators can win potential allies. After one of my presentations at an elementary school, I saw this happen as a result of how an African American principal responded to an irate African American parent.

As the principal and I were walking through the school office, we heard a loud voice, and realized that a parent was arguing with a secretary. The principal quickly intervened. In a very calm and professional tone, she told the woman that she was the school principal, and asked what was wrong. The mother was still very upset as she explained to the principal that she was angry because she'd been told that her two children would have to go to different elementary schools. One was already enrolled at the principal's school, but she had been notified that because of a boundary issue, her other child would have to attend another school. Although the mother's voice remained raised for some time, the principal kept responding in a very calm and respectful tone. She kept using the "broken record" routine of repeating over and over, "Ma'am, I understand that you are upset, and if you calm down, I'll be able to help you." Before long, the mother had calmed down, and she and the principal were able to discuss the problem in a civil and mutually respectful manner. If the principal had instead pulled a power play, as many principals would have done when dealing with an angry black parent, the situation could have escalated and ended in disaster. One of the main lessons that school administrators can learn from this story is that when people have been treated as stepchildren and second-class citizens all their lives, they have amassed a lifetime of incidents of maltreatment. For this reason, many walk around "armed" mentally and emotionally for battle and are quick to react defensively. However, when people treat these parents and their children respectfully, they usually find that they receive respect in return. This is something that principals should remember and convey to the other adults on campus.

Finally, school leaders should continue to work on their own professional development to learn additional ways to increase parent involvement; they should also offer related professional development workshops to their staff and teachers. The U.S. Department of Education's *Family Involvement in Children's Education* is a wonderful resource that contains lots of practical information that can be useful to school leaders. Administrators should continue to read the research on high-performing, high-poverty, high-minority schools. Dr. James Comer's School Development Plan is another important resource with which school administrators should become familiar.[14]

Teachers

To improve their relations with parents, teachers must first deal with their own negative beliefs and decide how they really feel about parents—especially the parents of America's stepchildren. Too many teachers waste time judging and criticizing these parents because they don't understand these groups and have negative opinions of them. It is so easy for teachers to judge the home lives of students whom they know little about and don't understand. But I've also come to realize that a lot of the teachers who judge students' parents harshly do so because they are frustrated by their own inability to teach these students effectively. Some of these teachers have very weak teaching skills, are underqualified, and have poor classroom management skills, yet instead of facing their own teaching inadequacies, they find it easier to criticize parents for being uncaring and students for being lazy and unmotivated. To form positive relationships with students' parents, teachers must conduct an honest self-assessment.

Teachers must also work on their communication skills and on becoming more assertive. Like many school administrators, teachers can fear outspoken and assertive parents. Teachers who are fearful of vocal black parents and other outspoken parents need to face their fears and get professional help in this area. Having said this, however, I also caution teachers to be wise in their dealings with parents. During my own junior high and high school teaching years, for example, I learned that in some cases it was a good idea to have an administrator present during parent conferences. When parents have indicated that they believe they can speak to the teacher in a disrespectful manner or behave in other intimidating or offensive ways, the teacher should plan ahead of time to request the presence of an administrator at any conferences with this type of individual. Teachers should also be aware of their rights and contact authorities if any parent threatens them.

One of the best strategies that I used to improve my relations with my students' parents was to find creative ways to send them positive messages. Most parents hear from teachers only when teachers have a complaint about their child's behavior or poor academic progress. When I taught high school, I realized that it's easy for a teacher to concentrate her energy on the students who are behaving badly or working below their potential. In fact, I was spending a considerable portion of my planning period making phone calls to parents to tell them about these problems. One day, it dawned on me that I was ignoring the well-behaved students and their parents by spending so much time communicating with the other parents. From that point on, I vowed that I would devote part of each planning period to telephoning the parents of well-behaved students and students who were earning decent grades. When I made the first few telephone calls, I was amazed at how grateful and surprised the parents were. Most said that no teacher had every contacted them to relay good news about their child. In addition to telephoning the parents of well-behaved and hardworking students, I also asked my husband to make computer-generated greeting cards for me that said "Thanks for raising a well-behaved child," or "Your child is a good student," and so on. Both my students and their parents were thrilled to receive these cards.

Another simple strategy that I used was to learn some Spanish by listening to tapes on my way to and from work. My years of French study in high school and college came in handy when I was a Peace Corps volunteer in Zaire and Cameroon, but in California, French didn't help me at all. Because many of my students' parents didn't speak any English, I thought it would be useful to learn Spanish in order to communicate with them. Although I only learned some very basic sentences while listening to audiotapes in my car, when I greeted Spanish-speaking parents in their native language on Back to School Night or at Open House, they were clearly pleased, and so were my high school students. When they returned to school the following day, they shared positive messages that their parents had asked them to give to me. From what I gathered, my attempts to speak with the parents in their native language sent a message to them that I wanted to communicate with them and that I respected their language enough to try to learn it—even though I know I sounded awful!

Another point that teachers should keep in mind is that they shouldn't assume that parents don't care about their children's education just because the parents aren't visible at school functions. Sometimes parents are assisting their children academically at home in ways that teachers know nothing about.[15] Moreover, sometimes parents are so overwhelmed by life's challenges, trying to make ends meet and to feed, clothe, and house their children, that getting their kids to attend school on a regular basis is the best that some parents feel they can do.[16]

A related point, one of the most important that I will stress in this book, is that educators and policymakers shouldn't punish children for the home lives, communities, and parents from which they come. I didn't choose my parents, and no one else has had that luxury either. This simple truth is one that educators and policymakers seem to forget or ignore. Some educators assume that certain kids have parents who don't care about their education, and use it as an excuse to shortchange students academically and to subject them to other forms of inequality of educational opportunity. This is a sad, destructive, and widespread practice. I hope that the following story will reinforce this point.

A few years ago, I was in a Chinese restaurant ordering take-out food for my family when a loud voice behind me caught my attention. A man was scolding someone loudly enough for the entire restaurant to hear. When I turned around to see what was happening, I was dismayed: the noise was coming from a table in the corner of the restaurant where two women, a man, and an infant sat. The man had propped the infant, who was too young to sit up alone, at the table in a sitting position, and it was the *infant*, not the women, who had incurred his anger. Each time the baby whimpered, he yelled "Be quiet!" or "Cut it out!" After each command, either the man or the younger woman at the table would place a bit of Chinese food in the baby's mouth. As I tried hard to mind my own business and to hide my obvious disgust, two thoughts came to mind: first, I thought that "some people should never become parents, and this man was clearly one of them." Not only was he scolding an innocent baby who couldn't understand his anger or his commands, but he and the woman were feeding her table food at a time when her digestive tract was unable to digest it properly. Second, I thought, "This is the very reason that it's a waste of time for teachers to indulge in the blame game, wasting their time complaining about parents and assuming that parents don't care about their children's education." Some parents are truly unfit to raise children properly, and some may not care about their children's education (although I'm convinced that most do), but most parents have not been trained to teach children in the way that teachers have been trained. They have not earned teaching credentials, and they have not taken child development classes. Therefore, it is an unfortunate but obvious truth that many children will arrive at school with less information and fewer skills than they should have, and suffering from symptoms of poor or inadequate parenting. However, these students shouldn't be punished by teachers for having inadequate, abusive, or otherwise ineffective parents. It's not the kids' fault. Instead of penalizing children for the homes from which they come and wasting time complaining about what parents haven't done, teachers need to do what they are paid to do: to offer every single student—including America's stepchildren—a quality education.

Finally, teachers should also keep in mind that some parents don't feel comfortable being at school. They may have had negative schooling experiences themselves, they may feel unwelcome at the school, or they may be embarrassed for other reasons, as the following story illustrates.

After I gave a presentation at a local university, a biracial (black and Native American) elementary school teacher stayed to talk with me. This woman, who taught English Language Learners at a predominantly Latino school, was excited about her work. She spoke proudly of the wonderful writing projects that her students had done. But she also wanted advice about how to get their parents more involved in the children's education. She had invited parents to visit her classroom and had shared strategies they could use to assist their children. She was disappointed, however, that few had accepted her offer to visit her classroom. "One parent told me that she was too embarrassed to come because she couldn't speak English well," the teacher said. She had also learned that many of her students' parents truly didn't know how to be advocates for their children at school. "Their kids get taken advantage of because the parents don't know what to do," according to the teacher.

As this story suggests, many parents have their reasons for not being visible at school, but this doesn't necessarily mean that they don't care about their children's education. Teachers should keep this in mind when they're wasting time blaming parents and accusing parents of not caring. Indulging in the blame game doesn't change anything; it merely causes teachers to misuse valuable time and energy that they could be spending searching for alternative solutions to increase parent involvement and to improve their own teaching efficacy.

Parents

One of the best ways that parents can improve their relations with teachers is to provide as much support for their children's education as possible. They can ask teachers for specific strategies, attend school events and parent-teacher conferences, visit classrooms, and use various strategies at home, including

- Letting their children know that education is important and a top priority
- Checking over homework
- Talking with their children about how their school day went

- Finding ways to help their children master subjects with which they are struggling, by finding tutors, buying workbooks, and asking the school about intervention programs and other types of assistance for struggling students
- Helping children manage their time well
- Knowing their children's friends and helping them make wise choices in selecting friends
- Taking their children on educational family outings
- Visiting bookstores and libraries with their children
- Quizzing their children before tests
- Proofreading writing assignments
- Limiting and monitoring TV viewing on school days
- Playing educational games (such as Scrabble, Boggle, Trivial Pursuit, Mastermind, and Upwords)
- Finding positive ways to motivate their children, especially boys and middle school and high school students, to keep doing well in school

Part of parents' job is also to ensure that their children lead balanced lives. They should be careful not to place too much pressure on their children, which can cause depression, suicide attempts, cheating, resistance, and other problems. Parents should also exercise caution in not becoming so involved that they end up cheating for their children by actually doing their homework for them.

Policymakers

Policymakers can do their part to improve the relations between parents and educators and to increase parent involvement in at least two ways. First, they can ensure that schools have adequate funding to create programs that have been shown to increase parent involvement. The most effective are programs based on holistic approaches that also address systemic problems and problems in the wider community that prevent parents from becoming highly involved in their children's education.

A second way that policymakers can help is to require mandatory parenting classes, starting in middle school. Most parents don't take formal classes to learn how to be good parents. Many follow the patterns of their own parents—even if those parents were abusive or ineffective. Others decide to go to the opposite extreme from how their parents reared them. The result is that children are often treated like guinea pigs and are reared through trial-and-error methods. If all students were required to take parenting classes, starting in middle school and continuing through high school, I believe this would improve parenting skills and reduce child abuse rates and teenage pregnancy rates. Just as cooking and sewing courses used to be required, parenting classes should become a standard part of the secondary school curriculum. This would improve parent-educator relations in the long run, because more parents would understand how to be good parents and would see the important role that parents play in their children's education.

A Final Word

In April 2004, I met another unforgettable individual. This African American woman had taught ninth grade for two years and third grade for four years before she quit teaching in the public school system entirely. As she shared her experiences, they resonated with me because, in my opinion, her story is so typical of many teachers in urban schools and in schools with predominantly low-income and black and Latino students.

This teacher was highly educated. She had a bachelor's degree in sociology and a master's in social work. During California's teacher shortage that stemmed from a reduction in class sizes, this woman got an Emergency Credential and left her job in the aerospace industry to accept a position to teach history courses to high school freshmen.

The clash between the teacher and her mostly black and Latino students started almost immediately. She had gone into teaching with a set of assumptions that contrasted sharply with the realities she faced. Most of these assumptions were based on her own upbringing and experiences while attending schools in northern Louisiana. "When I was growing up," she said, "we never challenged those teachers. We were black and the teachers were white, so we knew better." When she first started teaching, one of her biggest surprises was that her own students didn't automatically defer to her, obey her, or treat her with the level of respect that she'd assumed would be her right as a teacher.

A second source of disappointment for her was the widespread student apathy in her classes. She had expected the students to do their work and to do it enthusiastically. However, she admitted that her own lack of teacher training contributed to this and other problems that she faced. She stated: "Even though I had the education, I had no training. I had no delivery skills. There was no coaching, no mentoring for me. The students ate me alive. I take ownership because I didn't have the training. Not only did I shortchange them, but I think that when you don't have the skills, they know it. I was afraid and they knew it."

Despite this admission, however, she was still totally disillusioned by the students' lack of interest in her courses. She was also disappointed that their parents weren't involved as much as she thought they should have been. When she became a teacher, she'd expected parents to be visible at school functions, receptive to her concerns, and more active in their children's schooling. What she found was the opposite: "I got no support from the parents," she repeatedly stated during our conversation.

Although these problems contributed greatly to her growing sense of disgust, the lack of support from administrators and the strong pressure from the school principal to pass low-achieving and nonachieving students through the system became the catalysts that prompted her to finally leave the school. She explained,

The administrators would want me to push kids through the system. I'm a real stickler with grades. I would get a lot of flack from parents also. I tried to explain to them that we were not helping students [by giving them grades they didn't earn]. Some of them couldn't read. I flatly refused to do it, and I got my hands slapped so many times because I wouldn't do it. I don't agree with it. I think the straw that broke the camel's back was when I was told by the principal, "This kid has to go on." He was an African American boy. I knew we were doing him a disservice. It should've been a crime. The principal told me, "With or without you, we're going to do it," and they did. He had been absent a lot and never did any assignments. I called the parents, and his mom said she didn't know what to do with him and asked me for advice. I had no clue how to raise any teenager because I wasn't a mom. I was angry. That's when I decided that I couldn't do that anymore.

Even though this teacher felt that she wasn't "cut out" to teach ninth grade, when she left the high school, she decided to give teaching another try. Perhaps another school district in a more affluent and conservative county would be the answer. When she began teaching third grade in this less urban district, she went in with the same mind-set: the students would be eager to learn, the parents would be actively involved in their children's schooling, and she'd receive strong administrative support.

Some of her assumptions proved to be correct. Her third graders were very enthusiastic. They wanted to learn. They were respectful and weren't apathetic. Furthermore, she received administrative support. But the problem was *the parents*. Most couldn't speak English, they rarely attended school functions, and many weren't able to help their children with homework. "When I went to the elementary school," she said, "I still had some of the issues that I had before, but I didn't have the issue of 'Let's push them through the system.' But I did have the issue of no parent involvement."

After four years of teaching at the elementary school, this woman abandoned teaching altogether. Today she works as a vocational counselor for adults who are trying to enter the workforce.

She loves her job and believes that she is making a positive difference. Regarding her years as a teacher, she says, "I would not advise anyone [who doesn't have proper teacher training] to do it."

This teacher's story illustrates that good intentions aren't enough. I believe that even if she had received the proper training in her subject area, her mind-set would have continued to make it difficult for her to become an effective teacher. She couldn't relate to her students or to their parents. More important, she couldn't accept that the world is a different place than it was when she went to school. Today's adolescents, especially many in urban schools, expect their teachers to earn their respect, to make the curriculum culturally relevant, and to present it in interesting ways.[17] This teacher's mind-set made it difficult for her to understand the realities that successful teachers must accept. At her second school site, she had support from administrators and she had enthusiastic students, but she continued to be disillusioned by the perceived lack of parent involvement. In other words, like many teachers, she became preoccupied with an aspect of students' lives that was totally outside her control. Instead of changing her mind-set and focusing on what *she* could do to help students during the five days per week that she had them as a captive audience, she focused her attention elsewhere. Soon, this one source of disappointment began to overshadow all other facets of her job. The lessons in this story are important ones that teachers and administrators should keep in mind as they seek to improve schools.

10

"They Should Worry More About Our Future"

Why America's Stepchildren Need a College Preparatory Curriculum

Francisco Jimenez grew up in a family that was so poor that he often had to miss school to work in the farm fields of central California. In his autobiography, *The Circuit*, he described a nomadic childhood, one in which clean drinking water, decent lodgings, decent shoes, and a warm jacket to wear were luxuries that his family usually couldn't provide for him. Attending school on a regular basis was another luxury for Jimenez.[1]

Like Jimenez, Ben Carson, an African American, also grew up in poverty. Although he didn't have to miss school to work in fields, he experienced many hardships. Periodically, these hardships and the stress of raising two sons alone took their toll on his mother. Sometimes she would go away, leaving the boys in the care of a family friend. Years later, Carson learned that during the periods when she went away, his mother had been checking herself into a mental health facility until she was able to take care of her children and herself.[2]

In spite of their difficult and impoverished childhoods, both Carson and Jimenez became successful adults. Unlike many individuals who grow up in poverty, both were able to drastically improve their socioeconomic status. The main reason was that they earned college degrees. Jimenez later became a university professor, and Carson became a surgeon who earned international fame for his skill at separating conjoined twins. Their stories illustrate what the U.S. Census Bureau has repeatedly shown: in general, regardless of race, ethnicity, or gender, income is positively correlated to educational attainment. In other words, individuals who earn college degrees typically have higher incomes than those who receive less education.[3]

Because African Americans and Latinos are overrepresented among the individuals who live below the poverty level,[4] for them earning a college degree can take on a new meaning and even a sense of urgency. It can become their ticket out of poverty. Contrary to popular opinion about America's stepchildren, countless students from low-income backgrounds and many African American and Latino youths dream of attending college. For example, in *Getting Ready to Pay for College*, the U.S. Department of Education reported that in its study, most of the middle school and high school students and their parents from all racial and ethnic groups believed that the students would attend college.[5]

Although many students want to attend college in order to attain a professional goal or to improve their economic status, various factors often prevent them from fulfilling this dream. One obvious barrier is caused by financial problems. Some students simply can't afford to attend college after they leave high school. Another problem can stem from cultural expectations. For example, I've met several women who said that as a result of strict cultural expectations for females, they were expected to get married and start a family after they graduated from high school. Two of the women who went against this norm were actually disowned by their fathers. One who went all the way through graduate school wept when she described the emotional price she'd paid for going to college against her father's wishes.

Another deterrent to college attendance is the belief prevalent in many low-income and urban communities that attending college or having a college degree won't necessarily lead to employment. For example, one of my former African American graduate students told our class that she had enrolled in a doctoral program because she wasn't able to find a job in her field after earning a bachelor's degree. An African American mother whom I interviewed for a previous book project said that although she hoped her two children would eventually decide to go to college, she was somewhat ambivalent about the importance of college because she knew people who had college degrees but were unemployed. In communities where unemployment rates are high, many people believe this, and when kids grow up in these communities, they may think attending college is a waste of time.

Another deterrent to college attendance is pressure from parents in low-income families for their children to start working full-time as soon as possible. When I was a high school teacher, two of my favorite students, a girl and a boy, faced this problem. Both were Latinos who came from first- or second-generation immigrant families. Both were hardworking tenth graders who earned good grades, yet at different times, each came to me to say he or she was being pressured to drop out of school. In the case of the girl, one day she arrived at school and told me that she'd run away from home after her parents had told her that she should drop out of school and start working full-time. Although she was already working part-time in a local garment district, if she worked full-time she'd be able to help the family even more. Because her parents hadn't been able to attend school for as long as she had, they felt that she'd received more than enough education. The daughter, however, disagreed. Her desire to stay in school and eventually attend college was so great that she'd left home. After a lot of drama, a member of the extended family allowed her to move in and promised her that she'd at least be allowed to finish high school.

In the second case, the highest-ranked student in one of my tenth-grade classes came to school one day and told me that he was dropping out. Before he even began to explain the reasons, the look on his face told me that he was in extreme emotional pain. We'd often discussed college, and I knew that he had every intention of going. Like Francisco Jiménez, Ben Carson, myself, and countless others, he was going to escape poverty through a college education. So when he came to tell me that it would be his last day in school, for a moment I was speechless. I'd been certain that of all of my students, he would become a success story. Never in my wildest dreams did I think that he'd not only fail to go to college but also drop out of high school in tenth grade. Then he told me why, and everything became clear: even though he was already working full-time after school and until late at night, he would now have to get a part-time job in addition to the full-time one he already had. The only other wage earner in the household, his uncle, had just died. Now this tenth grader would be solely responsible for the financial welfare of the entire household, and on top of this, he needed extra money to pay for his uncle's funeral.

My heart went out to him. There was no way that I could change his family's dilemma or remove the heavy burden that had been placed on this boy's shoulders. The one thing I could try to do was to keep him from dropping out of school. So I asked him to please give me an opportunity to speak with his counselor before he left school that day. Thankfully, he had a wonderful counselor who found a way to keep him in school. Upon hearing his story, she decided that the only option was to transfer him to the local continuation school, which had a shorter school day than the regular high schools in the district. That way, the boy would get out of school early enough each day to still have time for more work hours. Unfortunately for me, after this student transferred to the continuation school, I never heard from him again. But I've never forgotten him, and I've often wondered whether he was eventually forced by poverty to drop out of school before graduation or if he eventually made it to college.

In addition to nonschool factors, the school system itself can also become a deterrent to college attendance for America's stepchildren. One of the most obvious ways is through low teacher expectations that result in students' having weak academic skills. Many students from low-income backgrounds, especially African American, Latino, and Southeast Asian American students, are passed through the K–12 system even if they can't read well, lack basic math skills, and have weak writing skills.

In her autobiography *Life Is Not a Fairy Tale*, Fantasia Barrino, an *American Idol* winner, described how she made it all the way to ninth grade without being able to read well. In ninth grade, she finally dropped out of school completely. Later, as a teen mother, she was embarrassed that she couldn't even read children's books to her daughter, let alone fill out a job application.[6] A similar example pertains to an African American high school senior whom I interviewed several years ago. This student didn't learn how to read until she was in high school. Because she was dyslexic, most of her teachers didn't know how to help her. Eventually, one teacher taught her how to decode words, and unlike Fantasia, this student ended up going to college. Good reading skills are crucial to students' academic success not only during their K–12 schooling but also in college; students who enter college with weak reading skills are less likely to graduate and earn degrees.[7]

Through the questionnaire data and during the focus group discussions, the students at American High School were able to voice their opinions about many issues pertaining to college, including whether or not they felt that their teachers and counselors had adequately prepared them for college and whether or not they felt that pursuing a college education was worthwhile.

What the Students Said

The teachers at American High School shared their views related to their students and college through their survey responses. Half the teachers stated that they believed that most of their students would go to college, but nearly 40 percent didn't believe that all students deserve a college preparatory curriculum, and more than one-fifth believed that most of their students didn't have the aptitude or skills to succeed at college.

Although only half the teachers believed that their students would attend college, the majority of students who completed the student questionnaire said they planned to attend some type of postsecondary institution after high school. In fact, 86 percent of blacks, 78 percent of whites, and 64 percent of the Latino questionnaire respondents said this.

Racial and gender differences surfaced among the student responses. White females were more likely than any other group to say they planned to attend college after graduation, and Latino males were least likely. Whereas there was little difference between the percentages of black males and black females who planned to attend college, the differences between the percentages of Latino males and Latinas and between white males and white females were greater. There are numerous possible explanations for these racial and gender disparities. As I mentioned in Chapter Seven, for example, a high percentage of the black males in the study were athletes. It is therefore possible that some planned to attend college in order to pursue their dreams of becoming an NFL or NBA professional. Also, in many instances, males in general tended to be doing worse academically in comparison to their female counterparts.

Another explanation might pertain to the students' academic track. Those who were in AP and college preparatory courses should have been more likely to have college in mind than those in lower-ranked academic tracks. A higher percentage of black students who participated in the study were enrolled in honors and college preparatory courses than white participants and Latinos. Some focus group participants believed that students in higher-ranked tracks received more information about college, and several complained that AP and honors students received more information and better services from counselors. For example, one student said:

> The counselors are more worried about helping those in honors and AP classes. I was in nonhonors classes my freshman year because of a mistake. I got into my honors classes during my tenth and eleventh grade year and it's a big difference how they teach, and how the counselors come in and actually tell you things. I've known since my sophomore year that we were supposed to have an art [class]. So that means that the

counselors only pay special attention to certain groups or certain classes. The graduation requirements are different from the college requirements. They make it like, "Okay, you graduate, but you don't have to go to college." They make sure you graduate so that they can say that everybody graduated, but they don't care if you go to college to further your education.

Another possible explanation also pertains to the quality of counseling that students received. During the focus group discussions, several counseling-related reasons surfaced to explain some of the factors that affected students' post–high school plans. For example, many focus group participants complained that counselors at American High School were failing to provide them with adequate advice, especially about prerequisites for college. According to one student, "If you ask, then they give you the wrong information." Another student explained, "I asked the counselor about foreign language, and I'm still confused because some are saying that we need three years of foreign language to get into a four-year college. Then I asked again, and they said we need two years." A third focus group participant said, "Counselors aren't up-to-date on what we need. One minute they're telling us one thing, but actually we get more information from our math teachers. They don't even tell us what classes to take in order to get into a good college. It's our math teachers that tell us that next year, they're going to be requiring four years of foreign language. The counselors, they don't even know. They're miseducated about everything. They're like, 'Uh, uh, maybe you should take that.'"

An African American student said, "I think we need more black counselors that are going to help us. It's not like they're taking their time to help us. They will help us if we ask, but it's not like they're really concerned. It's like 'whatever' for them." However, another African American student disagreed: "I don't think it even has to do with the counselor's color. If you ain't a good counselor, you just are not a good counselor."

A more common belief among students was that there was a schoolwide climate in which less important issues overshadowed more important ones, such as adequately informing students about college requirements. As one focus group participant put it:

> This school worries about what we have on, more than
> our grades or whether or not we're going to college. I went
> to our counselors, and I asked them what requirements we
> have for college. I just found out this year, my senior year, that
> you have to have a visual and performing arts [class] to go to a
> four-year college in California. Nobody told me that. I've had
> counselors come in my classrooms from the ninth grade up
> until now, and none of them have said until this year that you
> have to have visual and performing art. So now I don't have all
> of the requirements to go to a four-year university, and I passed
> my English class with a D, but a D doesn't make me eligible to
> get into college. So what am I supposed to do? I can't take it
> over because I passed the class. Instead of worrying about what
> we're wearing, they should worry more about our future,
> college, trying to get us to college. I know a lot of kids that
> go to this high school do not go on to college. If they do,
> they go to the local community college. They should worry
> more about our education than what we're wearing to school.

Another explanation that surfaced pertained to economic factors. Several focus group participants believed that by going directly into the military after they graduated from high school, they would be able to earn money and get a fully funded college education at the same time. For example, a Latina student said she felt that there were "better opportunities" in the army, "because I will be going to school and having a job at the same time." Another Latina said that by going into the military, she would be following in her grandfather's footsteps, be able to travel, and get a college education at the same time, while receiving medical benefits. "I know it's a better opportunity," she explained, "because they pay for your college. When you work for them, they give you medical, dental, and vision [coverage] for free. It's just a good thing."

There were also differences among students who planned to go directly to a four-year institution rather than a two-year college. Black students were a lot more likely than whites and Latinos to say they planned to attend a four-year institution immediately after high school. Latino students were more likely than whites and blacks to say they planned to go directly to a two-year college. Once again, many focus group participants pointed the finger at school counselors to explain why some students were more likely to plan to go directly to a two-year versus a four-year institution. According to one focus group participant, "My counselor said that going to a community college for the first two years is the same thing as going to a university, except it's cheaper." A white male focus group participant said he'd heard that "Community college is cheaper. You get the same core classes that you would get at a four-year. You will get them done in the same way, and you get the same amount [of education] at a community college." But some students said they wanted to attend a two-year rather than a four-year institution because it was all they needed for a certain profession. For example, a white male focus group participant said that he planned to become a firefighter, so all he needed were two years of community college.

Tying It All Together

Even though many of their teachers didn't believe that most of them would go to college, that they deserved a college preparatory curriculum, or that they were smart enough to succeed in college, most of the students in my study at American High School planned to attend college after graduation. This discrepancy between the teachers' low expectations and the students' high ones for themselves is common at underperforming schools nationwide. The fact is, like many teachers at American High School, a lot of adults in the United States believe that America's stepchildren don't deserve a college preparatory curriculum and can't do well in college. To these teachers and other like-minded adults, I say, don't play God with other people's children, for you are not the master of their fates.

I believe that *every* student deserves a college preparatory education and the *right to decide* whether or not he or she will attend college. In other words, teachers should equip *all* their students with the tools to succeed in college, and if a student *decides* not to attend college, that's his or her choice. I'm aware that there are people who disagree with me and argue that it's better to sort kids into vocational and college preparatory tracks early in their schooling in order to prepare non-college-bound students for a trade or vocation that will allow them to find employment after high school. But as a black mother of three children (including two daughters who are currently in college, one as an undergraduate, the other as a doctoral student who is married to another African American doctoral student at a prestigious university), children who have always known that their parents expected them to attend college, and as a former child from a low-income family and a challenging neighborhood, I'm a strong advocate for the "college preparatory curriculum for all" model. Of course, for this approach to be effective, all the problems that I've mentioned throughout this book that prevent America's stepchildren from getting a quality K–12 education must be eradicated. In the recommendations section of this chapter, I offer specific suggestions to adults. But first, I want to share several stories that explain why I'm so adamant about the importance of a college preparatory curriculum for *all* students—including America's stepchildren. The first story is about my own experiences.

In January 1984, I hit rock bottom. I was the single parent of a six-month-old baby and was working only part-time. I had no medical benefits and no car, and was living with a couple who had marital problems. When it seemed that things couldn't get any worse for me, two cataclysmic events occurred. The first was that I became very ill with pneumonia.

When I dragged my feverish body to a clinic for the poor, I was told that I needed to find someone to take care of my baby to prevent her from getting sick. The problem was that I had no relatives or friends in the city to which I had relocated. I also couldn't afford to miss any days from work, because as a substitute teacher, I had no job benefits nor any guarantees that I'd be working from one day to the next. So no matter how sick I was—horrible cough, fever, and exhaustion notwithstanding—I had to force myself to get out of bed each day, dress and feed my baby, get her to the sitter's, and then drag myself to work.

The second event was worse than the first. One day, while I was still recovering from pneumonia, I received a call from a relative who informed me that a small child in our family had been sexually abused. This news not only increased my depression but also made me feel hopeless about life in a world in which people do horrible things to children. Soon my depression got so bad that I was seriously contemplating suicide. Each night as I lay in bed, I thought how much easier it would be if I were just to end it all. For me—a coward when it comes to physical pain—an overdose of some type of prescription drug seemed to be the easiest way to die. But each time I thought about killing myself, I remembered my baby. I had brought her into this world, and it would be selfish for me to take my life and leave her behind. Taking my baby's life never entered my mind, but taking my own was a constant temptation. However, imagining all the things that might happen to my child if I left her behind to be reared by extended family members convinced me not to kill myself. No matter how bad things were, I had to live for my child and try to give her a good life.

Instead of opting for suicide, I eventually resorted to a coping strategy that had sustained me throughout childhood, adolescence, and young adulthood: prayer. One night, I got on my knees and prayed for wisdom and for help. When I got up and climbed into bed next to my baby, I had a glimmer of hope for the first time since I'd learned of the sexual abuse of the little family member, and my life did begin to improve. In fact, within a few months, I had my own apartment in a low-income complex, and the following September, I was offered a full-time teaching job.

In February 2006, I was reminded of those difficult days long ago, after I gave a talk at a church where I had been invited to be a speaker for Black History Month. A member of the audience approached me. This soft-spoken Latina told me that she had been inspired by my presentation, "You Are a Fearfully and Wonderfully Made *Survivor* with a Purpose." But I soon learned that what she really needed was encouragement. It turned out that at age thirty-two, she wanted to go to college. Her life had been filled with turmoil, but her dream of attending college had never died. Growing up with two drug-addicted parents who eventually began to use heroin couldn't kill her dream. Having to leave home at age fourteen to face the world on her own after home became unbearable couldn't kill her dream. Being assaulted in front of her high school by her boyfriend one day, while bystanders refused to intervene, could not kill that dream. Becoming a mother at age seventeen couldn't kill that dream. Learning at age thirty, during a heated argument, that the woman who'd "raised" her until age fourteen was not her biological mother couldn't destroy that dream. And that woman's death two years later hadn't destroyed that dream.

As we stood on the sidewalk outside the church talking, I learned that the woman who had "raised" her had been dead for only one month, and the thirty-two-year-old was still grieving. But as she spoke about her childhood and the fact that most of her teachers had never realized what her home life was like or had never "gone the extra mile" to make a positive impact on her, her desire to attend college kept coming up in the conversation. She spoke of a police officer who once told her that she'd end up becoming a "slut and a drug addict" even though she was only a child at the time. She also spoke of her determination during childhood never to use illegal drugs. "I never wanted to be like my parents," she told me. As she continued to weave the tapestry of her life with words, I kept inferring that what she really needed was encouragement and "permission"; for some reason, she needed to hear me say that it wasn't too late to pursue her dream. "But am I too old to go back to college?" she asked. "I went to community college for one semester, and I loved it." Throughout the conversation, I kept reassuring her and sharing bits and pieces of my own life story, and in the end, I felt that she was mentally ready to return to college.

For several days after I met her, this woman's story stayed on my mind. In many ways our stories were similar. We had both come from low-income, minority backgrounds and dysfunctional families. Although I was an adult when I had my first child, we both had been single parents. Since childhood, both of us had dreamed of going to college one day. In spite of these similarities, there was one huge difference between us: I had gone straight to college after high school, because when I was in sixth grade, Mrs. Tessem, the teacher who changed my life, told me I'd better go to college, as if I had no choice. Prior to that time, no one at school had viewed me as anything more than a discipline problem and an academic failure. Because I had gone to college and earned a bachelor's degree by the time I became a single parent, when I fell on hard times, I had some options that the Latina didn't have. A college degree meant that the odds were against my remaining in poverty indefinitely.

Less than one week after I met this soft-spoken woman, I met two other women who shared their stories with me. Each woman remained behind to speak with me after I conducted reading workshops for new teachers in the Los Angeles Unified School District. Both were Latinas, one middle-aged and the other apparently in her twenties. The middle-aged woman surprised me by saying that although she was a brand-new teacher, she had never earned a high school diploma! In fact, she had dropped out of high school during her senior year. At that time, her home life was difficult, and she had little direction in her life. Then, during her senior year, after being insulted by a math teacher, she decided that she'd had enough of school. Even though she had thought about going to college, few, if any, educators saw any potential in her. However, several years later, she learned about a program that was designed to help minority students go to college. Through this program, she was admitted to a community college. Later she earned a bachelor's degree. On the day that I met her, she said that she was seriously considering going on to graduate school.

The younger new teacher whom I met that day also told me a heartwarming story. Unlike the middle-aged Latina, she had been an outstanding student throughout her K–12 schooling. She worked hard, earned good grades, and was well behaved. Although her mother was proud of her efforts, one day she gave her daughter sad news: "I can't afford to send you to college," she told her. In one sentence, the child's hopes were dashed. "No one ever told me that I could apply for financial aid," the woman told me, "and my mother didn't know about it." To compound matters, during her high school years, her school counselor spoke to her only once. "He called me in one day," she said, "and began to yell at me. He said, 'Maria, you need to pull up your grades and get your act together.' I said, 'Who's Maria?'" It turned out that her counselor had mistaken her for another student, a Latina who was an underachiever and a discipline problem!

Like the middle-aged Latina, this young woman eventually attended college, earned a degree, and became a teacher. Because of her own experiences and the fact that she almost didn't make it to college, she made a commitment to start developing a college-going mind-set in her students as early in the school year as possible. In addition to constantly talking to them about the benefits of attending college, she also created "mock graduations." She'd have each student stand in front of the class and pretend that he or she was earning a bachelor's degree, as their classmates cheered. Then the student had to pretend that he or she was earning a master's degree. Finally, each student had to envision himself or herself earning a doctorate. "I want them to see themselves with a Ph.D.," this teacher said. Surprisingly, her students were only in the fifth grade, at an age when most teachers wouldn't have thought about instilling a college-going mind-set in them.

Both of these stories were inspirational to me, and the second one reminded me of a story that my husband told me about his own schooling experiences. Throughout his entire K–12 schooling, not one counselor spoke to him about attending college, even though he earned decent grades and was a well-known student athlete. The only time his counselor ever called him to the office was to scold him. Once again, it was a case of mistaken identity. In my husband's case, however, there was an African American educator, Mr. Redd, at his high school. Mr. Redd was well aware of the institutional racism and tracking in the school district that prevented many promising young African American students from attending college. Therefore, like the fifth-grade Latina teacher, Mr. Redd made a commitment each year to develop a college-going mind-set in the African American students—even those who weren't his own pupils. Because of Mr. Redd's advice, my husband decided to attend college, and Mr. Redd taught him how to apply.

Unfortunately, the feedback from the students at American High School indicates that the stories I just described are common: many students—especially America's stepchildren—dream of attending college, but often factors in and outside school can keep them from attaining these dreams. A recurring message from the students at American High School was that they didn't receive enough support from their counselors. Students complained of being given the wrong information about courses they needed to take in order to be eligible for college, of not being given enough information, and of being dissuaded from attending four-year institutions even though it is a well-known fact that in California, students of color who attend two-year institutions have very low transfer rates to four-year institutions.

Tying It All Together

In the next sections, I offer suggestions to administrators, counselors, teachers, parents, and policymakers.

Administrators

School administrators can create a college-going mind-set in students through numerous activities. The research on high-achieving, high-poverty, high-minority schools indicates that in these exemplary schools, administrators create a climate of high expectations for students, teachers, staff, and parents.[8] When high expectations permeate the entire school, the educational disparities created by the common tracking system that sorts students into "college-bound" versus "non-college-bound" categories can be reduced, if not alleviated altogether. Traditionally, college-bound students have received the best teachers and the best preparation for a professional career during adulthood, whereas non-college-bound students, especially low-income students and students of color in urban schools, have often been subjected to low expectations, grade inflation, and a substandard curriculum.[9] The report *Gaining Traction, Gaining Ground* revealed that some schools that improved student achievement reversed the long-standing practice of giving the best students to the most experienced teachers. In these schools, the best teachers worked with the lowest-performing students.[10] This makes sense. After all, why should the neediest kids be stuck with the worst teachers year after year?

In addition to promoting high expectations and expecting excellence from the entire school community, administrators can form partnerships with local colleges and universities, sponsor college fairs, and fund field trips to local colleges for students. Inviting college students to serve as tutors and to give presentations about college life and tips on how to survive at college are other simple strategies that administrators can use. Administrators can also offer workshops in which parents are given information about college funding, the college admission process, and how they can help their children prepare academically for college. Offering SAT and ACT preparation workshops for students and providing adequate funding for teachers to purchase SAT and ACT workbooks for their students can also be helpful. As I emphasize in the next section, administrators should also hold school counselors accountable for providing *all* students with correct and extensive information about college requirements, deadlines, financial aid, and the process of applying to college.

Counselors

School counselors play an important role in whether or not students go on to college. Counselors receive information about financial aid, scholarships, application deadlines, and college fairs. One way that counselors can help is to ensure that *all* students receive this information in a timely manner. Counselors should also visit classrooms to inform students about deadlines and fee waivers and to give students checklists of what they need to do in order to apply for college. Counselors should also make sure that students are receiving correct advisement about which high school courses are required for college. In spite of the fact that many counselors are overwhelmed by scheduling duties and discipline problems, every high school counselor should make a commitment to devote a portion of his or her day to counseling students about college, and this should include students who may not appear to be "standard college material." In other words, counselors should make a strong effort to encourage underachievers and students in non-college-preparatory classes to consider attending college. Sometimes just hearing that someone believes that you have the potential to excel in an area in which you've never received encouragement can make all the difference in the world. As the stories in this chapter illustrate, I've met too many adults who told me that although they dreamed of going to college when they were younger, no one ever discussed college with them when they were in K–12 schools.

Teachers

Like school principals and counselors, teachers can play an important role in motivating students to go to college. Teachers can talk about the benefits of a college education by showing actual statistics from the U.S. Census Bureau which explain that the average person with a college degree earns more than someone who doesn't have one. This is something that I did when I taught high school, and my students were quite surprised to see the actual dollar differences.

Teachers can also tell students why they themselves decided to go on to college and share stories about their college experiences with students. When I was working on my doctorate, for example, I would bring my textbooks into my high school classroom and tell students about the books and about the courses I was taking, as well as why I was pursuing a Ph.D. Several of my female students said that after hearing me speak about my quest for the doctorate, they had decided that they wanted to earn one as well. Most of these girls would be first-generation college students, yet they were motivated to go beyond the bachelor's and master's degree, just because someone took the time to explain to them how earning a Ph.D. might be beneficial to them.

Teachers can also devote a considerable amount of their instructional time to teaching students how to write different types of essays. Because college applicants are required to write a personal essay, giving students plenty of opportunities to practice writing personal essays is a great way to help them prepare. Focusing on SAT and ACT preparation is another very important way that teachers can help students prepare for college. In many affluent school districts, students receive lots of help from their teachers that is designed to prepare them for the SAT. For my own students at the predominantly Latino urban-fringe high school at which I taught for eleven years, I purchased several SAT workbooks and encouraged students to borrow them and do all the practice tests in the booklets. I also offered extra credit to students who purchased their own SAT workbook or who checked one out of the public library, and I assigned vocabulary exercises from the SAT workbooks.

Parents

As I mentioned earlier, when I was collecting data for one of my previous book projects, I conducted interviews with African American parents. Although most of the interviews were interesting, among the most memorable was the interview I conducted with a retired pediatric nurse. This woman had adopted a drug-addicted baby who was in fourth grade at the time of the interview. Throughout the interview, the woman spoke of the challenges she had faced as this boy's parent, but she also spoke about her dreams for him. She wanted his future to be bright, and she wanted him to rise above the circumstances of his birth. For her, his attending college was the solution. So even though the child was only in elementary school, she had already started saving money for his college education, and during summers she would take him to visit Historically Black Colleges. What she was doing was developing a college-going mind-set in this child.

As I mentioned in the introduction of this chapter, most parents want their children to go to college, even if they didn't go themselves. However, many parents— especially those who didn't go themselves—may not know how to go about developing a college-going mind-set in their children. Ideally, as the case of the retired pediatric nurse indicates, parents should start when children are very young by talking with them about college and conveying the message that the parents expect them to attend college. Some parents make it clear to their children that just as attending elementary school, middle school, and high school are not options, attending college isn't either; it's mandatory.

Parents can take their children to visit colleges and help them identify the colleges to which they should apply. Parents can also help their children figure out what areas they should major in, depending on the child's strengths and interests. Several magazines are published annually that focus on the "best" colleges and universities, and they contain information that can make it easier for parents to assist their children in selecting a college.

Parents can also help their children explore financial aid options. Many websites and booklets devote considerable space to this topic. Speaking of booklets, parents can also help their children prepare for college by buying them SAT and ACT workbooks or checking them out of the library. Encouraging their children to read the workbooks and complete the accompanying practice tests is a very useful strategy that I used with my former high school students and with my own children.

Parents should also become familiar with Internet resources. For example, the College Board website (collegeboard.com) provides useful information about writing essays and planning for college. The "Planning for College" section includes tips to help students develop an action plan, become familiar with options they should consider, develop good study habits, and deal with math anxiety, along with other college survival tips.

Although there are a lot of great ways for parents to motivate their children to go on to college, I do want to caution parents about putting too much pressure on their children. Several related stories come to mind. One involves an acquaintance who attended the same high school that I had attended. This gifted artist had a nervous breakdown after being pressured by her mother to over-achieve. Another story that comes to mind pertains to a "gifted" child in the Midwest who started attending college at a much earlier age than most students. Although he excelled academically at most subjects, he eventually committed suicide. I read about this child prodigy case right around the time that I learned of the suicides of two students who lived in dorms at the university that one of my own children attends. I kept wondering if too much outside pressure to be perfect or to overachieve had played a role in their deaths. So although it's important for parents to want the best for their children and to do all they can to help their children be prepared for college, there must also be balance and common sense.

Policymakers

Once again, policymakers can help more of America's stepchildren get to college by doing their part to improve the K–12 schools these students attend and the neighborhoods in which they live. Adequate funding must be available to eliminate systemic problems, institutional racism, and all the factors that create inequality of educational opportunity. There must also be enough funding for

- Scholarships and grants to assist low-income college-bound students
- Low-income K–12 schools to sponsor field trips to colleges
- Low-income K–12 schools to pay for guest speakers
- Low-income high schools to offer SAT and ACT workshops and to buy class sets of SAT and ACT workbooks
- Low-income high schools to offer enough AP courses

- Low-income high schools to offer fee waivers for college applications and AP exams
- Low-income middle schools and high schools to have an adequate number of *well-trained* counselors

---

A Final Word

At the end of a presentation I gave for teachers who were attending a local university, a Latino high school teacher raised his hand and asked, "How do I motivate my students to go to college when they don't even care and they accuse me of acting white?" He went on to add that his students lived in a very poor community and seemed to be apathetic about everything he tried to do. As I responded to his question, one of the main points that I emphasized was the importance of understanding why his students appeared to be apathetic, resistant, and unconcerned about attending college. "If you look at the adults in your family and most are unemployed or earning low wages," I replied, "it might be hard to feel hopeful about the benefits of school. Some of their family members also went through the entire K–12 school system, and it doesn't appear to have helped them financially."

My goal was to explain to him that the cycle of poverty and high unemployment rates in their community may make it difficult for students to truly believe that education will benefit them. This is where storytelling, statistics, guest speakers, and a relevant and empowering curriculum can make a difference. I told the teacher, "Many of your students have been brainwashed through low expectations, an irrelevant curriculum, and societal factors that include widespread poverty in their community. Now you have to *reprogram* them by constantly repeating the message that a good education can really make a difference."

I remain convinced that in spite of the widespread racism and second-class treatment that many of America's stepchildren will be subjected to throughout their lives, a college education is one option that can help them improve the quality of their lives.

11

The Truth Can Set Us Free!

Seven Lessons I've Learned About School Reform in America

In early March 2006, as I was driving to work listening to Dr. Laura Schlessinger's radio program, one particular caller's story captured my attention. The caller, who was in her early twenties, told Dr. Laura that she had telephoned the show for advice a few years earlier. She had called the first time to talk about her mother's live-in boyfriend, a man who had sexually assaulted her when she was still a child. Evidently, when she called the first time, Dr. Laura had told her to contact the police immediately. According to the young woman, she had followed Dr. Laura's advice, but by the time the police arrived, the boyfriend had disappeared, and her mother told them that he'd never return. In other words, she promised the police that her daughter and other children would be safe from then on.

Unfortunately, the mother lied. At the time when the young woman called Dr. Laura's show in 2006, her mother had not only permitted the boyfriend to move back in but also had had a child by him. The young woman was once again seeking Dr. Laura's advice. She was planning to move out of her mother's house, but was concerned about the safety of her younger siblings. Like many callers, she wasn't prepared for Dr. Laura's response. In addition to telling the young woman to contact the Department of Social Services on behalf of her younger siblings, Dr. Laura told her that she needed to stop fantasizing. "Your mother is evil," she said bluntly. The young woman began to cry and defend her mother, claiming that she was a good woman who had merely stayed with the boyfriend for financial reasons. But no matter what she said,

Dr. Laura kept emphasizing that her mother was just as evil as her child-molesting boyfriend.

As I drove to work that day, this story resonated with me for two reasons. The more obvious of the two is that I've read or heard about too many cases in which mothers passively stood by while their children were being abused. Like Dr. Laura, I agree that these mothers are evil. Less obvious is how this story reminded me of some of the main conclusions I've drawn about school reform in America. In fact, the first of the seven lessons I discuss in this chapter is directly related to the caller's story.

Lesson One: Lies, Subterfuge, and Denial Are "Weapons of Mass Destruction" That Impede School Reform and Harm Many Students, Especially America's Stepchildren

In 2005 and 2006, many Americans grew increasingly disillusioned with the U.S. government's "spin" on why our troops needed to remain in Iraq. By then, most Americans had realized that the initial justification for the war—to rid Iraq of weapons of mass destruction—was a lie. There weren't any weapons of mass destruction in Iraq at the time that U.S. troops were sent there, and apparently many high-ranking U.S. government officials knew this. Because of one lie, thousands of fatalities and injuries have occurred and continue to occur as of this writing.

It has now become clear that just as the war in Iraq was based on a lie, so too was the latest school reform venture, No Child Left Behind. Some of the so-called evidence of the miracles that occurred in Texas schools stemmed from deceitful practices, such as forcing many low-performing students to drop out of school. As I mentioned in the introduction to this book and in Chapter Three, the high-stakes testing that is the foundation of NCLB has also led to widespread cheating by teachers and students in other states besides Texas.

Even before NCLB became law, reporter Jim Lehrer interviewed a teacher, Stacy Moscowitz, who taught third grade at P.S. 90 in the

South Bronx. According to Lehrer, Moscowitz and some of her colleagues gave their students the correct answers to New York City exams. Even more surprising was Moscowitz's insistence that "her school's former principal had encouraged cheating."[1]

In another 2000 report, journalist Matthew Robinson revealed that teachers in Los Angeles and Austin, Texas, had also been caught cheating for their students. Furthermore, P.S. 90 wasn't the only school in New York at which teachers had cheated. In fact, when it came to cheating, Robinson accused New York State of being "the biggest offender." Investigators charge that teachers and principals at thirty-two schools gave students answers to the Empire State's standardized tests."[2] Robinson ended his report with a warning: "The education establishment does not want reform, and it will go to great lengths to avoid it. As politicians scramble and educators grapple with increased scrutiny, expect more cases like those in New York, Texas, and California."[3]

Robinson was right. Two years later, more cases of cheating surfaced. One report indicated that from 2002 to 2004, Arizona officials had investigated "twenty-one allegations of teachers or principals cheating on standardized tests."[4] By 2004, California officials had investigated four hundred teachers,[5] and teachers in Louisiana, South Carolina,[6] Wisconsin, Pennsylvania, Massachusetts, Washington, and Illinois[7] had been accused of cheating for their students. In a *BusinessWeek* article, reporter Brian Grow questioned whether NCLB's insistence that test results be tied to school funding was "a recipe for deceit."[8]

But as I came close to completing the first draft of this book—in fact, on the very morning I listened to Dr. Laura tell that young woman that her mother was evil—I saw another example of the lying and subterfuge that NCLB has created.

The incident started with an e-mail that I received from a school employee. This woman had been kind enough to invite me to speak to a group of educators, and the e-mail was intended to finalize the plan before my presentation took place a few days later. In the e-mail, the employee was extremely polite and professional, but there was one little sentence that unnerved me: the woman's supervisor, the director of instruction for the district where I'd be giving my presentation, had told her to warn me not to say anything about a particular academic program that the district was using. Even though I hadn't been planning to mention the program in the first place, before long, my feeling of being unnerved turned into full-fledged outrage: "How dare they try to tell me—a grown woman, wife, parent, scholar, author, and educator with more than twenty years of teaching experience—what I can and can't say!"

To alleviate my growing anger, I fired off an e-mail reply to the woman who had sent me the warning. I asked for the name of her supervisor and told her the positive and negative details that I knew about the particular program that I wasn't supposed to mention in my upcoming talk. I also stated that I'd heard complaints about the program from several teachers in the district and that one of my graduate students, a professor at another university, had just submitted a dissertation that was based on a study involving this same program. Furthermore, I said that during my experiences as a workshop and conference presenter throughout the nation, no one had ever tried to tell me what I could and couldn't say.

But sending that e-mail wasn't enough for me. Anger still consumed me, so I decided to telephone the woman. I explained to her that I knew she was caught in the middle and only following her supervisor's orders, yet it was still quite offensive to me to be told to censor my presentation merely because the district had invested millions of dollars in a program that was producing mixed results. In fact, the test scores of upper elementary school students and secondary school students in the district were pitiful, and the district has one of the nation's highest dropout rates for black and Latino students.

During our phone conversation, the woman was very gracious, and we ended the call on a milder note. Nevertheless, the message didn't escape me that this district was doing what so many others throughout the nation have done. The bottom line, I learned, wasn't whether or not the program was effective in helping students.

The bottom line was that the school superintendent and others who had invested millions of dollars in the program wanted to look good.

The other troubling aspect of the district's decision to adopt this program was that in so doing, the "powers that be" created a climate of fear. Aside from censoring people like me, they pressured administrators to follow the party line. I learned that administrators were warned that if they didn't support the program and force their teachers to use it "religiously," they could lose their jobs or be demoted. In this climate of fear, teachers were policed to ensure that they were sticking to the program, and administrators were forced to police them. Some of the individuals who did the policing also were forced to serve as spies and to let officials know if professional development presenters were "bad-mouthing" the program, so that they could be blackballed from the district. Meanwhile, in the midst of this climate of fear, students continued to fall through the academic cracks.

This situation reminds me of the famous children's story "The Emperor's New Clothes." An emperor was duped into paying lots of money to two scam artists posing as tailors, who promised to make him a new wardrobe. During each fitting, when the tailors would brag about how good the emperor looked in his new outfits, the emperor was too ashamed to admit that he couldn't actually see the clothing, so the charade continued. In the end, it took a small child to speak truth about power in a way that many administrators have become too fearful to do. As the emperor strutted naked down the main street of his town with his head held high, the child blurted out, "But the emperor has no clothes on." All the townspeople, no doubt secretly relieved, ridiculed the emperor. Every single one of them knew that the man was naked in the first place, yet no one had had the courage to say it out loud.

Too many administrators and policymakers know that investing in expensive programs won't solve the many problems that plague America's schools, for no program can suffice for outstanding teaching and children are not robots. In the past, the latest fad or program didn't close the achievement gaps, and today, expensive programs won't solve the problem. A program that is used by an underqualified, culturally insensitive, racist, or disillusioned teacher and that requires students to be "programmed" like robots is merely going to waste money. That's one of the very problems that is occurring in the school district that tried to censor my presentation. It's also one of the main findings from the study I conducted at American High School. At that low-performing school, too, district officials had invested a huge sum of money in a reading program. Teachers were being forced to use the program, to require students to read certain books, and then to test them on these books and tie their grades to their reading test scores. However, students were still finding ways to cheat.

As I said in Chapter Three, the feedback that I collected from the teachers and students at American High School suggests that when people are "forced" to do things with which they don't agree or that seem to offer no clear benefits, they find ways to express their displeasure. Until policymakers and school district decision makers are willing to face some of the deeply entrenched problems that are prevalent in schools, test scores will continue to remain low for many students, high school dropout rates will remain ridiculously high in some districts, and money will continue to be wasted on programs instead of being invested in people. When we know and accept the truth and are willing to speak truth, the truth can set us free. When we are cowardly and in denial, we will strut around like the naked emperor—looking ridiculous.

Lesson Two: Some People in High Places Don't *Really* Want the Achievement Gaps to Be Closed

As I emphasized in the previous section, one of the lessons I've learned about school reform has to do with the deception involved. But I've also learned that like the bottom lines of most organizations, systems, and societies, the bottom line in school reform is that it's all about politics. Everything is political. And in the case of the latest school reform venture, NCLB, I learned that the politics can often be pretty dirty.

In his best-selling book *Confessions of an Economic Hit Man*, economist John Perkins repeatedly emphasizes that ". . . men in power are corruptible."[9] So are some women, I've learned! I've also learned that many influential people—policymakers, school district officials, school administrators, and even some teacher specialists— don't really want to see the achievement gaps between blacks and whites, blacks and Latinos, Latinos and whites, and the poor and the nonpoor eradicated. Moreover, many are actually benefiting from the gaps. For example, an educator recently informed me that a principal in his school district didn't want to see the English Language Learners at her school redesignated as "English proficient" students because doing so would cause the school's rank, which is based on standardized test scores, to suffer.

I've also heard that instead of providing adequate support to help low-performing students do well on standardized tests, some principals actually encourage them to stay home when the tests are given. One reason is that the principals don't want to run the risk of these students' scores having a negative effect on the school's academic rank; the other is that they don't want these kids to perform *better* because the school will lose some of its federal funding if there are fewer Title 1 students enrolled in the school. This may be one of the reasons why so much of the money that has been invested in Title 1 programs hasn't produced dramatic and positive results for the groups of students who have traditionally underperformed in school.

Related to what I've learned about the role of dirty politics in impeding true school reform is the realization that job security and perks are also connected to those politics. Some educators go along with bad decisions and bad programs, and accept ineffective and counterproductive policies and practices that are dictated from "higher ups" simply because they fear they'll lose their jobs. This is a legitimate concern, and it is human nature to want job security. But the pressure on administrators and other educators to accept bad programs and policies that are forced on them has created a large cadre of weak, cowardly, and unethical school leaders.

In the case of legislators and other policymakers, I wonder what their motive truly is. When state lawmakers force school districts to accept programs that cost millions of dollars yet produce mixed results, I wonder if these policymakers are benefiting in some financial way. Are they getting kickbacks? A white veteran second-grade teacher recently told me she has learned that whenever there's pressure to remain silent about expensive ineffective programs and go along with the status quo, "Somebody is getting a lot of money from it." The recent corruption scandals involving Enron and other major corporations show how easy it is for people in high places, policymakers, and others in leadership positions to use their power to amass wealth at the expense of those with the least amount of power.

Lesson Three: Too Many Influential People Still Don't Believe That America's Stepchildren Are Capable of Academic Excellence

Whenever I mention such terms as *race*, *racism*, and *color-blind racism* in my presentations to racially mixed audiences of educators (be it in K–12 settings or in higher education), the same thing usually happens: some people become visibly upset or uncomfortable. They clearly want me to shut up, and their body language, facial expressions, and sometimes even their comments suggest that I'm behaving in a politically incorrect manner. In this current conservative political era, it's not okay to speak boldly and directly about the role that racism and privilege play in fostering inequality of educational opportunity. But the uncomfortable looks and negative body language fail to achieve their goals with me. God gave me a big mouth for a reason, and I open it whenever I feel it necessary. So even though it's not politically correct to talk about the role of racism and privilege in impeding true school reform, I'm going to do so in this section anyway.

One of the main lessons I've learned about school reform is that many reformers are big hypocrites: they don't really "walk the talk." How can they, when most of these same individuals—educators and policymakers—don't want to live in neighborhoods containing too many African American and Latino families, attend places of worship with too many of them, or send their own children to schools in which too many of them are enrolled? More important, although these individuals claim to want to reform schools and close the achievement gaps, many of them don't really believe that African American and Latino students are capable of academic excellence. On the contrary, they actually believe that these groups are less intelligent than white students and some Asian American students. In other words, they really believe that no matter how often we try to reform schools, "those people will never get it. They are lazy, inferior, incapable," and so on. National studies have shown that such stereotypes are widespread in America and that most Americans are socialized to believe that whites are superior to blacks and Latinos.[10] Yet when it comes to discussions about education reform, most people pretend that these stereotypes don't exist, and are in full-fledged denial with regard to their own beliefs about blacks and Latinos.

The biblical scripture "A house that is built upon sand will not stand" applies to this lesson I've learned about school reform: individuals who fundamentally believe that blacks and Latinos are too dumb to do well academically will be incapable of creating viable programs and implementing reform efforts that will close the achievement gaps. Their reforms, which are usually based on hypocrisy, arrogance, and cultural ignorance, will at best become self-fulfilling prophecies. Two very fragile but widely believed notions are woven tightly into American society: the notion that whites are superior to most other groups, especially blacks and Latinos, and the belief that whites deserve to be on top in this society because they are more intelligent and they work harder. These beliefs become self-fulfilling prophecies in organizations, including schools, and they drive many school reform practices. These practices perpetuate institutional racism in the form of tracking students of color into low-level academic tracks and white students into college preparatory tracks, low expectations for students of color, grade inflation, and other manifestations of the theory of structural inequality. This theory maintains that schools perpetuate the class differences that exist in the larger society, and that school practices will keep whites on top and blacks, Latinos, and low-income children at the bottom economic rungs of society even after they finish their K–12 schooling.[11]

Lesson Four: Oppressive School Settings, Inadequate Teacher Preparation Programs, and a Lack of Support Will Continue to Drive New Teachers Out of the Profession

In his autobiography *The Ragman's Son*, actor Kirk Douglas described an incident during his childhood in which he was injured by a vehicle. When the child went crying to his father, expecting comfort, a hug, or sympathy, he got another "wound" instead: "That's what you get for playing in the street," his father scolded.[12] Just as his father blamed the victim in this case, a lot of victim-blaming goes on in school settings and when decisions are made about school reform. Students are blamed, parents are blamed, and teachers are sometimes blamed for institutional and systemic problems that aren't their fault.

As I worked on this book, time and time again I saw evidence of new teachers' asking for support and being criticized and made to feel that they were at fault. A 2004 *Los Angeles Times* article about the trials of a first-year local teacher illustrates how difficult teaching can be when a teacher feels overwhelmed. According to the article, thirty-four-year-old Ricardo Acuna was inspired by his wife, a teacher, to abandon his career as a full-time writer to become a teacher. As a participant in a "special program for mid-career professionals and college graduates without education credentials," he received an intensive six-week crash course before he began to teach at a Los Angeles high school in 2003.[13]

Although Acuna would have to take education courses for several more years before earning his credential, he went into his first classroom with high hopes. Acuna ". . . particularly had in mind kids who were like he had been: poor kids, struggling kids, kids on the margins. But he found problems he had never imagined."[14] Besides student apathy and misbehavior, he learned that many students had weak academic skills and family problems. Furthermore, the mentoring program that had previously been in place to assist new teachers in his school district had been drastically reduced as a result of budget cuts. "Moreover, [to Acuna,] asking for help would've been embarrassing. Instead, he struggled, fretting over what to teach and how to manage students."[15]

The stress resulted in nightmares and marital discord for Acuna. Despite the fact that he had grown fond of his job and some of his students, the question that loomed large in his mind was "Could he stick it out? Would he be like the 68 percent of teachers hired by L.A. Unified in 1997–98 who were still in the classroom five years later? Or would he be like the other 32 percent who left, some for other school districts and others who quit teaching altogether?"[16]

One of the main ways to alleviate some of the problems that Acuna faced and that drive so many teachers out of the profession is for teacher preparation programs at universities and at school sites to ensure that every new teacher is equipped with knowledge and skills related to preparing effective lesson plans, working with culturally diverse students, working with students from challenging backgrounds, working with students whose skills are below grade level, and managing the classroom effectively. Many teacher training programs, especially those at colleges and universities, fail to do a good job of preparing new teachers to work in urban and low-performing schools, and when teachers reach the actual school site, they often don't know where to turn for help. Postsecondary institutions must do a better job of preparing new teachers. This means that professors must be knowledgeable about the skills and information that new teachers need. In other words, they can't be ignorant about what is really going on in K–12 schools.

At the actual school site, every new teacher should automatically be assigned a mentor who is an exemplary veteran teacher—not just someone who is collecting an extra stipend without doing the extra work. Administrators and district officials should hold mentors accountable for providing ongoing assistance to new teachers. Administrators should also meet with new teachers periodically throughout the year to ask them if they need additional assistance. They should also ensure that new teachers attend professional development workshops throughout the school year and have access to books and journals about teaching fundamentals. In other words, new teachers need extensive support. Of course, this would require adequate funding from policymakers.

Lesson Five: As Long as Their Voices, Needs, and Concerns Continue to Be Ignored, Teachers and Students Will Find Creative Ways to Derail School Reform Efforts

One of the most obvious lessons I've learned about school reform that is a strong recurring theme from the American High School study is that teachers and students can find ways to derail education reforms when they feel ignored and feel that their needs and concerns aren't being addressed. A good example is a story that a new teacher shared with me after I'd done a presentation for a large school district.

This teacher worked at a school that is approximately 75 percent Latino and 25 percent black. According to this young white teacher, her district had recently invested a large sum of money in a language arts program for high school students. She was not only required to use this program with her high school students but also forced to put related standards, lesson plans, and exercises on the board on a daily basis, so that a school official could monitor whether or not she was "following the program." Each day, the official would peer into her classroom to see if the correct daily assignment from the mandated program was in the proper place on the chalkboard. It always was. The teacher made sure that she followed that particular rule.

The problem, however, was that the teacher believed that the program was flawed and counterproductive. Her students didn't like it, and neither did she. She felt that there were better ways to motivate her students to become good readers and good writers. So instead of following the program, she merely fooled the official by letting him think that she was complying. She put the information on the board, but really "did her own thing."

Throughout this book, I've mentioned that there is a strong need for decision makers to be more inclusive in their efforts to reform schools. The research on the high-performing, high-minority, high-poverty schools indicates that one of the most effective strategies that school leaders use in reforming low-performing schools is to create an inclusive community. The views and concerns of parents, teachers, support staff, and students are taken into consideration.[17] When policymakers and decision makers take the time to ask teachers, parents, and students, and especially America's stepchildren, how they feel about school policies and proposed changes, they may be surprised to learn that these groups have many great suggestions that the policymakers never even thought of. Unfortunately, as things currently stand, few policymakers believe that these groups have anything of value to say. As long as this attitude persists, too many schools throughout the nation will be plagued by the problems that I described throughout this book.

Lesson Six: At Best, School Reforms That Are Based on High-Stakes Testing Will Produce "Tuna" That Looks Like Star-Kist but Is Not the Real Thing

During my childhood, the TV commercials for Star-Kist tuna were among my favorites. These popular commercials featured two animated tunas—one that was plump and attractive but actually a fraud, and one that was attractive but also the "real thing," a quality tuna. The gist of the commercials was that looks can be deceiving; a good-looking tuna might end up being bad tasting or even rotten at its core. Only Star-Kist guaranteed that the consumer would get a superior product.

One of the lessons I've learned about school reform reminds me of these commercials. The lesson is that at best, school reforms based on high-stakes testing will produce something that *looks* good—high standardized test scores—but that might not actually be good at its core. In other words, students may earn high test scores, but that doesn't necessarily mean that true learning has occurred. In the *Unschooled Mind*, Howard Gardner wrote about how the nation's schools were producing students who could recite facts, figures, and other information that they'd been trained to memorize, but weren't able to apply this information to other contexts.[18] In other words, they lacked critical thinking skills. The same thing is happening today with the overemphasis on test scores.

Although high test scores may indicate that "learning" really occurred, they may also be indicative of other things. For example, they might really mean that a student memorized the test content. When I taught high school, we once had a problem that illustrates this point. At that time, the district required all students to pass a district-created exam that included a writing component. Students had to demonstrate that they could write a grammatically correct simple paragraph. It soon became clear that many of the English Language Learners (ELLs) had difficulty passing the writing component of the exam. At this point, two interesting events occurred. The first was that some of the teachers who were hired to score the writing section of the exam began to lower their standards and make excuses. They decided to hold ELLs to a lower standard than native English speakers and overlooked grammatical errors. The other thing that happened was that some high school students began to cheat. Administrators learned that in some cases, students who had previously failed the exam permitted friends or relatives to come to the test site and take the exam for them. From then on, testing officials were forced to require students to bring in a photo identification card.

Another well-known example of cheating in that same school district involved a student who "cheated his way into the valedictorianship." This student became valedictorian of his high school graduating class, not because of hard work, but by cheating. According to numerous students at the school including the school salutatorian, this student enrolled in the same classes taught by the same teachers that his older sister previously had. His sister allegedly gave him all of the assignments, tests, and quizzes that she had completed when she took these classes. All her brother had to do was to memorize his sister's work. His "ingenious" plan worked. On graduation day, his parents and relatives beamed proudly as he gave the valedictory speech.

This story is similar to one that Janice Hale recounted in *Learning While Black*.[19] She learned that her son's classmates at the elite private elementary school he attended had received unfair educational advantages. These children knew information that Hale's son did not know and earned better grades because they had received the workbooks and assignments ahead of time at home. Their parents had kept their older children's work and were able to prepare their younger children for forthcoming lessons and assignments long before the teacher introduced them to the rest of the class. In the case where a child, such as Hale's son, hadn't had siblings who previously attended the school, it often appeared that the other children—the white kids—were much smarter and learned the new information faster than Hale's African American son. The truth was that, like the cheating valedictorian, they had merely been exposed to the information beforehand, and this helped them to perform well on tests, homework, and class work.

High test scores can also mean that the students had teachers who devoted more class time to test preparation and attended schools in which more support was given to help students do well on tests. Many students who participated in the American High School study attributed their low test scores to inadequate preparation by their teachers. Some students complained that the curriculum wasn't aligned to the standardized tests they were required to take and that teachers barely devoted any time to preparing them for the tests. Students also complained that they got the impression in some classes that their teachers weren't serious about the tests, and that the classroom environment wasn't conducive to doing well on the tests.

High test scores might also mean that the students who did well were serious about doing well on the test. When people believe that something is important to them, they are more likely to take it seriously. At American High School, for example, many students said that they didn't have a serious attitude about the standardized tests. Many viewed them as a waste of time, and many failed to see how they would benefit from doing well on the standardized tests. As one of the African American focus group participants said, "I didn't take it seriously, because it didn't have anything to do with me as an individual. The school gets points, so the school won't get shut down. But, it's like, sometimes you feel that the school don't care about you, so why you gonna care about the school?"

High test scores might also indicate that the students who did well felt comfortable about their ability to do well. The research on stereotype threat that I mentioned in Chapter Three suggests that some groups, such as African Americans, Latinos, and females, are more likely to be affected by negative stereotypes, and the resulting anxiety can have a detrimental effect on their test performance. Some, such as my late sister Tammie who was studying for the bar exam when she died, can become so immobilized by fear and anxiety that they forget everything that they've studied in preparation for the test. Others may merely become so apathetic or passive-aggressive that they make only a halfhearted attempt to pass the test. Some may not even try to pass the test at all. LeVelle, the African American third or fourth grader whom I described in Chapter Seven, is a good example. In explaining why he wasn't even going to pick up his pencil and attempt to take the test, he told the principal, "I ain't giving that white woman one more reason to say I'm dumb."

I believe that the high-stakes testing movement is dangerous and counterproductive. No test— especially a test that contains measurement flaws, that is culturally biased, "normed" on middle-class white students, and that measures socioeconomic status rather than what students have been taught in school—can truly illustrate what students know. Therefore, as I've said previously, I believe that multiple types of assessments, including portfolios, writing samples, oral reports, projects, and so on, should also be used. I learned this the hard way when I taught junior high school long ago, as the following example illustrates.

When I first became a teacher, my own pet peeve was related to writing. Because I'd had such a humiliating experience during my first year of college after being told that I had extremely poor writing skills, when I became a teacher I vowed that *all* my students would have to develop good writing skills in order to pass the class. So I assigned a lot of essays, and students' essay grades were weighted more heavily than all other assignments. The problem was that students who had already developed good writing skills *before* they came to my class could easily earn a high grade on their report card, but the students who had never been taught how to write a decent sentence, let alone an essay, not only had to learn this information but also needed a lot of practice to understand the basics of grammar and composition before they could actually write good essays. In other words, the students who arrived in my class with weak writing skills were at a disadvantage from day one in comparison to their classmates who were already outstanding writers. After I eventually realized that some of the hardest-working students in the class would continue to earn low grades on their report card as long as I continued to weigh the writing assignments more heavily than all other assignments, I decided to find other ways to measure what the students had learned. Once I started to give more weight to their projects, oral reports, quizzes, and tests, so that the essay grades didn't overshadow the others, I saw that students' confidence increased, more students earned higher grades, and more students seemed to be interested in class activities.

I think that policymakers should consider doing the same thing: using multiple means to assess what students have learned.

As I stated in Chapter Three, countless students—especially America's stepchildren—at all levels of the U.S. education system will have their brilliance overlooked and their potential underestimated as long as they are judged solely by test scores and as long as schools fail to provide them with strategies to help them manage test anxiety and with adequate exposure to the subject matter covered on the required tests.

Lesson Seven: Because of Resistance and Racial Prejudice, It Is Difficult for African American and Latino School Administrators to Improve the Status Quo in K–12 Schools

Another lesson I've learned about school reform is how difficult it is for black and Latino school administrators to change the status quo at the school district level and at underperforming school sites. Often these administrators are met with strong opposition from their white superiors, white teachers, white parents, school board members, and sometimes even white students. But the story doesn't end there; sometimes the opposition comes from other people of color as well. For example, an African American principal told me that she was constantly being criticized by a negative group of black teachers at her elementary school. These teachers resisted the changes that she tried to implement at the school. Although the principal believed that raising expectations and holding teachers accountable would be extremely beneficial to the students at the school, this group of teachers was defiant and resistant. They not only caused her considerable grief but also made her job a lot harder than it had to be. They also hurt her feelings, because she had expected cooperation from members of her own race.

Another African American principal told me that he had recently come under attack by Latino parents. These parents were so upset with him that they were insisting that he be fired. This turn of events had been totally unexpected by the principal because he had been very popular with parents at the beginning of his principalship.

The school was predominantly Latino, and the principal had instituted several reforms that benefited Latino students. Although his reforms had a positive effect on Latino students' test scores, he eventually realized that he also needed to devote more attention to improving black students' scores. That's when "all hell broke loose." As soon as the principal attempted to focus on black students as well as Latino students, parents and teachers began to accuse him of racism. They complained to the school board about him and even stirred up community activists to insist on his ouster. At the time that he shared this story with me, his fate was uncertain. He didn't know if the school board would give in to the pressure and fire him, but the emotional toll that the ordeal had taken on him was obvious to me.

Although these situations may be common in low-performing schools at which teachers have been permitted to do as they pleased and have been conditioned by a climate of low expectations, the complaints that I've heard more often concern the opposition that black leaders face from whites. For instance, a white middle school Special Education teacher told me about her African American principal's dilemma. This man had become principal of a predominantly black and Latino school at which most of the teachers were white, in a school district that has one of the nation's lowest graduation rates. According to the Special Education teacher, her colleagues criticized everything the principal did. I told her I wasn't surprised. After all, these teachers have been socialized in a society in which they are taught almost from birth that black people are inferior to whites and that whites deserve the best of everything, including most leadership positions. It is therefore difficult for many whites to accept the leadership of an African American or Latino. On top of this, most whites grow up believing that blacks aren't very smart, so many will assume that when a black person is in a position of leadership, he is unqualified, got there because of Affirmative Action, and knows less than they know. But the teacher's response surprised me. "I think there's another reason why they don't want to listen to him," she said. She told me that fear was linked to their resistance. "Because black people have been mistreated historically by whites," she said, "white teachers fear that a black person who is their boss will retaliate against them and not treat them fairly." This was a new one for me, and I was quite surprised.

A related story concerns an African American school superintendent who repeatedly met widespread opposition from white teachers who criticized the improvements that she tried to make in a low-performing, predominantly black and Latino school district. "She plays the race card," the teachers accused. "She's only out to help blacks," others complained. In the face of widespread opposition from a huge block of white teachers in the district, the superintendent held her head high and continued to forge ahead with her plans. However, she was always aware that she was surrounded by enemies—white teachers who were watching her every move and reporting anything and everything they could to the school board.

These stories are a reminder of how deeply entrenched racial prejudice is in U.S. society. One of the recommendations that I've made in most of the previous chapters is that school administrators, teachers, parents, and policymakers need to engage in self-examination to uncover their negative mental baggage. As long as so many influential people—parents, who are the leaders in the home; policymakers, who make decisions that affect the nation; teachers, who make important decisions involving countless children; school district officials and K–12 administrators, who are supposed to serve as leaders of schools; and university professors who train teachers—fail to deal with their baggage, America will remain a nation that fosters hypocrisy. This nation will continue to spend huge amounts of money to "rescue" third world countries and do "humanitarian" deeds abroad, yet neglect the schools the nation's stepchildren attend and the communities in which they live. The one theme that connects each of the seven lessons I've described in this chapter is that of hypocrisy.

The Real "Final Word" of This Book

One of the most fascinating books I've read recently is called *The Pity of It All: A History of Jews in Germany, 1743–1933*. In this book, Amos Elon provides a detailed historical account of the widespread oppression of Jews that occurred in Germany during a period of nearly two hundred years. Elon does a superb job of describing the policies and practices that were implemented in Germany and other European countries for centuries in order to keep Jews in slavery-like bondage. At the same time that legal and political mandates denied Jews the civil rights that most other Germans enjoyed, Jewish appearance, culture, religion, family life, aptitude, and integrity were routinely criticized as being inferior and in some cases even evil. In fact, many Germans and other Europeans actually believed that Jews were subhuman. Almost with regularity, Jews were scapegoated for the economic problems in the wider society, and pogroms and anti-Jewish riots erupted periodically to keep Jews in a constant state of fear and to remind them of their second-class status.[20]

As I read this book, I was often reminded of some of the lessons I've learned about school reform and inequality of educational opportunity. Although there can be no comparison between what I've learned about school reform and the atrocities that Jews have experienced historically, there are a few parallels. One of these is that government officials, educators, social scientists, and others have historically blamed Jews and denigrated everything about them at the same time that oppressive and exclusionary policies and practices were enforced against them. Instead of blaming these policies for many of the social problems that European Jews experienced, the "victims" were blamed for their own fate. This is similar to the way that black and Latino parents and students are often blamed for the students' poor academic performance. But in Overcoming Our Racism: The Journey to Liberation, Wing Sue reaches a different conclusion. According to Wing Sue, there are "standard operating procedures" (SOPs) in the United States that are designed to keep whites on top through unearned privilege and institutional racism. In schools, the SOPs that are harmful to students of color include segregation, a substandard curriculum, a Eurocentric curriculum, testing practices that use middle-class whites as the norm, educators' deficit-oriented mind-sets, tracking, and inequitable school financing.[21] In other words, just as the SOPs in the larger society are designed to perpetuate white superiority, the same is true of schools.

As long as these SOPs continue to exist in schools and the wider society, true school reform will never occur. Many African Americans, Latinos, Native Americans, Southeast Asians, and other stepchildren will continue to underperform in schools, and the achievement gaps will continue to exist. Countless extremely bright and talented students from these backgrounds will start elementary school with high hopes. By fourth grade, many will have been tracked for academic failure by being placed in Special Education courses and labeled as discipline problems.[22] By ninth or tenth grade, many will have dropped out of school. Among those who remain in school will be a group of optimists who still believe in the "system" and that education can improve the quality of their lives. However, too many who remain in school will have "dropped out" psychologically because they realized that the American Dream was never meant for people like them, society's stepchildren.

I believe that instead of continuing to play the games that have been played in the past and either merely giving lip service to their desire to reform schools or only using their power and influence to promote expensive programs that will benefit them personally, policymakers need to answer an important question: "Do policymakers, especially white ones, really want to close the achievement gaps, improve urban schools, and eradicate inequality of educational opportunity?" Those who answer yes must consider whether or not they are willing to have more black, Latino, Native American, and Southeast Asian students competing with white middle- and upper-class students for college admission slots and higher-paying jobs. To answer yes means they are admitting that instead of supporting the current school and societal inequities that make it more likely that America's stepchildren will end up working at Wal-Mart, McDonald's, or other low-paying jobs, these policymakers are really willing to level the playing field.

—————

When I think about the lessons I've learned about school reform, dirty politics, and the ways in which America's stepchildren continue to be set up for failure, I sometimes wonder if I'm wasting my breath conducting professional development workshops and wasting my time writing books to improve social conditions. Recently, one of my African American graduate students asked me about this. "How can you continue to have hope that things will get better after all you've been through?" she asked. I told her that although it is true that I often feel hopeless about the racism, hypocrisy, white privilege, and denial that are common in the United States, I keep doing the work I do for two reasons.

First, I believe that I owe it to my ancestors and to all of the African Americans who had dogs sicced on them, high-power water hoses sprayed on them by law enforcement, and the doorways of schools blocked to them (even by governors), and who were thrown in jail, lynched, and mistreated in other ways, so that I could have a better life. I have benefited from their struggles, and although I too have struggled, my hardships have been small in comparison to theirs.

Second, I believe I have a moral obligation to use my writing talent, public speaking opportunities, and knowledge to try to make a positive difference in this world. In 2005, the many obituaries and tributes I read about Kenneth Clark reminded me of how important this work is but also of the enormity of the opposition against improving schools and social conditions.

Clark, who became one of the nation's most famous social scientists and the most eminent black social scientist, together with his wife, Mamie, conducted studies about racial prejudice that were instrumental in prompting the U.S. Supreme Court to outlaw segregation in public schools. After the Brown v. Board of Education ruling, Clark was "brimming with optimism that segregation would disappear within a matter of years. But the next decades would prove a great disappointment." During the 1960s and 1970s, he was hired to improve public schools in Harlem and Washington, D.C., but "his proposals were vetoed by the superintendent and the teachers union." By the 1980s, Clark had lost his optimism about race relations and had begun to feel that his life had been a "lost cause."

He had underestimated the "intractability of racism in the North." Sadly, fifteen years before his death in 2005, Clark viewed his life as "a series of glorious defeats."[23]

On the surface, it appears that Clark's work and the Supreme Court ruling failed, in that today, schools still tend to be segregated, primarily because most white people don't want their children attending schools that have too many African American, Latino, Native American, and Southeast Asian students. In his latest book, *The Shame of a Nation*, Jonathan Kozol does an excellent job of exposing the many guises of inequality of educational opportunity. Kozol writes extensively about the inequitable funding that is prevalent between the schools that America's stepchildren attend versus those attended by middle- and upper-class whites, and he talks about the diligence of many white parents and even policymakers in ensuring that schools will remain segregated, thereby guaranteeing that America's stepchildren will receive an inferior education.[24]

Today things have gotten so bad that in several states there are campaigns to reinstate legally sanctioned segregation in schools. But in my opinion, the work of Kenneth Clark and other trailblazers, such as Thurgood Marshall and many others, wasn't in vain. Their efforts will forever be credited with influencing the highest court in the most famous nation in the world to outlaw segregation in schools. They have also left behind a model of social justice activism that should galvanize others to take action.

Even though the Supreme Court ruling didn't prevent *de facto* segregation from continuing, it did outlaw *de jure*, or legally sanctioned, segregation. This is a very important point for all Americans to keep in mind as certain policymakers in Omaha, Nebraska, and other places slowly surrender to racist public pressure to turn back the hands of time. These individuals want to return to the days when lawmakers openly condoned and created policies that clearly ensured that America's stepchildren would get the crumbs, scraps, old and outdated textbooks, raggedy desks, and other discards and castoffs from the tables, homes, and schools of middle- and upper-class whites. If this book has not caused parents and equity-minded policymakers and educators to rise up in righteous indignation and shout "enough!" this insidious campaign to reverse any progress that has been made in the past should do so. I end this book with a call to action to parents, teachers, school administrators, and policymakers to make a commitment to do everything within their power to improve low-performing schools and the social conditions that create second-class citizens and societal stepchildren. This commitment must start with truth-seeking about one's own negative mental baggage and truth-telling about the lies, cover-ups, and intricate ways that inequality of educational opportunity is *allowed* to exist in one of the world's wealthiest and most powerful nations. I conclude with three quotes from Noguera, and one from Hilliard:

It is important to remember that we remain a long way from achieving equality of educational opportunity in the U.S.[25]

Public schools . . . remain profoundly unequal.[26]

In the absence of a national effort to pursue equity in other areas [outside of schools] it is unlikely that schools will ever succeed on their own.[27]

The issue of will is certainly broader than the schools. It's a political issue about whether we care about everybody.[28]

Notes

Introduction

1. Lehrer, J. (2000, April 26). Cheating teachers. *Online NewsHour*. www.pbs.org/newshour. Retrieved February 17, 2005.

   Robinson, M. (2000, January 31). Wave of cheating teachers hits southern California coast. www.conservativenews.org. Retrieved February 17, 2005.

   Kossan, P. (2004, July 11). Cheating or misunderstandings? *The Arizona Republic*. www.azcentral.com. Retrieved February 17, 2005.

   Grow, B. (2004, July 5). A spate of cheating—by teachers: No Child Left Behind links test results to school funding. Is that a recipe for deceit? *BusinessWeek Online*. www.businessweek.com. Retrieved February 17, 2005.

2. Rather, D. (2004, January 7). *The Texas miracle*. www.cbsnews.com. Retrieved February 17, 2005.

3. California Department of Education. Data and Statistics. (2004). www.cde.ca.gov./ds/. Retrieved August 17, 2004.

4. California Department of Education. (2004). *California High School Exit Examination (CAHSEE): 2004 CAHSEE Results*. www.cde.ca.gov/nr/ne/yr04/yr04rel72attb.asp. http://www.cde.ca.gov/nr/ne/yr04/yr04rel72attb.asp. Retrieved November 18, 2006.

5. California Department of Education. (2004). *O'Connell releases 2004 Star and CAHSEE results*. www.cde.ca.gov/nr/ne/yr04/yr04rel72.asp. Retrieved November 18, 2006.

6. Richard, A. (2004, August 11). Edison Alliance hired to help struggling S.C. district. *Education Week*. www.edweek.org./ew/articles/2004/08/11/44allendale.h23.html. Retrieved August 25, 2004.

7. Ibid.

8. Cholo, A. B., & T. Dell, A. (2004, June 23). 100 new schools to be created. *The Chicago Tribune*, sec. 2, p. 1.

9. Charter schools said to lag on test scores: National findings are cited in study. (2004, August 17). *The Boston Globe*. www.boston.com/news/local/articles. Retrieved August 26, 2004.

10. Kingsbury, K. (2004, August 13). Charter schools remain subject of debate. www.cnn.com/2004/Education/08/13b2s. Retrieved August 26, 2004.

11. Ibid.

12. Charter schools said to lag on test scores, 2004.

13. Coleman, J. (2004, August 15). Charter school closing starts scramble. *The Oakland Tribune*. www.oaklandtribune.com. Retrieved August 26, 2004.

Chapter One

1. Thompson, G. L. (2004). *Through Ebony Eyes*. San Francisco: Jossey-Bass.

2. White teachers fleeing black schools. (2003, January 13). www.cnn.com/2003/EDUCATION/01/13/resegregation.teachers.ap/index.html. Retrieved November 18, 2006.

3. Cruickshank, D. R., & Haefele, D. (2001, February). Good teachers, plural. *Educational Leadership*, 58(5), 26–30.

4. Darling-Hammond, L. (1999). *Teacher quality and student achievement: A review of state policy evidence*. University of Washington: Center for the Study of Teaching and Policy.

5. Haycock, K. (1998). Good teaching matters . . . a lot. *Thinking K–16*, 3(2), 3–14.

6. Grosso de Leon, A. (2001). *Higher education's challenge: New teacher education models for a new century*. New York: Carnegie Corporation. www.carnegie.org. Retrieved January 5, 2005.

7. U.S. Department of Education. (2003). *Meeting the highly qualified teachers challenge: The secretary's second annual report on teacher quality*.

www.ed.gov/about/reports/annual/teachprep/2003title-ii-report.pdf. Retrieved October 8, 2003.

8. Keller, B. (2005). N.D., Utah dispute federal findings on teacher quality. *Education Week, 24*(18). www.edweek.org. Retrieved February 3, 2005.

9. U.S. Department of Education. *No Child Left Behind: Highly qualified teachers and paraprofessionals.* www.ed.gov/admins/tchrqual/learn/hqt/edlite-slide027.html. Retrieved February 3, 2005.

10. Darling-Hammond, 1999, *Teacher quality and student achievement.*

11. Grosso de Leon, 2001, *Higher education's challenge*, p. 2.

12. deCourcy Hinds, M. (2002). *Teaching as a clinical profession: A new challenge for education.* New York: Carnegie Corporation. www.carnegie.org/pdf/teachered.pdf, p. 3. Retrieved January 5, 2003.

13. Haycock, 1998, Good teaching matters . . . a lot, p. 10.

14. Haberman, M. (1995). *Star teachers of children in poverty.* West Lafayette, LA: Kappa Delta Pi.

15. Schwarzenegger, A. (2005, January 5). *State of the State Address*, p. 2. http://gov.ca.gov/index/php?/speech/2408

16. Seibert, T. (2005, February 1). Bredesen's goal: Pull schools out of cellar. *The Tennessean, 101*(2), 1A.

17. Stutz, T. (2005, February 2). Will teacher merit pay make the grade? *Dallas Morning News.* www.dallasnews.com. Retrieved February 3, 2005.

18. Samuels, C. A. (2005, January 19). Bush promotes plan for high school test: President indicates that education is still high on his agenda. *Education Week.* www.edweek.org/ew/articles/2005/01/19/19bush.h24.html. Retrieved February 5, 2005.

19. Kannapel, P., Clements, S. K., Taylor, D., & Hibpshman, T. (2005). *Inside the black box of high-performing high poverty schools: A report from the Prichard Committee for Academic Excellence.* Lexington, KY: Prichard Committee for Academic Excellence, p. 3.

20. Comer, J. P. (2004). *Leave no child behind: Preparing today's youth for tomorrow's world.* New Haven, CT: Yale University Press.

Carter, C. S. (2000). *No excuses: Lessons from 21 high-performing, high-poverty schools.* Washington, DC: Heritage Foundation.

Leighton, M. S. (1996). *The role of leadership in sustaining school reform: Voices from the field.* Washington, D.C.: U.S. Department of Education.

21. Simon, W. E., Jr., & Izumi, L. (2003, April 23). High-poverty but high-performing schools offer proof that minority students from poor families can thrive. *The Orange County Register.* www.pacificresearch.org/press/opd/2003/opd_03-04-23li.html. Retrieved June 7, 2005.

Yau, R. (2002). High-achieving elementary schools with large percentages of low-income African American students: A review and critique of the current research. In S. J. Denbo & L. Moore Beaulieu (Eds.), *Improving schools for African American students: A reader for educational leaders* (pp. 193–217). Springfield, IL: Thomas.

22. Kunjufu, J. (2002). *Black students/middle class teachers.* Chicago: African American Images.

23. De Becker, G. (1997). *The gift of fear: Survival signals that protect us from violence.* New York: Little, Brown.

Chapter Two

1. O'Faolain, N. (1996). *Are you somebody: The accidental memoir of a Dublin woman.* New York: Henry Holt.

2. Noll, J. W. (Ed.). (1999). *Taking sides: Clashing views on controversial educational issues.* (10th ed.). New York: McGraw Hill/Dushkin.

3. Viadero, D. (1990, November 28). Battle over multicultural education rises in intensity. *Education Week, 10*(13), 1, 11, 13.

4. Thompson, G. L. (2004). *Through ebony eyes: What teachers need to know but are afraid to ask about African American students.* San Francisco: Jossey-Bass, p. 191.

5. Corwin, M. (2001). *And still we rise: The trials and triumphs of twelve gifted inner-city students.* New York: HarperCollins.

6. Ibid, p. 84.

7. Ibid, p. 84.

8. Ibid, p. 203.

9. Ibid, p. 203.

10. Ibid, p. 210.

11. Collins, M. (1992). *Ordinary children, extraordinary teachers.* Charlottesville, VA: Hampton Roads.

12. Gay, G. (2000). *Culturally responsive teaching: Theory, research, and practice.* New York: Teachers College Press.

13. Delpit, L. (1995). *Other people's children: Cultural conflict in the classroom.* New York: New Press.

    Ladson-Billings, G. (1994). *The dreamkeepers: Successful teachers of African American children.* San Francisco: Jossey-Bass.

    Cross, B. (1995). The case for a culturally coherent curriculum. In J. Beane (Ed.), *The coherent curriculum.* Alexandria, VA: Association for Supervision and Curriculum Development.

    Hilliard, A. G., III. (2003). *No mystery: Closing the achievement gap between Africans and excellence.* In T. Perry, C. Steele, & A. G. Hilliard III (Eds.), *Young, gifted, and black: Promoting high achievement among African-American students* (pp. 131–165). Boston: Beacon Press.

    Gay, 2000, *Culturally responsive teaching.*

    Hale, J. E. (2001). *Learning while black: Creating educational excellence for African American children.* Baltimore: Johns Hopkins University Press.

14. Ladson-Billings, 1994, *The dreamkeepers.*

15. Cross, 1995, *The case for a culturally coherent curriculum.*

16. Gay, 2000, *Culturally responsive teaching.*

17. Gray, W. S. (2003). *Storybook treasury of Dick and Jane and friends.* New York: Grosset & Dunlap.

18. Ibid.

19. Thompson, 2004, *Through Ebony Eyes.*

20. Cross, 1995, *The case for a culturally coherent curriculum.*

    Ladson-Billings, 1994, *The dreamkeepers.*

Chapter Three

1. Kohn, A. (2000, September 27). Standardized testing and its victims. *Education Week*. www.edweek.org. Retrieved February 17, 2005.

2. Popham, W. J. (2004, November). A game without winners. *Educational Leadership*, 62(3), 46–50.

3. Thompson, G. (2004). *Through Ebony Eyes*.

4. Gould, S. J. (1996). *The mismeasure of man*. New York: Norton.

5. Gould, Ibid.

6. Popham, 2004, p. 46.

7. Fair Test. (n.d.). *Norm-referenced achievement tests*. Cambridge, MA: Fair Test: The National Center for Fair & Open Testing. www.FairTest.org. Retrieved January 15, 2005.

8. Popham, 2004, A game without winners, p. 49.

9. Ibid, p. 48.

10. Kohn, 2000, Standardized testing and its victims, p. 5.

11. Hilliard, A. (2006). Assessment equity in a multicultural society. *New Horizons for Learning* (pp. 18–20). www.newhorizons.org/strategies/assess/hilliard.htm. Retrieved December 6, 2006.

12. Kohn, 2000.

13. Olson, L. (2000, July 12). Poll shows public concern over emphasis on standardized tests. *Education Week*. www.edweek.org. Retrieved January 15, 2005.

14. Samuels, C. A. (2005, January 19). Bush promotes plan for high school test: President indicates that education is still high on his agenda. *Education Week*. www.edweek.org/ew/articles/2005/01/19/19bush.h24.html. Retrieved February 5, 2005.

15. Comer, J. P. (2004). *Leave no child behind: Preparing today's youth for tomorrow's world*. New Haven, CT: Yale University Press, pp. 8, 9.

16. Archer, J. (2005, August 22). Conn. files long-awaited lawsuit challenging No Child Left Behind Act. *Education Week*. www.edweek.org. Retrieved August 30, 2005.

17. Comer, 2004, *Leave no child behind*.

18. Aronson, J. (2004, November). The threat of stereotype: To close the achievement gap, we must address negative stereotypes that suppress student achievement. *Educational Leadership, 62*(3), pp. 14–19.

Steele, C. (2003). Stereotype threat and African-American student achievement. In T. Perry, C. Steele, & A. G. Hilliard III (Eds.), *Young, gifted, and black: Promoting high achievement among African-American students* (pp. 109–130). Boston: Beacon Press.

19. Aronson, 2004, The threat of stereotype, p. 2.

20. Duke, N., & Ritchhart, R. (n.d.). No pain, high gain: Standardized test preparation. http://content.scholastic.com/browse/article.jsp?id=4006. Retrieved August 30, 2005.

21. U.S. Department of Education. (2001). Family involvement in children's education: An idea book (Abridged version). Jessup, MD: Office of Educational Research and Improvement.

22. Corwin, M. (2001). *And still we rise: The trials and triumphs of twelve gifted inner city students*. New York: HarperCollins.

Chapter Four

1. 5-year-old cuffed, arrested in Florida. (2005, March 18). http://abclocal.go.com/wls/story?section=News&id=2887093. Retrieved November 18, 2006.

2. Five year old arrested at school in Jacksonville. http://teachers.net/chatboard. Retrieved April 26, 2005.

3. Ibid.

4. Ferguson, A. A. (2001). *Bad boys: Public schools in the making of black masculinity*. Ann Arbor: University of Michigan Press.

5. Thompson, G. L. (2004). *Through ebony eyes: What teachers need to know but are afraid to ask about African American students*. San Francisco: Jossey-Bass.

6. Ibid.

7. Delpit, L. (1995). *Other people's children: Cultural conflict in the classroom*. New York: New Press.

8. Benard, B. (2004). *Resiliency: What we have learned*. San Francisco: WestEd.

Chapter Five

1. Federal Bureau of Investigation. (2004, November). *Hate crime statistics, 2003*. Washington, DC: FBI Uniform Crime Reporting Program. (Hate crime statistics for various years are available at www.fbi.gov/ucr/ucr.htm.)

2. Ibid, p. 7.

3. Thompson, G. L., & Louque, A. C. (2005). *Exposing the culture of arrogance in the academy: A blueprint for increasing black faculty satisfaction in higher education*. Sterling, VA: Stylus.

4. Oakes, J. (1999). Limiting students' school success and life chances: The impact of tracking. In A. C. Ornstein & L. S. Behar-Horenstein (Eds.), *Contemporary issues in curriculum* (2nd ed., pp. 224–237). Needham Heights, MA: Allyn & Bacon.

5. Landsman, J. (2004, November). Confronting the racism of low expectations. *Educational Leadership, 62*(3), 28–32.

6. Skiba, R., & Peterson, R. (1999). The dark side of zero tolerance: Can punishment lead to safe schools? *Phi Delta Kappan* online. www.pdkintl.org/kappan/kski9901.htm. Retrieved November 18, 2006.

7. Kohn, A. (2000, September 27). Standardized testing and its victims. *Education Week*. www.alfiekohn.org/teaching/edweek/staiv.htm. Retrieved February 17, 2005.

8. Thompson, G. L. (2004). *Through ebony eyes: What teachers need to know but are afraid to ask about African American students*. San Francisco: Jossey-Bass.

9. Wing Sue, D. (2003). *Overcoming our racism: The journey to liberation*. San Francisco: Jossey-Bass.

   Thompson, 2004, *Through ebony eyes*.

10. Boghossian, N., & Sodders, L. M. (2005, June 19). School hate crimes spike: LAUSD police report that incidents have quadrupled in past decade. *Los Angeles Daily News*. www.dailynews.com. Retrieved July 19, 2005.

11. Ibid.

12. FBI, 2004, *Hate crime statistics, 2003*.

13. Ibid.

14. Devoe, J. F., & and Kaffenberger, S. (2005, July). *Student reports of bullying: Results from the 2001 School Crime Supplement to the National Crime Victimization Survey*. Washington, DC: National Center for Education Statistics.

15. Barton, P. E. (2004, November). Why does the gap persist? *Educational Leadership, 62*(3), 8–13.

    Thompson, 2004, *Through ebony eyes*.

16. West, C. (1994). *Race matters*. New York: Vintage.

17. Thompson, 2004, *Through ebony eyes*.

18. Thompson & Louque, 2005, *Exposing the culture of arrogance in the academy*.

19. Ladson-Billings, G. (1994). *The dreamkeepers: Successful teachers of African American children*. San Francisco: Jossey-Bass.

20. Hale, J. E. (2001). *Learning while black: Creating educational excellence for African American children*. Baltimore: Johns Hopkins University Press.

21. De Becker, G. (1997). *The gift of fear: Survival signals that protect us from violence*. New York: Little, Brown, p. 179.

22. Corwin, M. (2001). *And still we rise: The trials and triumphs of twelve gifted inner city students*. New York: HarperCollins.

23. Maynard, J. (2006, January 26). CNN picks up Bennett after Novak departs. www.washingtonpost.com. Retrieved June 5, 2006.

Chapter Six

1. Devoe, J. F., & and Kaffenberger, S. (2005, July). *Student reports of bullying: Results from the 2001 School Crime Supplement to the National Crime Victimization Survey*. Washington, DC: National Center for Education Statistics.

2. Welker, K. (2006, April 4). Female teacher allegedly raped boy 28 times. www.nbc10.com. Retrieved May 27, 2006.

3. Associated Press. (2006, April 14). Alabama teacher accused of sex, murder plot. MSNBC.com. Retrieved May 22, 2006.

4. Eggen, P., & Kauchak, D. (2001). *Educational psychology: Windows on classrooms* (5th ed.). Upper Saddle River, NJ: Prentice Hall.

5. U.S. Departments of Education and Justice. (1999). *Indicators of school crime and safety*. Washington, DC.

6. Thompson, G. L., & Louque, A. C. (2005). *Exposing the culture of arrogance in the academy: A blueprint for increasing black faculty satisfaction in higher education*. Sterling, VA: Stylus.

   Thompson, G. L. (2003). *What African American parents want educators to know*. Westport, CT: Praeger.

7. Noguera, P. (1999). How student perspectives on violence can be used to create safer schools (p. 19). www.inmotionmagazine.com/pnlist1.html. Retrieved December 8, 2006.

8. Hale, J. E. (2001). *Learning while black: Creating educational excellence for African American children*. Baltimore: Johns Hopkins University Press.

   Simmons, R. (2002). *Odd girl out: The hidden culture of aggression in girls*. Orlando, FL: Harcourt.

   Thompson, G. L. (2004). *Through ebony eyes: What teachers need to know but are afraid to ask about African American students*. San Francisco: Jossey-Bass.

9. Thompson, 2003, *What African American parents want educators to know*.

   Canada, G. (1995). *Fist stick knife gun: A personal history of violence in America*. Boston: Beacon Press.

10. Salter, A. (2003). *Predators: Pedophiles, rapists, and other sex offenders*. New York: Basic Books.

    De Becker, G. (1997). *The gift of fear: Survival signals that protect us from violence*. New York: Little, Brown.

11. Stout, M. (2005). *The sociopath next door*. New York: Broadway Books.

12. Blass, T. (2004). *The man who shocked the world: The life and legacy of Stanley Milgram*. New York: Basic Books.

13. Goldensohn, L. (2004). *The Nuremberg interviews*. New York: Knopf.

14. Blass, 2004, *The man who shocked the world*, p. 215.

Chapter Seven

1. Thompson, G. L. (2002). African American Teens Discuss Their Schooling Experiences. Westport, CT: Praeger.

2. Thompson, G. L., & Louque, A. C. (2005). *Exposing the culture of arrogance in the academy: A blueprint for increasing black faculty satisfaction in higher education.* Sterling, VA: Stylus, p. 167.

3. Perry, T. (2003). Achieving in post-civil rights America: The outline of a theory. In T. Perry, C. Steele, & A. G. Hilliard III (Eds.), *Young, gifted, and black: Promoting high achievement among African-American students* (pp. 87–108). Boston: Beacon Press, p. 97.

4. Ibid.

5. Ferguson, A. A. (2001). *Bad boys: Public schools in the making of black masculinity.* Ann Arbor: University of Michigan Press.

6. Foster, M., & Peele, T. B. (1999). Teaching black males: Lessons from the experts. In V. C. Polite & J. E. Davis (Eds.), *African American males in school and society: Practices and policies for effective education* (pp. 8–19). New York: Teachers College Press.

7. Moore, M. (2001). *Stupid white men: And other sorry excuses for the state of the nation!* New York: HarperCollins.

8. Ferguson, 2001, *Bad boys,* p. 116.

9. Thompson, G. L. (2003). *What African American parents want educators to know.* Westport, CT: Greenwood.

10. Noguera, P. (2002). *The trouble with black boys: The role and influence of environmental and cultural factors on the academic performance of African American males* (p. 17). www.inmotionmagazine.com/er/pntroubl.html. Retrieved December 8, 2006.

11. Corwin, M. (2001). *And still we rise: The trials and triumphs of twelve gifted inner city students.* New York: HarperCollins.

12. Ibid, p. 36.

13. Ibid, p. 198.

14. Noguera, 2002, *The trouble with black boys.*

15. Noguera, P. (2001). *The role and influence of environmental and cultural factors on the academic performance of African American males* (p. 2).

www.inmotionmagazine.com/pnaamale1.html. Retrieved December 8, 2006.

16. U.S. Department of Education. (2005, September). *Pocket projections: Projections of education statistics to 2014*. Washington, DC: National Center for Education Statistics.

17. Tyre, P. (2006, January 30). The trouble with boys. *Newsweek*, pp. 44–52.

18. Kunjufu, J. (2005). *Keeping black boys out of special education*. Chicago: African American Images.

19. Ibid.

20. Noguera, 2002, *The trouble with black boys*, p. 18.

21. Noguera, 2001, *The role and influence of environmental and cultural factors on the academic performance of African American males*.

22. Kunjufu, J. (1984). *Developing positive self-images and discipline in black children*. Chicago: African American Images.

23. Kunjufu, J. (1990). *Countering the conspiracy to destroy black boys (vols. 1–3)*. Chicago: African American Images.

24. Noguera, 2001, *The role and influence of environmental and cultural factors on the academic performance of African American males*, p. 4.

Chapter Eight

1. Strauss, V. (2004, November 18). Amid disrepair, students 'just can't think': Sweltering heat, faulty bathrooms top list of woes. *The Washington Post*, p. DZ10. www.washingtonpost.com/wp-dyn/articles/A57498-2004Nov17.html. Retrieved November 18, 2006.

2. Gewertz, C. (2003, February 12). Bathroom blues: School restrooms are often dirty, dank, and depressing. But a lone crusader is proving that they don't have to be. *Education Week*. www.edweek.org/ew/articles/2003/02/12/22bathroom.h22.html. Retrieved May 31, 2005.

3. Strauss, 2004, Amid disrepair, students 'just can't think.'

School sanitation. (n.d.). Wisconsin Council on Children & Families. www.wccf.org/pdf/schoolsanitation.pdf. Retrieved May 31, 2005.

Dirty lessons. (2003, January 30). www.cbs2.com/consumer/local_story_13420295. Retrieved May 31, 2005.

Thomas, J., & Witenko, V. (2004, December). Overcrowding squeezes learning; also the great toilet paper debate. www.gothamgazette.com/article//20041222/6/1225. Retrieved November 18, 2006.

McKay, G. (2000, February 28). Bathrooms a reflection of school's climate. www.post-gazette.com/regionstate/20000228 bathrooms2.asp. Retrieved May 31, 2005.

Williams, J. J., IV. (2005, May 28). School's bathrooms are raising a stink: Teachers, parents complain of shoddy conditions, slow response. www.nola.com/news. Retrieved May 31, 2005.

4. Thomas & Witenko, 2004, Overcrowding squeezes learning.

5. Dirty lessons, 2003.

6. Ibid.

7. McKay, 2000, Bathrooms a reflection of school's climate.

8. Yan, E. (2005, February 13). Strict limits on school bathrooms. www.nyNewsday.com. Retrieved May 31, 2005.

9. Dirty lessons, 2003.

10. Gewertz, C., 2003, Bathroom blues.

11. Yan, 2005, Strict limits on school bathrooms.

12. California Senate Bill 892. (2003, February 21). www.opsc.dgs.ca.gov/SABPrograms/DMP_Clean_Restroom.htm. Retrieved May 31, 2005.

13. 21st Century School Fund. (2003, July). DCPS students successfully campaign for better bathrooms. *Better Buildings: Better Schools.* www.21csf.org/csf-home/publications/emails/BetterSchoolsEmail Update13.asp. Retrieved November 18, 2006.

14. Quoted in Strauss, 2004, Amid disrepair, students 'just can't think.'

15. Quoted in Gewertz, 2003, Bathroom blues.

16. Ibid.

17. McDougal, D. (1996). *In the best of families: The anatomy of a true tragedy.* New York: Warner Books.

Chapter Nine

1. Crain, W. (1992). *Theories of development: Concepts and applications.* Upper Saddle River, NJ: Prentice Hall.

2. U.S. Department of Education. (2005). *Parent and family involvement in education: 2002–03.* Washington, DC: National Center for Education Statistics.

3. U.S. Department of Education. (2001). *Efforts by public K–8 schools to involve parents in children's education: Do school and parent reports agree?* Washington, DC: Office of Educational Research and Improvement.

4. Ibid, p. 32.

5. Markow, D., & Martin, S. (2005). *The MetLife survey of the American teacher: Transitions and the role of supportive relationships.* Warwick, RI: MetLife, p. 72.

6. Ibid, p. 73.

7. Comer, J. P. (2004). *Leave no child behind: Preparing today's youth for tomorrow's world.* New Haven, CT: Yale University Press.

8. U.S. Department of Education. (2001). *Family involvement in children's education: An idea book* (Abridged version). Jessup, MD: Office of Educational Research and Improvement.

9. Thompson, G. L. (2003). *What African American parents want educators to know.* Westport, CT: Greenwood.

10. Markow & Martin, 2005, MetLife survey of the American teacher, p. 32.

11. Thompson, G. L., Warren, S., & Carter, L. (2004). It's not my fault: Predicting high school teachers who blame parents and students for students' low achievement. *High School Journal, 87*(3), 5–14.

12. Thompson, 2003, *What African American parents want educators to know.*

13. Ibid.

14. Comer, 2004, *Leave no child behind.*

15. Thompson, 2003, *What African American parents want educators to know.*

16. Clark, R. (1983). *Family life and school achievement: Why poor black children succeed or fail.* Chicago: University of Chicago Press.

17. Thompson, G. L. (2004). *Through ebony eyes: What teachers need to know but are afraid to ask about African American students.* San Francisco: Jossey-Bass.

Foster, M., & Peele, T. B. (1999). Teaching black males: Lessons from the experts. In V. C. Polite & J. E. Davis (Eds.), *African American males in school and society: Practices and policies for effective education* (pp. 8–19). New York: Teachers College Press.

Delpit, L. (1995). *Other people's children: Cultural conflict in the classroom.* New York: New Press.

Chapter Ten

1. Jimenez, F. (1997). *The circuit: Stories from the life of a migrant child.* Albuquerque: University of New Mexico Press.

2. Carson, B. (1999). *The big picture: Getting perspective on what's really important in life.* Grand Rapids, MI: Zondervan.

3. U.S. Census Bureau. (n.d.). *The big payoff: Educational attainment and synthetic estimates of work-life earnings. www.census.gov/prod/2002 pubs/p23-210.pdf.* Retrieved December 13, 2006.

4. Ibid.

5. Horn, L. J., Chen, X., & Chapman, C. (2003, September). *Getting ready to pay for college: What students and their parents know about the cost of college tuition and what they are doing to find out.* Washington, DC: Institute of Education Sciences.

6. Barrino, F. (2005). *Life is not a fairy tale.* New York: Fireside.

7. U.S. Department of Education. (2004). *The condition of education 2004 (Indicator 18: Remediation and degree completion).* Washington, DC: National Center for Education Statistics. http://nces.ed.gov/programs/coe/2004/section3/indicator18.asp. Retrieved November 18, 2006.

8. Carter, C. S. (2000). *No excuses: Lessons from 21 high-performing, high-poverty schools.* Washington, DC: Heritage Foundation.

Yau, R. (2002). High-achieving elementary schools with large percentages of low-income African American students: A review and critique of the current research. In S. J. Denbo & L. Moore Beaulieu (Eds.), *Improving schools for African American students: A reader for educational leaders* (pp. 193–217). Springfield, IL: Thomas.

9. Landsman, J. (2004, November). Confronting the racism of low expectations. *Educational Leadership*, 62(3), 28–32.

Thompson, G. L. (2004). Home to school to work transitions for African Americans: Eliminating barriers to success. In D. Halpern (Ed.), *Changing the metaphor: From work/family balance to work/family interaction* (pp. 117–133). Mahwah, NJ: Erlbaum.

Council of Chief State School Officers. (2002). *Expecting success: A study of five high performing, high poverty schools.* www.ccsso.org. Retrieved June 5, 2005.

10. The Education Trust. (2005). *Gaining traction, gaining ground: How some high schools accelerate learning for struggling students.* Washington, DC: Author.

Chapter Eleven

1. Lehrer, J. (2000, April 26). Cheating teachers. *Online NewsHour.* www.pbs.org/newshour. Retrieved February 17, 2005.

2. Robinson, M. (2000, January 31). Wave of cheating teachers hits southern California coast. www.conservativenews.org. Retrieved February 17, 2005.

3. Ibid.

4. Kossan, P. (2004, July 11). Cheating or misunderstandings? *The Arizona Republic.* www.azcentral.com. Retrieved February 17, 2005.

5. Ibid.

6. Ibid.

7. Grow, B. (2004, July 5). A spate of cheating by teachers: No Child Left Behind links test results to school funding. Is that a recipe for deceit? *BusinessWeek Online.* www.businessweek.com. Retrieved February 17, 2005.

8. Ibid.

9. Perkins, J. (2004). *Confessions of an economic hit man*. San Francisco: Berrett-Koehler, p. 105.

10. Wing Sue, D. (2003). *Overcoming our racism: The journey to liberation*. San Francisco: Jossey-Bass.

11. Gould, S. J. (1996). *The mismeasure of man*. New York: Norton.
Wing Sue, 2003, *Overcoming our racism*.

12. Douglas, K. (1988). *The ragman's son*. New York: Pocket Books.

13. Hayasaki, E. (2004, December 19). Beginning a new chapter in his life. *Los Angeles Times*, pp. A1, A48.

14. Ibid, p. A48.

15. Ibid.

16. Ibid.

17. Carter, C. S. (2000). *No excuses: Lessons from 21 high-performing, high-poverty schools*. Washington, DC: Heritage Foundation.
Comer, J. P. (2004). *Leave no child behind: Preparing today's youth for tomorrow's world*. New Haven, CT: Yale University Press.
Yau, R. (2002). High-achieving elementary schools with large percentages of low-income African American students: A review and critique of the current research. In S. J. Denbo & L. Moore Beaulieu (Eds.), *Improving schools for African American students: A reader for educational leaders* (pp. 193–217). Springfield, IL: Thomas.

18. Gardner, H. (1991). *The unschooled mind: How children think and how schools should teach*. New York: Basic Books.

19. Hale, J. E. (2001). *Learning while black: Creating educational excellence for African American children*. Baltimore: Johns Hopkins University Press.

20. Elon, A. (2002). *The pity of it all: A history of Jews in Germany, 1743–1933*. New York: Henry Holt.

21. Wing Sue, 2003, *Overcoming our racism*.

22. Kunjufu, J. (1985). *Countering the conspiracy to destroy black boys*. Chicago: African American Images.

23. All quotations are from Woo, E. (2005, May 3). Kenneth Clark, 90; His studies influenced ban on segregation. *The Los Angeles Times*, p. B10.

24. Kozol, J. (2005). *The shame of a nation: The restoration of apartheid schooling in America*. New York: Crown Publishers.

25. Noguera, P. (2005). *It takes more than pressure to improve failing high schools* (p. 1). www.inmotionmagazine.com/er/pn_pressure.html. Retrieved December 8, 2006.

26. Ibid.

27. Ibid, p. 4.

28. Hilliard, A. (1997). Maintaining faith in a teacher's ability to grow: An interview with Asa Hilliard. *Journal of Staff Development, 18*(2), 1–3. www.nsdc.org/library/publications/jsd/jsds97spks.cfm. Retrieved September 16, 2006.

Appendix A: Teacher Demographics

During the period when the teachers completed the questionnaire, 136 teachers were employed at the participating high school. Therefore, the 121 teachers who completed the questionnaire represented 89 percent of the teachers at the school. Seventy-five percent of the questionnaire respondents were white, and 54 percent were males. Nine percent of the participants were working under an Emergency Credential, 42 percent had a full credential, and the remainder had some other type of teaching credential. The average questionnaire respondent had taught for nine years, and the majority planned to still be teaching at the same school three years from the time when they completed the questionnaire. Forty-three percent of the respondents taught basic courses; 25 percent taught college preparatory, honors, or AP courses; and 18 percent taught Special Education classes.

Appendix B: Student Demographics

Of a total school population of approximately 3,200 students, 268 completed the questionnaire and 146 participated in the focus groups. Although more than half the students were in regular classes, a substantial percentage was in college preparatory and AP classes. Twenty percent had a 3.5 or higher GPA, 5 percent had a 1.6 or lower GPA, and 35 percent were failing one or more courses.

Questionnaire Respondents

Blacks   38%

Latinos   33%

Whites   19%

Asians   2%

Unspecified race/ethnicity   8%

Focus Group Participants

Blacks   43%

Latinos   38%

Whites   19%

Appendix C: Additional Information About the Student Questionnaire Respondents

Questionnaire respondents ranged in age from 13–14 years old (10 percent) to 17–18 years old (30 percent), but the largest age group consisted of 15–16 year olds (56 percent). Seniors accounted for the smallest group of questionnaire respondents (13 percent); an almost equal percentage of ninth, tenth, and eleventh graders completed questionnaires. When I disaggregated the data by academic track, Special Education students (4 percent) and vocational education students (4 percent) made up the smallest groups of questionnaire respondents. The majority of the questionnaire respondents were involved in at least one extracurricular activity at the school. Nearly 40 percent were athletes, but only 2 percent participated in student government. More than one-fifth of the questionnaire respondents participated in "other" extracurricular activities that they didn't specify.

Appendix D: Teacher Questionnaire Results

One hundred and twenty-one teachers participated in the teacher phase of the study. Because not all teachers responded to every statement, some percentage totals are less than 100.

Teachers' Attitudes About the School in General (by %)

Statement	Strongly Agree	Agree	Disagree	Strongly Disagree
Three years from now, I will probably still be teaching at this school.	42	34	9	10
I consider my current school site to be one of the best public schools in this district.	31	37	27	2
I consider my current school site to be one of the best public schools in the state.	9	22	48	17
I would not want my own children to attend this school.	10	19	38	33

Teachers' Beliefs About Their Colleagues (by %)

Statement	Strongly Agree	Agree	Disagree	Strongly Disagree
I believe that most of the teachers at this school are outstanding educators.	17	57	23	3
I do not believe that most of the educators in my department are outstanding educators.	3	23	45	29
Some of my colleagues do not have high expectations for their students.	23	57	16	4
Most of my colleagues do not have low expectations or a negative attitude about students.	12	55	30	3

Teachers' Beliefs About Their Students' Parents (by %)

Statement	Strongly Agree	Agree	Disagree	Strongly Disagree
I believe that parents or guardians are largely to blame for students' low achievement.	12	52	31	5
The majority of my students do not have parents or guardians who are concerned about their academic welfare.	3	31	51	15
I would like to have more interaction with my students' parents.	26	48	23	3
The majority of my students come from decent homes.	13	53	33	1

Teachers' Beliefs About Their Students (by %)

Statement	Strongly Agree	Agree	Disagree	Strongly Disagree
Most of my students do not enjoy coming to my classes.	5	10	51	34
I do not believe that all students have the potential to be academically successful in my classes.	9	14	33	44
I do not believe that Special Education students can handle a rigorous curriculum.	4	28	51	17
I believe that all students deserve a college preparatory curriculum.	24	36	26	13
I believe that some students are incapable of passing my classes.	6	18	30	46
I believe that students from poor economic backgrounds have the aptitude to succeed in my class.	55	40	3	1
I care about my students' academic and personal welfare both inside of and outside of school.	54	43	3	0
I believe that most of my students will become successful adults.	31	50	17	1
By the end of the current academic year, most of my students will not meet the grade level standards for my content area.	7	19	43	31

Statement	Strongly Agree	Agree	Disagree	Strongly Disagree
I expect that most of my students will pass my class with a "C" or higher grade.	36	46	15	3
I believe that students who do poorly in school are largely to blame for their failure.	13	38	42	7
When students fail to pass a test or fail an assignment, they are largely to blame.	13	44	37	6
Most of my students do not want to succeed academically.	1	11	56	32
Most of my students are well behaved during class.	28	54	15	3
I do not believe that most of my students will go to college.	13	36	36	15
I believe that students' race/ethnicity has some bearing on their aptitude.	3	14	24	59
The majority of my students cannot read at grade level or above.	23	40	33	2
I believe that students from poor economic backgrounds do not have the aptitude to be academically successful.	2	3	32	63
I believe that most of my students cannot succeed academically at college.	2	20	46	32

Teachers' Attitudes About Teaching (in %)

Statement	Strongly Agree	Agree	Disagree	Strongly Disagree
Three years from now, I will most likely be a public school teacher.	65	26	4	5
I love my teaching job.	60	31	8	1
I believe that teachers' attitudes and expectations affect the quality of instruction that students receive.	64	33	3	0
I believe that my curriculum and instructional practices will improve the quality of my students' lives.	46	47	6	1
I want all of my students to succeed in my classes.	83	16	0	1
I believe that I have received adequate training to effectively teach the majority of my students.	36	43	18	3
Sometimes, I have to lower my standards because many of my students cannot handle a rigorous curriculum.	8	31	40	21

Teachers' Beliefs About Their Teaching Efficacy (by %)

Statement	Strongly Agree	Agree	Disagree	Strongly Disagree
I am an outstanding educator.	33	54	13	0
Most of my students would rate me as an outstanding educator.	26	60	13	1
Most of my students would consider me to be one of the best teachers they ever had.	20	52	21	0
I have done an outstanding job of providing my students with the best quality of instruction that I can give.	28	66	4	1

Teachers' Instructional Practices (by %)

Statement	Strongly Agree	Agree	Disagree	Strongly Disagree
My students know that I am available to give extra help during class on a regular basis.	56	41	3	0
I use multiple strategies to present my subject matter to students.	48	49	3	0
I often permit my students to work collaboratively.	51	38	7	0
I treat my students the way I would want my own children's teachers to treat my children.	62	34	2	2
I spend the majority of most class sessions on instruction instead of on discipline.	41	48	8	3

(Continued)

Statement	Strongly Agree	Agree	Disagree	Strongly Disagree
I do not encourage my students to ask questions in class.	1	3	27	69
I utilize multiple strategies to check for comprehension during class.	41	55	4	0
I use multiple methods to assess my students' subject-matter knowledge, instead of only using tests.	40	55	3	2
I make the curriculum relevant to my students' lives.	36	55	9	0
I do not use enough innovation and creativity in my lesson plans.	4	23	53	17

Appendix E: Student Questionnaire Results

Students were asked to respond to most questionnaire items by using a four-part Likert scale consisting of strongly agree, agree, disagree, strongly disagree. There were also a few fill-in-the-blank items, yes or no items, and a section for additional comments. The following results indicate the percentages of black, Latino, and white students who strongly agreed or agreed with questionnaire items.

Statement	Blacks (%)	Latinos (%)	Whites (%)
I like this school.	65	70	68
Most of my teachers are good teachers.	70	79	84
I learn a lot of useful information in most of my classes.	61	79	62
Most of the homework that is assigned is not very useful to me.	50	47	52
I am often confused by the work that my teachers assign.	41	46	36
Most of my classes are boring.	66	57	48
Most of my teachers treat me fairly.	78	81	86

(Continued)

Statement	Blacks (%)	Latinos (%)	Whites (%)
Most of my teachers are willing to give me extra help during class if I need it.	67	67	86
Most of my teachers are unwilling to answer questions if I don't understand an assignment.	32	28	4
Most of my teachers aren't very patient when I don't understand an assignment.	35	28	18
Most administrators treat me fairly.	68	78	72
Most security treat me fairly.	71	75	66
If I ever have children, I would want them to attend this school.	32	44	34
I'm not sure that I'll graduate on time.	16	20	10
I have the right number of credits for my grade level.	76	79	94
I'm failing at least one class at this point.	36	48	20
I am lacking some credits that are necessary for me to graduate on time.	34	38	12
Most of my teachers believe I have the potential to be a good student.	93	91	92
Most of my teachers don't believe I'll become a successful adult.	22	17	20
At this school, I've never experienced any racism from students.	46	52	32

Statement	Blacks (%)	Latinos (%)	Whites (%)
At this school, I've never experienced any racism from teachers.	55	63	76
At this school, I've never experienced any racism from administrators.	72	72	74
At this school, I've never experienced any racism from security.	73	66	64
Students are usually treated fairly at this school by most adults.	58	56	56
I'm doing my best in most of my classes.	85	84	80
Often, my personal problems prevent me from earning good grades and doing well on tests.	52	65	50
In most of my classes, I haven't learned as much as I would like to learn about my own culture.	62	49	42
I've never been suspended from this school.	62	74	74
I've received at least one referral to the office for misbehavior.	34	36	44
I wish that most of my classes were more challenging.	33	43	40
I'm well behaved in most of my classes.	83	85	90
I wish I had better teachers.	58	54	38

(Continued)

Statement	Blacks (%)	Latinos (%)	Whites (%)
I wish I could learn more about my own culture in my classes.	75	57	36
Most of my teachers are fair about discipline.	51	58	66
Most of my teachers won't give extra help during class time.	34	38	28
Often, I'm too embarrassed to ask teachers for extra help.	37	48	12
I believe that most of my teachers care about me.	56	57	70
Most of my teachers don't like me.	27	20	14
Most of my teachers think I'm a troublemaker.	21	25	18
I would get better grades if I spent more time on my homework.	70	73	70
I would get better grades if I spent more time on my class work.	68	76	56
I don't usually take my classes as seriously as I should.	50	52	28
I often feel unsafe at this school.	30	39	42
I've never been in a fight or physical altercation at this school.	67	71	76
I get along with most of my teachers.	78	78	90

Statement	Blacks (%)	Latinos (%)	Whites (%)
I get along with most students at this school.	72	78	74
I treat most adults on campus respectfully.	83	85	88
Most adults at this school treat me respectfully.	70	79	72
My parents/guardians are very concerned about my education.	86	85	90
Most of my classes aren't really preparing me for the "real world."	60	61	50
Most of my classes aren't really teaching me what I need to know to survive in my community.	52	50	42
I take state tests like the SAT 9 very seriously.	62	65	64
Most of my teachers do a good job of preparing me for state tests like the SAT 9.	49	54	58
In the past, I didn't do my best on the SAT 9 because I believed that it was a waste of time.	49	47	34
My SAT 9 scores weren't very high because I haven't been taught most of the information on the test.	45	58	42
Most of my teachers have done a good job of preparing me for the High School Exit Exam.	44	53	56

(Continued)

Statement	Blacks (%)	Latinos (%)	Whites (%)
I believe that I will pass the High School Exit Exam.	75	71	92
My reading skills are good.	89	88	88
I can read and understand most of my textbooks.	86	88	92
Last year, I could read and understand most of the information on the SAT 9.	77	73	72
My math skills are good.	68	57	72
I understand most of my math assignments.	66	66	66
Last year, I understood most of the SAT 9 math problems.	43	49	54
The discipline policies at this school are used fairly.	46	50	46
If I get good grades, I'm afraid that people might think that I'm a "nerd."	23	18	16
Most of my friends want me to earn good grades.	78	73	88
I am an outstanding or good student.	80	67	84
I always complete my homework on time.	32	37	56
I spend one hour or less on homework each night.	66	62	70
I spend one hour or less studying for tests each night.	72	82	82
My schoolwork is very important to me.	57	46	60

Statement	Blacks (%)	Latinos (%)	Whites (%)
Getting good grades is very important to my friends.	46	35	32
I always do my best to get good grades.	46	47	62
Getting good grades is very important to me.	81	70	74
My education is very important to my parents.	84	85	88
Most teachers are doing a good or adequate job of preparing me for my future goals.	75	72	76
Last year, passing the SAT 9 was very important to me.	26	30	32
This year, passing the state tests is very important to me.	49	55	60
Passing the High School Exit Exam is very important to me.	72	72	76
Most of my friends earn good grades.	75	64	76
I plan to attend a four-year college/university immediately after graduation.	68	39	56
I plan to attend a community college immediately after graduation.	18	25	22

(Continued)

Statement	Blacks (%)	Latinos (%)	Whites (%)
Most of my teachers explain assignments well.	57	66	76
Statement	Yes	Yes	Yes
If before or after-school tutoring were available to help you prepare for state tests like the SAT 9 and High School Exit Exam, would you attend tutoring sessions?	56	53	42

Appendix F: Classroom Management Exercise 1

I have used this exercise as a homework assignment following classroom management presentations that I've given to new teachers. Administrators, support teachers, mentors, and others who conduct classroom management professional development workshops may find it beneficial to use with new teachers. Both new and veteran teachers can use this activity as well as the one in Appendix G on their own.

Homework Assignment

1. Read chapter 3 of *Through Ebony Eyes*. . . .

2. Measure your own classroom management effectiveness against the recommendations on pp. 98–100.

   - Which of these areas are your strong points?

   - In what areas do you need to improve?

3. Identify two of your students whom you view as discipline problems.

   - Which of their behaviors bother you the most?

   - What classroom management strategies have you used with them?

Appendix G: Classroom Management Exercise 2

1. Identify your most unruly class or the class where you have the highest number of misbehaving students.

   • Write one or two sentences about each student, starting with the phrase, "In my opinion, _____ is . . ."

   • What you write should be an honest description of how you feel about the student.

2. After at least a twenty-four-hour period, read what you wrote about each student.

   • Determine what your responses reveal about how you view these students.

   • Determine whether or not your perceptions may be affecting the way that you interact with certain students.

   • Determine whether or not your perceptions may have some bearing on the students' behavior in class.

   • Determine whether or not you need to change the way in which you view and interact with students about whom you've formed negative opinions.

3. Select one student in this class about whom you've formed a negative opinion.

   • For twenty-one consecutive school days, force yourself to view and treat this student as if he or she were the brightest student in your class. This means that you will treat this student respectfully and in a manner that a teacher would treat a brilliant child.

   • Document what you learn from this exercise.

Index

Sex crimes, 159
Sexual abuse of, 166
Sexual predators, single mothers and, 174
Shame of a Nation (Kozol), 289
Slavery, taught in classes, objections to, 44–45
Sociopathy, 175–176
Staff, racial and ethnic diversity of, 54
"Standard operating procedures" (SOPS), 286–287
Standardized tests, 65–96; administrators and, 88–89; community resources, 91; flaws in, 67; four-pronged approach to improving test scores, 87–94; high test scores and intelligence, 92; Internet, information regarding, 91–92; parents and, 91–93; preparing students of, 66; student/teacher feedback regarding, importance of, 85–87; teachers and, 89–90; test bias, 68–69
Stanford Achievement Test (SAT), 67, 70; preparation workshops, 260, 262
State-mandated tests: diverse teaching strategies: need for, 83–84: importance of the tests, stressing, 84; math sections, preparing students for, 82–83; relevant information provided for, 82; student recommendations about teachers' help in preparing for, 81–84; teacher patience, 83; test preparation, time spent on, 81–82; tutoring, 81
Steele, C., 90
Storybook Treasury of Dick and Jane, 50
Storytelling: safety and, 171
Stout, Martha, 175–176
Student questionnaire: caring teachers, 23–24; good teachers/teaching, 19; results, 319–326; teacher perception, 22–23; teacher quality, 20–22; teachers' instructional practices, 24–27
Students: on college attendance, 249–253; community, beliefs, concerns, and interests, 15; connection between poor reading skills, math skills, and test scores, 75; creating a college-going mind-set in, 259–260; demographics, 292; effort, 65–96; failing courses, 71–72; on High School Exit Exam (HSEE), 77–79; misbehavior, looking for messages in, 117–118; preparation for, 79–81; SAT 9 and CAT 6 State-Mandated Tests, attitudes about,

72–74; preparation for, 75–77; on school's physical environment, 209–213; on standardized tests, 70–71; state-mandated tests, teachers' help in preparing for, 81–84
Subject-matter mastery, 15
Suspension, 103–105, 116, 193

T

Taking Sides (Noll), 39
Tammie, 94–96, 281
Teacher demographics, 309
Teacher quality, 15
Teacher questionnaire results, 312–318
Teachers, 235–236; African-American males and, 189–191, 199; assertiveness, 235–236; classroom patterns; looking for messages in, 118–120; college preparatory curriculum and, 261–262; communication skills, 235–237; culturally relevant education and, 55–60; culturally relevant teaching methods; use of, 147; discipline and, 116–120; evaluations, 31; hiring of, 30; inclusiveness, 55; as leaders, 116; marginalization and, 55; "mental baggage," 31–32; mind-set of, 36, 55, 63; negative, 30–32, 35; on-site professional development library; access to, 114–115; parental involvement in schools and, 235–239; physical environment of school and, 214–215; professional development workshops, 30–31, 53, 88; race relations at school, 146–147; racism from, 141–142; safety, 166–170; school rules; discussion of, with parents, 122–123; standardized tests and, 89–90; and student academic performance, 31–33; student misbehavior; looking for messages in, 117–118; teaching around "big ideas" strategy, 55–56
Teacher support, 28, 275–277
Teaching excellence, 14–15; definition of, 15; models of, 15
Tessem, Susan, 14–15, 18, 37
Test-taking strategies, 91–92
"Test Taking Tips for Families" (Practical Parenting Partnerships), 91
Through Ebony Eyes . . ., 32, 39–40, 66–67, 98, 101, 116–117